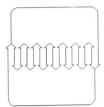

THE EXECUTIVE ARCHITECT

THE EXECUTIVE ARCHITECT

Transforming Designers into Leaders

John E. Harrigan, Ph.D.

Paul R. Neel, F.A.I.A.

with contributions by

Douglas H. Austin, F.A.I.A.
Jim Brecht, A.I.A.
Paul S. Chinowsky, B.Arch, Ph.D.
Fred L. Foote, F.A.I.A.
David Gensler, M.B.A.
M. Arthur Gensler, F.A.I.A.

Jeffrey Heller, F.A.I.A.
Charles Luckman, F.A.I.A.
Judy L. Rowe, F.A.I.A.
Don Willcox, Executive
Larry Wolff, A.I.A.

JOHN WILEY AND SONS, INC.
New York   Chichester   Brisbane   Toronto   Singapore

Library of Congress Cataloging-in-Publication Data
Harrigan, John E.
    The executive architect : transforming designers into leaders /
John E. Harrigan and Paul R. Neel.
        p.   cm.
    Includes bibliographical references and index.
    ISBN 0-471-11352-2 (cloth : acid free paper)
        1. Architectural practice—United States—Management.
    2. Architectural services marketing—United States.
    3. Architecture—United States—Decision-making.   I. Neel, Paul R.
    II. Title.
    NA1996.H32   1996
      720′.68—dc20   95-44028

Printed in the United States of America

10 9 8 7 6 5 4 3 2 1

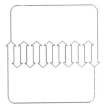

CONTENTS

1 | THE EXECUTIVE ARCHITECT   1

   To the Readers   2
     The Professional Reader   *3*
     The Student Reader   *3*
     The Faculty Reader   *4*
     The Corporate Reader   *4*
   The Two Pathways: Insights and Methods   5
     Insights   *6*
     Methods   *8*
   The Transformation of Professional Practice   9
     A Practical Strategic Prescription   *10*
   Application Possibilities   13
     Hidden Assets   *14*

  Insights: Charles Luckman, F.A.I.A.   16
   Read Critically   20

2 | LEADERSHIP   25

   Unlimited Opportunity Is the Most Promising Vision   25
   Build a High-Performance Practice   26
   Renew Your Intellectual Capital   27
   Consider Carefully What People Can Do
   and What People Are Willing to Do   27

Appreciate the Importance of Teamwork as a Pooling
of Experience and Expertise   28

Be Willing to Hustle   28

Be Willing to Answer All Questions Related
to Cash Flow and Profit Margins   29

Insights: M. Arthur Gensler, Jr., F.A.I.A.   31

Interview Highlights   31

The Interview   32

Insights: Jeffrey Heller, F.A.I.A.   43

Interview Highlights   43

The Interview   43

Method No. 1: Critical Thinking   52

The Goal of Realizing Our Potential   54

Mapping the Challenges Ahead   56

A Unique Challenge   58

3 | STRATEGY   59

Architects Are Respected for Their Creativity
and Contributions to Quality of Life   60

The Challenge to Strategy Is to
Identify Needed Innovations   60

A Competitive Strategy Places a Firm
Ahead of Conventional Wisdom   61

Strategy Does Not Consist of Simple Choices
Between Clear-Cut Alternatives   61

Insights: Jim Brecht, A.I.A.   62

Interview Highlights   62

The Interview   63

Method No. 2: Thorough Analysis   75

Anchor Points   76

First Anchor Point: Benchmarks   *77*
Second Anchor Point: Action Plans   *81*
Third Anchor Point: Assets   *81*

Fourth Anchor Point: Design Guidelines   *84*
Fifth Anchor Point: Financial Analyses   *84*
Innovation   85

4 | CLIENT RELATIONS   87

Focus on Your Client's Risks and Critical
Success Factors   87

Respond to Your Client's Evolving Needs   88

Remain Alert to Changing Goals by Working
with Clients as "Insiders"   89

Insights: Don Willcox, Corporate Executive   90

Interview Highlights   90

The Interview   91

Method No. 3: Client Assessment Strategy   106

Opportunities for Client Engagement
and Professional Service   108

Entering a New Market   111

Learning from Clients   113

International Enterprises   115

Honoring a Tradition   *116*
Contributing to a New Enterprise   *118*
Perfecting a Design Center   *119*
*Quality of Life at Work, at Home, and
in the Community*   *120*

Safeguards   121

Shoulder to Shoulder   *122*
Information Resources   *123*

5 | WORKING WITH CLIENTS   125

Make Client Representatives Feel Essential   125

Provide Time for Give and Take   126

Detect Barriers to Project Success   126

You Can Easily Change the "Why"—
The Challenge Is to Change the "How"   126

Insights: Fred L. Foote, F.A.I.A.   127

    Interview Highlights   127

    The Interview   128

Method No. 4: Knowledge Base System   144

    Basic Strategy   145

    The Knowledge Base System Logos   148

    Design Guidelines   157

       Programming Has Too Many Shortcomings   *157*
       The Emphasis on Fad and Fashion   *159*

    Commentaries   159

       1.0 Quality of Life Challenge   *159*
       2.0 Facility Life Characteristics   *161*
       3.0 Family Life Characteristics   *164*
       4.0 Community Life Characteristics   *165*
       5.0 Critical Circulation Patterns   *166*
       6.0 Interior Architectural Spaces   *168*
       7.0 Workstations   *174*
       8.0 Communication and Information Systems   *174*
       9.0 Facility Space Arrangements   *175*
       10.0 Facility Design Image   *177*
       11.0 Facility Site Plan   *178*
       12.0 Community Master Plan   *180*

6 | QUALITY OF LIFE   **183**

    We Must Thoroughly Understand
    What People Need and Want   184

    We Don't Provide Buildings; We Provide Experiences   184

    Verify Every Objective   185

    Avoid Haphazard Design in Which
    Everything Is Style and Fad   185

Insights: Judy L. Rowe, F.A.I.A.   186

    Interview Highlights   186

    The Interview   187

Method No. 5: Field Studies   206

    Case Study Archives   206

    Basic Elements of Field Studies   207

1: The Human Touch   *207*
2: Learning about Clients   *208*
3: Points of View   *209*
4: Situational Factors   *209*
5: Dilemmas and Conflicts   *210*
6: Financial Analysis   *210*
7: Market Analysis   *211*
8: Supplemental Information   *211*

Example One: Office/Home Design Center   212

*"Bring Life to a Building before There Is
a Building"*   *212*

Example Two: Worker Performance and Satisfaction   226

Key Workers and Their Associates   *227*
Organization Dynamics   *228*
Worker Activities   *229*
Work Culture   *231*
Workstations   *232*
Communication and Information Systems   *235*
Software as an Insight   *237*
*The Organization's Concern for Skilled
Job Performance*   *238*

Example Three: Understanding a Client's Situation   241

Initial Field Study Findings   *241*
The Growth Plan   *242*
The Organization   *243*
Store Development Costs   *244*
Infrastructure   *246*
Capital and Cash Flow Requirements   *246*
GDI Field Study Conclusion   *247*
Confirm Customer Needs and Desires   *247*
Develop Design Guidelines   *248*
Use Modular and Factory-Finished Casework   *250*
Identify New Store Locations   *250*
*Create Lease Specifications
and Standard Specifications*   *251*
Adapt Store Model Prototype   *251*
Set Up Design and Construction Team   *252*
Schedule and Track Progress Growth Plan   *253*

7 | KNOWLEDGE DEVELOPMENT   255

Knowledge Establishes a Sense of Direction   255

Keep a Keen Eye on the Accomplishments
of Entrepreneurs   256

Develop Appropriate Knowledge Bases   256

Realize the Potential of Technology   256

Insights: Paul S. Chinowsky, B. Arch., Ph.D.   257

Interview Highlights   257

The Interview   258

Insights: David Gensler, M.B.A.   264

The Interview   265

Method No. 6: Research Techniques   280

A Typical Two Weeks of Research   281

Group Identification Techniques   281

     Progressive Survey   *283*
     Directed Group Identification Techniques   *292*

Study Sessions   293

Interviews   297

Preference Assessment   299

Activity Analysis   307

     The First Step in Activity Analysis Is to Determine
     Which Facility Users Must Be Given Special
     Consideration   *307*
     The Second Step in Activity Analysis Is to
     Determine Which User Activities Are Important   *308*
     The Final Step in Activity Analysis Is to Depict
     How Activities Vary by User, Event, and Space   *308*
     Communication Matrix   *310*

Systematic Observation   310

Questionnaires   314

     Development Considerations   *315*

8 | VALUE, PERFORMANCE, AND IMAGE   317

Insights: Douglas H. Austin, F.A.I.A.   318

Interview Highlights   318

The Interview   319

Method No. 7: Decision Support Systems   339

"Open Entry, Open Exit" Project Scenario   339

Two Faulty Scenarios   *341*
A More Promising Scenario   *342*
Decision Support System: Expert Choice   344
Selecting a Facility Concept   *345*
Site Selection   *349*
Cost/Benefit Analysis   *349*
Defining Quality of Life   *351*
Decision Support System: Relational Database   351
Virtual Databases   *353*

Insights: Paul R. Neel, F.A.I.A.   356
Comment   356

Insights: John E. Harrigan, Ph.D.   360
Comment   360

References   363

Name Index   367

Subject Index   369

CHAPTER ONE

THE EXECUTIVE ARCHITECT

We will argue in this book that what goes on outside the office, the world of our clients, is more important than what goes on inside the office. This book promotes the premise that competitive success in America and throughout the world requires new strategic thinking, marketing sophistication, innovative professional services, and effective client relations skills. There is a sense of concern in this writing. We, as architects, do not often realize how important we are and how insignificant we can be. We are important when we thoroughly understand the challenges facing our clients and client organizations, and when we deliver effective solutions of notable value. We become insignificant when we do not realize that potential fully, and when we respond to the world outside the office in a superficial manner. This book emphasizes the client side of professional practice to promote a dramatic improvement in the relationship between architects and clients.

Clients are restructuring for the future, looking for the ideal organization, investing their professional, service, technical, and production personnel with the responsibility for creating the road to success. Competing within a challenging economy, clients and client organizations are creating their own lifestyles and cultures. The way clients are looking to the future requires that we study our client's situation more than we have ever done before. If we are to succeed, we must learn a great deal about how clients are organized and what strategies underlie their way of doing business. As client organizations improve their corporate and business practices, we have to make similar progress. We have to see ourselves as executives as much as we see ourselves as architects. To help achieve this, we have created the figure of the "executive architect": the person with the responsibility to increase profits, be a performance leader, and establish a competitive image of the firm and its professional services.

We face a world of unlimited opportunity. Cultures are evolving, economies are expanding, technology is advancing, the daily life of people is becoming more complex, and the need for perfected physical settings and planned developments is becoming more pressing. In an economy where every region of the world is expanding simultaneously, the desire for a high quality of life at work, at home, and in the community has intensified. To make economic, social, and cultural evolution our opportunity, we must look beyond the everyday aspects of professional practice and seek to learn as much as possible about the client's world. How do we attain the management sophistication needed to gain new commissions and contracts? How do we develop our potential for future growth and establish a market reputation for the opportunities we are in practice to attain? The answers are always found in the world of our clients.

To the Readers

The executive architect concept will help you live outside your office, studio, or classroom and enter the world of clients, investors, and stakeholders. To do this you must study these pages as if you were learning a new language, with all the emphasis on vocabulary, structure, and comprehension. As you study the chapters of this book, think about a recent building design or land development project. How would application of the executive architect concept have improved this work? Think about a future project—how would you apply the concept? Please, take this point to heart. You must modify and improve the basic material presented here.

Let's present one word two ways:

life   and   生 命

The first presentation was formed mechanically, by pressing keys. The second presentation was formed by hand. This difference between mechanical forms and ideograms is the basic premise of the executive architect concept. Nothing here is impersonal. Everything requires your skill, perceptions, and unique characterizations.

The Professional Reader

Our goal is to motivate you to think as your clients think. The future of the professional practice of architecture is predictable. We will go in as many directions as our clients and client organizations go. Responding to the opportunities and challenges created by clients, we must expand the current boundaries of professional practice, providing every service necessary for the achievement of building value, performance, and image. Don't underestimate the challenge. Searching for opportunity, many architects have the feeling they are going down an unknown river with many bends and a lot of white water, or sailing with a chart that doesn't show reefs and shoals, or worse, shows them in the wrong place. It seems that marketing sophistication and effective business development strategies are needed. Clients are becoming increasingly knowledgeable and sophisticated about their investments in the built environment. How well we understand these new demands will determine our future.

Gilbert D. Cooke, A.I.A., Cal Poly's director of architecture, a dedicated reader of the manuscript, concluded that the concept of the executive architect has always been part of the history of the profession. From his perspective, we have stressed enduring fundamentals that, in one form or another, are common within the professional practice of architecture. He recognizes that the original aspect of this work is the degree of organization achieved and the efficiency with which client and client organization challenges are met. He suggests that the reader may see what is presented as merely common sense and as something you already know and do all the time. This may be true. However, Professor Cooke and the authors suggest that common sense and daily work without a guiding vision, a high degree of organization, and the means to develop a knowledge base of experience is not good business, nor is it good service to clients, investors, and stakeholders.

The Student Reader

This book prepares you to deal with the challenging world of practice. Although the professional practice of architecture combines business, design, and technology, architecture is taught primarily as an artistic endeavor. Your professional education has not profited sufficiently from advances in corporate and business management practices, nor from the experiences of the men and women who are in practice today. This book will enable you to think realistically about your professional responsibilities and understand the demands that will be placed on you. What you learn here will make you both a better designer and a leader in the building industry.

The Faculty Reader

What happens when architectural graduates enter professional offices? In a very short period of time, they are placed in positions of responsibility that require sophistication in attracting clients and distinguishing the firm in the eyes of prospective clients. This is something for which they receive little training. The needed capabilities are eventually learned, but learning how to lead is too often an expensive and stressful experience. We want your graduates to avoid management by trial and error. We want them to start their professional careers with a notable degree of organization and efficiency supported by the best of insights and methods. When client opportunities are addressed, we want to see common sense combined with methodology. These are some of the lessons we believe are found in this book and presented in a manner that facilitates a thorough understanding of the world of our clients. These lessons belong in the professional practice curricula, fourth- and fifth-year design studios, and professional and executive graduate programs.

During his first reading of this book, Gilbert D. Cooke, A.I.A., cautioned that some professors might hesitate to address the complexities of engaging clients and client organizations, believing that students have enough to learn. On the other hand, he firmly believes that architecture majors are talented people with remarkable potential. He sees them as career-oriented students with a high level of motivation. He knows they will respond to this work with accelerated professional growth.

The Corporate Reader

If you are a corporate, business, or institutional executive, we hope you will read this book, and go on to ask more from your architects. We want clients and client organizations to challenge our thinking regarding building value, performance, and image with the same regard for innovation that guides our work.

The Two Pathways: Insights and Methods

The principal themes of this book—to create a dramatic improvement in the relationships between architects and clients, to enhance and expand the spectrum of our services, and to learn how to present ourselves so that clients will accept fees that truly represent the value of our work—promote the transformation of the professional practice of architecture. This transformation process stresses the engagement of clients in terms of their strategic thinking and planning and every aspect of their endeavors, critical success factors, and investment risks. When we engage clients and client organizations in this fashion, we need the skills of both an architect and an executive. We need to understand executive leadership and action, how we should work and how our clients do work. To this end, the chapters of this book form a strategy for energetically engaging the world of the client. Each chapter presents insights and methods. The insights make it clear that there are things to be learned, trials to undertake, and skills to establish. The methods comprise a process of analysis that is the basis for achieving a sense of cooperation, collaboration, and shared responsibility between the client organization and the architect.

We use the word "insights" to suggest that our understanding of the transformation process can be enriched by the experiences of architects and clients. The insights presented in this book originate from interviews with principals of small, medium and large practices, corporate architects, architect/developers, developers of knowledge systems, and clients. The term "methods" refers to all the things we do to make our work clear and concise, complete and correct. Insights alone are not sufficient to transform a practice to one wholly engaged in the world of clients and client organizations. We need methods that help identify opportunities, create innovations, and evolve the strategies needed to achieve what we believe is promising or necessary. We need methods that help us find, understand, and keep clients. The principal theme of the methods presented is the translation of data and information into knowledge. To this end, as much care was given to the crafting of the methods presented in this book as was given to the formation of insights. The concern was not for perfecting exhaustive method applications, but for directing simple applications wisely.

Together, the insights and methods form a process for engaging clients with the greatest possible sense of partnership. We are approaching what Kenichi Ohmae (1990: 214) identifies as the time for opportunity, the time to explore the world "out there," to link our executive action to the the daily play of forces and activities and decisions within the world of our clients. Staying with the promise of unlimited opportunity, we must consider at this time not only the need to bring professional mastery to our practices, but also the need to stimulate the creative process, to test the ideas that emerge, to work out their strategy implications, and to invest in the development of high-potential ideas, as impossible as these may seem at the moment (Ohmae, 1982).

Insights

We have relied on professionals in the building industry to provide the insights needed to support the transformation of architectural practice. Each of our contributing architects —Charles Luckman, F.A.I.A.; Arthur Gensler, F.A.I.A.; Jeffrey Heller, F.A.I.A.; Jim Brecht, A.I.A.; Fred Foote, F.A.I.A.; Judy Rowe, F.A.I.A.; and Doug Austin, F.A.I.A.—is an outstanding professional well-versed in working with client organizations. Each exemplifies the concept of the executive architect, as well as being an accomplished designer. We have represented their professional work so we can appreciate that they are as invested in design as the very best of architects known primarily for their emphasis on building image. Professor Paul Chinowsky, Don Willcox, Executive Facility Manager, and David Gensler, M.B.A., provide exceptional service to clients, as demonstrated by their management views and research experiences. The emphasis in each interview is on a thorough way of thinking, the points and counterpoints of an expanding professional practice.

These interviews provided the topics for the chapters of this book. Many elements of executive leadership were identified by the professional firms we worked with while studying the dimensions of executive action. As a starting point, the authors presented the prospectus for this book to fifteen architectural firms. Individually and in groups, we reviewed the proposed topics of this book and their relevancy to the development of leaders for the building industry. These discussions were remarkable in that, within five minutes, everyone in the room was intensely involved in sharing insights and concerns. As a result of this experience, this book mirrors the world of professional practice, its concerns and opportunities.

Janet Harrigan, who managed the interview effort, suggests that it is very important that we do more than merely read the interviews. We must analyze them, distilling them into principles. Nothing is more practical than a good insight when it encompasses many situations and can be translated into action. A thoughtful study of the interviews will reveal the value of Charles Luckman's competitive strategies, Art Gensler's dedication to the people around him, Jeffrey Heller's recognition that there are design opportunities everywhere, Jim Brecht's proficient handling of all aspects of development, Don Willcox's skills in conceptual estimating, Fred Foote's capability to deal with project exigencies, Judy Rowe's competence in setting standards and specifications that serve as criteria of success, Paul Chinowsky's knowledge development expertise, David Gensler's ability to consider facility and real estate expenditures in terms of payoff to the client, and Doug Austin's ability to maintain his focus on architecture's three principal criteria: value, performance, and image. An aggragate of expertise like this is our ideal. When the building design and land development team is rich in experience and expertise and works wisely, a comprehensive and thorough response to our client obligations is possible.

Here are some of the questions to which our contributors responded:

- What are you doing to understand the challenge of changing markets?
- What do you see your competitors doing that seems to work?
- What are you doing to differentiate your firm in the eyes of potential clients?
- How do you evaluate a client's situation and views?
- How do you build up an association of trust?
- How about conflicting views? For instance, when a recommended design feature appears too costly to a client, how do you defend your view?

- Do you see opportunity in international projects and alliances? What are your guidelines for accepting such projects?
- Where do you get your business development and people management ideas? What do you read? Who do you listen to?

Methods

Insight that is not paired with appropriate methodology makes us vulnerable to the dangers associated with faulty assumptions and incomplete speculations. Likewise, methodology that is blind to purpose and intent is a danger. Another important aspect of methodology is that it must be practical in terms of the constraints of time, funds, and personnel that are the common limitations of professional practice. Our methods were verified as being useful and practical.

The methods presented in Chapters 2 and 3, critical thinking and thorough analysis, stress the importance of precise, thorough, and comprehensive thinking. Critical thinking is the most important of all the methods presented. It provides the foundation for leadership, for defining opportunity in your terms, and for the concepts needed to direct and expand the assets of your firm. Thorough analysis is linked to critical thinking. Without the progression from critical thinking to thorough analysis, critical thinking is only speculation, but when thorough analysis is paired with critical thinking, we are forced to consider opportunity and innovation in concrete terms. Thorough analysis is not a formalized process; it is an open process designed to help us think about the future and how best to approach it. Each client's project is worthy of the most intense critical analysis; we must apply argument to research findings and evidence to design proposals. Our work must combine information and methodology with insight and spontaneity, moving back and forth between fact and experimentation. This is an essential element for success.

Client assessment strategy, presented in Chapter 4, contains perspectives useful for learning from clients and learning about clients. This method suggests that we approach clients with the possibility that we will reject current standard ideas because that is exactly what sophisticated client organizations are doing. We want clients to see that we recognize opportunity and innovation as the heart of our service, in the same way that they consider these the essential core of enterprise. Chapters 5, 6, and 7 present a Knowledge Base System, field study undertakings, and research techniques that, in combination, provide a detailed understanding of the client's situation. In the last chapter, the discussion of decision support systems suggests formats for developing thorough problem-solving capabilities.

The use of these seven methods will assure clients that you are skilled in translating their expectations and requirements into design concepts, schemes, forms, and features. These methods will help you identify what clients, investors, and stakeholders see as the most important aspects of spaces, buildings, facilities, and planned developments. These methods promote a single-minded attention to achievement of a high quality of life at work, at home, and in the community.

The Transformation of Professional Practice

Our discussion of the insights and methods needed to transform our practices is often presented in a spirited fashion. At the same time, the concept is formed around a practical strategic prescription. Note that there is no paradox in combining the practical with the spirit of innovation. This is what the professional practice of architecture is all about, what makes our services unique. The authors and contributors feel that an architect's greatest responsibility is to create a new reality for people and our communities. While we recognize that this quest for new forms of architecture leavens our profession, it is not paradoxical to say that the world of our clients and client organizations demands practical executive action. This view was confirmed in an afternoon discussion that took place in Sacramento, California. We met with seven local architects at the office of John Stafford, A.I.A. It was a warm, sunny, California day, so we settled down on the patio. We had before us cool drinks and an article from *Progressive Architecture* entitled "Can This Profession Be Saved?" This article analyzes the reasons why there are fewer jobs for architects (Fisher, 1994). Our conclusion was that while the numbers were correct, these numerical analyses obscured the opportunities before us, as such analyses often do. In fact, we were all resentful of the title. While everyone admitted that the immediate demands of maintaining a successful practice were stressful and enormously competitive, each was ready to invest himself and his practice in an effort to grow as clients and client organizations placed new challenges before us.

A Practical Strategic Prescription

The Sacramento meeting generated one important consensus: we cannot continue to accept the view that when times are good we will prosper and when times are bad we will suffer. We examined the possibilities for improving and expanding client services in order to stablize our businesses. To achieve this, we must move from a business of commissioned services to one of direct participation in all of our client's endeavors, where productive participation establishes us as trusted partners, the currency for a continuing relationship.

Forming partnerships of trust with clients is the most demanding challenge facing the executive architect. The best results come when clients fully understand the extent to which architects can contribute to the resolution of their organization's most challenging problems. The only way to accomplish this understanding is to engage the client's entire organization. As depicted in Figure 1.1, we see ourselves as having something to contribute across the entire spectrum of client endeavors in terms of how their businesses are organized, what work customs and management philosophies underlie their way of doing business, their critical success factors, and the investment risks of which we must constantly be aware.

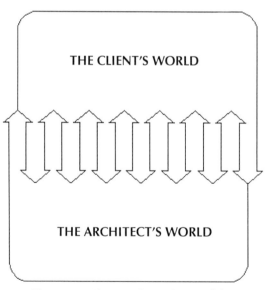

Figure 1.1. The transformation model.

The elements for transforming a practice to one wholly engaged in the world of clients and client organizations are developed in the chapters entitled Leadership, Strategy, Client Relations, Working with Clients, Quality of Life, Knowledge Development, and Value, Performance, and Image—a progression from the theoretical to the applied. When you study what is presented, remember that the full potential of the executive architect concept can be realized only when it is customized for your situation.

CHAPTER 2: LEADERSHIP

Leadership is the primary resource for transforming a practice. A competitive leader maintains a vision of unlimited opportunities. The search for opportunity never ends. It is what keeps you in business. Open to all possibilities, the executive architect experiments with ideas and methods and works to develop new capabilities within the firm.

CHAPTER 3: STRATEGY

Successful strategy for a professional practice takes what you are, where you want to go, looks to the outside for opportunity, plays with the idea of innovations, identifies required resources and skills, and produces action plans. An effective executive architect is alert to economic trends likely to transform market requirements and works to anticipate technological, social, economic, and environmental events that may provide opportunity. When you create such a focus you can concentrate on your unique identity. The goal is to differentiate your firm so you are positioned to control events rather than have events control you.

CHAPTER 4: CLIENT RELATIONS

This discussion is directed to the ground that was lost when architects became so unfocused that they allowed the intrusion of competitors who are, in fact, less knowledgeable about building value, performance, and image. We stress that a total focus on your client's risks and critical success factors is essential. What kind of executive action is this? The kind that builds a practice. When an organization finances a new government center or a new manufacturing facility, dedicating precious capital resources, risks are always involved. If you can demonstrate that you understand these risks, the client will soon become committed to your success.

CHAPTER 5: WORKING WITH CLIENTS

The strategy here is to make client representatives feel they are members of the project team and as responsible for project success as you are. If you allow client representatives to become spectators, you throw away the opportunity to put their knowledge, experience, and skills to use. Though groups of individuals have much in common, important individual differences always exist. The goal of collaboration with client representatives will always be to take the individual into the realm of judgment, to encourage the feeling that personal views are valuable and should not be held back.

CHAPTER 6: QUALITY OF LIFE

The most important aspect of improving quality of life at work, at home, and in the community is to determine what is important to your clients and the project stakeholders. Our contributors have made the study of people the core of their practices. They have learned to give weight to intangible variables and the consideration of the needs and wants of individuals. They experiment with the idea that we don't provide buildings, we provide experiences. You will find this a most useful thought. We argue that quality of life cannot be achieved without an understanding of the actual processes by which people live, as opposed to what we believe exists. Every step in a building design or land development project must be placed in the context of the client's thoughts and actions.

CHAPTER 7: KNOWLEDGE DEVELOPMENT

As the antecedent of opportunity and innovation, knowledge is the executive architect's most essential resource. Knowledge is what executive architects use to direct the crossovers between the world outside the office and the world inside the office. Working to establish opportunity for the firm, they look to the future, while carefully considering the assets of the firm and identifying where new assets have to be developed. If you identify the things to which your clients are paying attention, their challenge is your opportunity.

CHAPTER 8: VALUE, PERFORMANCE, AND IMAGE

The ability to provide services within the three-fold criteria of building value, performance, and image is the most marketable aspect of professional architectural services. To prevail over our competitors in the building industry, we must promote the extraordinary value of this professional service. This is the central endeavor as we lead the transformation of a professional practice.

Application Possibilities

Working with corporate and institutional clients presents one of the most promising opportunities to promote the transformation model. To help understand the implications of this, we can review one of the cases that helped us realize the value of working with clients as they think about facility development strategies. In this project, we confirmed the value of architectural services that verify project concepts and worth before capital is invested. We learned that we can exceed our client's expectations and revise possibly simplistic views of architectural services.

The project site was in a Japanese metropolitan center. The client's goal was to develop an Office/Home Design Center in which product manufacturers and professional service entities could lease space to display and market their products and services. In this instance, the client had already commissioned a building design, in which the ground floor scheme included only a reception area, lounge seating, and access to the elevators. This meant, from our point of view, that the most valuable customer service space was nothing more than a stylish setting. No advantage was taken of the opportunity to inform visitors about all the services available to them in the building. Likewise, the plan for the upper floors would have limited revenue to the simple leasing of space. Our service, based on an identification of the full potential of the enterprise, led to a ground floor with customer consultation services, a mutipurpose hall, several classrooms, a restaurant, and specialty retail stores. Each of the upper floors was centered around a service island linked to a network server providing access to product and service information. One floor was devoted to providing services to professionals in the building industry, including computer-aided design (CAD) workstations to be used by small professional firms in the area who could not afford such equipment. The result of our consultation was that, in addition to leased space, the client would gain revenue from the specialty retail stores, restaurant, roof-top lounge, rented spaces and equipment, and subscriptions from corporations, professional firms, and families wishing a close association with the activities occurring in the center. Just as significant for potential revenue was that this increased level of activity would permit higher lease rates. Without our full partnership with the client, these possibilities would have been unrecognized. A simple commission to design a building is always a mistake on the part of the client.

A VARIETY OF APPLICATIONS

The transformation of a professional practice means that we will engage clients with many different objectives, such as:

* Corporate and institutional executive boards formulating strategies for facility development and capital investment.
* Corporate and institutional project and facility managers responsible for managing their organization's undertakings.
* Institutions and corporations recycling buildings by means of extensive renovations.
* Land developers with a concern for the marketability and community acceptability of their projects.
* Architecture/Engineering/Construction corporations working on complex projects, such as the development of science cities and residential/industrial complexes.
* Home builders, both traditional contractors and prefabricated construction corporations.
* Investment bankers trying to determine the merit of a proposed development project.
* Corporate managers and engineers developing new building technologies.
* Manufacturers of home and office furnishings, fixtures, and equipment seeking to develop new products.
* International development corporations challenged by local lifestyle considerations and cultural concerns.
* Real estate executives selling options to interested investors.
* Public institutions responsible for local, regional, and national land development and community building projects.
* Neighborhood and community groups working to make their needs and concerns known to developers and government agencies.

Hidden Assets

Is it possible to present our services in such a way that clients will accept fees worthy of our value? The answer to this question is directly related to the assets created by the executive architect. When compared with large corporations, midsized companies, and even many small businesses, architectural practices generally have limited resources. This is true if you consider only highly visible, easily measured assets such as facilities, employee numbers, and market size. However, consider the other side of the coin, what Itami (1987) calls "invisible assets." Our greatest invisible assets are the values inherent in architecture and our professional sense of client and community responsibility. Foremost in the mind of the executive architect is the development of strategies for gaining the trust of prospective clients, another important asset, and establishing the strongest possible partnership between the architect and his or her client. Richard Young, A.I.A., notes that our usual situation—waiting for a request for services, competing with others for the job, and, all too often, accepting lower fees as a competitive strategy—must no longer be our common experience. What we can do for clients must be made known.

Participation as a trusted partner in a client's strategic thinking and planning is our goal. Certainly, your attempts to do this will be immediately appreciated by prospective clients. In many ways, our professional practices are ahead of our clients' way of doing business. Success for client organizations is related to the realization of the fullest possible benefits from the work of professionals, technicians, and staff. To achieve this, our clients seem to be heading in our direction; that is, toward the benefits associated with small, independent groups organized to realize their full potential. In this instance, clients can learn as much from us as we learn from them. We are a model of the kind of organization structure they need. The movement in corporate restructuring is about the values that maintain purpose and personal commitment. When we share our way of conducting business, our clients' future and the future of our profession become one.

Insights

Charles Luckman, F.A.I.A.

When we left Charles Luckman's office at the conclusion of our interview, we each had an autographed copy of his book, Twice in a Lifetime. *You should read this book before you read the one in your hands. When you share a day with Mr. Luckman, it is the education of a lifetime.*

A magna cum laude *graduate from the School of Architecture at the University of Illinois, Charles Luckman also became a candidate for Tau Beta Pi, the highest honorary engineering society in the nation. Mr. Luckman is one of only a few architects in the country to be invited into this society.*

As candidates for membership, Mr. Luckman and eleven engineering students were required to take a six-hour written examination that was both mind-boggling and backbreaking. Two weeks later it was announced publicly that the engineers had passed and Charles Luckman had failed. It was then decided that Charles should be given an oral examination. The hour and a half session involved questioning so technical in nature that Charles didn't know what the words meant, let alone what the questions meant.

The next morning it was publicly announced on the campus that he had failed the oral examination. Nonetheless, the Dean of Men personally invited him to attend the awards banquet, telling him to come with his head held high. When the dinner was over the Dean of the School of Engineering first returned the test envelopes so each candidate could see his mistakes. They were shocked to see that the envelopes had never been opened.

The Dean then explained to the audience that this had all been part of an initiation ceremony. Also, on certain occasions Tau Beta Pi decided that one electee would be given the "business" before admission to the society. Mr. Luckman rose and took his bow. The sound of laughter and applause was music to his ears. Upon graduation in June of 1931, Mr. Luckman had no job and three hopelessly nonnegotiable documents: a college diploma, a marriage license, and an architect's license.

Because of the lack of construction during the depression in 1931, Mr. Luckman took a "temporary" job with a large soap company, which advertised that it needed a young man who could draw for its advertising department. This turned out to be an eighteen-year detour from architecture and the beginning of a meteoric career in business.

He was soon transferred to sales, and rose rapidly from a store-to-store salesman to become president of Pepsodent Company at age 32 and president of all the American companies of Lever Brothers at age 37. In both situations, he inherited companies that were in serious trouble. Morale, sales, and profits were at an all-time low. Under his leadership, sales and profits of both companies reached record high levels.

During this time he contributed to our national culture in three ways: in 1937 he put "The Bob Hope Show" on the air for Pepsodent, in 1949 he formed the design concepts for Lever House on Park Avenue, and in 1950 he returned to architecture.

Creating such landmarks as the Los Angeles International Airport, Cape Canaveral Missile Test Center, Madison Square Garden, and Boston's Prudential Center, he was honored by election to the College of Fellows of the American Institute of Architects. Recognized by eight presidents from Harry Truman to Ronald Reagan as a man who would take on a nation's problems and succeed, and awarded France's Legion of Honor, England's Order of St. John, and Italy's Star of Solidarity, Charles Luckman has always served where needed.

Here is one instance that dramatically illustrates the many lessons to be found in *Twice in a Lifetime* (Luckman, 1988:291–292):

> Edwards Air Force Base was the biggest assignment, potentially, that had come our way. If our final master plan was approved, we would have the inside track to become the architects for the construction of the air base, which would cost $300 million.
>
> The key element in the assignment was not design—the military folks weren't concerned with the appearance of the new installation but with its function. The basic ingredient for us was research, and we spent many weeks conferring with the Air Force Research and Development people. I spent nights poring over books and technical journals to learn the lingo of jet aircraft so that I could talk intelligently with our client.
>
> We had to learn what the air force people thought would be built in the future in the way of jet and supersonic aircraft. We had to plan for planes that had not yet been built, and help determine the length and thickness of runways such planes would need; how to control the high level of noise on the field; where to place the storage tanks for safety and efficiency. Beyond that, we had to learn how best to

get the fuel to the planes; what kind of emergency equipment was needed; how extensive a communication network was required—all in addition to the usual planning of buildings, barracks, and hangers.

We set up a team of architects, designers, engineers, and consultants for the project. Two months later we had to present our detailed master plan for the project to General Patrick Partridge, the commanding officer of the Air Research and Development Command. It was with considerable trepidation that I walked into ARDC headquarters in Baltimore with my team of "experts" and faced General Partridge. His staff numbered some twenty colonels and majors.

Because that assignment was so important to us, I broke with the usual architectural practice of showing clients only the beautifully drawn final plan we were recommending. It seemed to me our clients would be better served if they saw all the alternatives we had tried and rejected before we came to our final recommendation. I didn't want a client wondering if we had explored all avenues. My premise was that we had to anticipate every alternative a client could imagine because if at the end of a presentation a client was able to ask a basic question, it meant we hadn't done our job adequately.

Explaining the forty large sheets of drawings, each showing a different approach to a master plan for the base, I was on my feet for almost two hours. I gave my "flip-flop" chart presentation of comparative analyses of all the alternatives, together with the pluses and minuses of each. I concluded with our final drawings, saying, "This is what we recommend . . . ." When I finished, General Partridge turned to his staff and said, "Gentlemen, I've seen everything I need and am ready to approve their plan."

Another significant opportunity created by the Luckman firm's investment in knowledge development is demonstrated in the following story (Luckman, 1988: 353).

As the second largest city in the country and the major tourist attraction on the West Coast, Los Angeles needed a new zoo by the beginning of the sixties. It was apparent to anyone that the rather mediocre prewar zoo did not compare to the one in San Diego, one of the finest in the world, but the voters had several times rejected bond issues for a new zoo.

To my mind it was simply presenting a new plan with a new idea for a zoo. Therefore, we decided to send a research team to study and analyze the major zoos in the country. We would then know enough to make recommendations for a master plan. In the autumn of 1962, Mayor Sam Yorty finally pushed through a bond issue to build a "Greater Los Angeles World Zoo," and we were well prepared. Competing with twenty-two other firms, our advance research work helped us to be named architects for that intriguing project.

Mr. Luckman's lessons are not limited to preparation, research, and presentation strategies. Returning to architecture from business, he introduced market research concepts to the field. He asked his architects to find out what workers in office buildings like and want, what patients in hospitals like and want, what spectators at sporting events like and want. His buildings reflect what the people want, not what architects think they should have!

Regarding the value amenities add to the client's investment, let's look at the case of Madison Square Garden. Some critics complained that "more than half the site was wasted on plazas, landscaping, trees, flowers, and fountains." Mr. Luckman's reply was, "In overcrowed New York City, this complex has given the people a great deal of open space with the amenities that they like. It will make those new buildings more valuable, and will pay financial benefits for a long, long time to come" (1988: 341).

This lesson was first seen in the design philosophy he created for the Lever House, where the entire ground floor is open space, filled with gardens for the people. Again, there were critics. "Who in his right mind would waste all that valuable Park Avenue ground-floor space?" developers asked. Nonetheless, Mr. Luckman has shown that amenities pay. Even when "creativity" was the vision, 94 percent of his projects have been completed within budget.

Mr. Luckman's views about professional growth can be found in his comments (1988: 343–344) that:

> One of the most difficult hurdles for an architect is to get that first assignment in a new field. The architect who does beautiful homes isn't given office buildings to design. The architect who does office buildings doesn't get churches or schools. We were primarily known for our master planning, our large government and military projects, our hospitals, office buildings, and sports facilities.
>
> When a prospective client from Philadelphia came in with $5 million to spend if we could come up with a new idea for a motel-hotel, we were intrigued and delighted. Assignments in new fields are the challenge and fun in architecture. They keep architects on their toes. It means more research, more learning. Something new is the best preventive medicine against fatigue in your work, your career, and your life.

Regarding executive leadership, Mr. Luckman advances the view that the human element is at the root of business success. Regardless of the sophisticated technology at the disposal of management, it is the enthusiasm of the people involved in making and selling things that determines the operating effectiveness of an organization. If managers want men and women to willingly use the latest advances that science and technology can provide, they must show them the benefits that will accrue to them in the process; that is, how they will make more money and have a more satisfying work life.

Mr. Luckman's final lesson is the keynote for all the following pages (1988:357):

> The art of marketing a product, a service, a person, or a company lies in determining and then advertising those things that are unique and distinctive. Whether you're selling toothpaste, soap, or an architectural firm, your special, individual experience is as important as any other single ingredient. You have to demonstrate to the public just what makes you different from, and better than, your competitors.

Read Critically

During this writing, we maintained a healthy skepticism about everything we developed. We are aware that theorizing often follows fad and fashion without serious thought, that it can be influenced by the ebb and flow of economic circumstance in a careless fashion. We know that there are more prayer books disguised as management readings in the business section of a transcontinental flight than are found in pews of churches. There are more medicine men on the stages of business seminars than in all the places of rite and ritual. On the other hand, there is wisdom out there in vast amounts and we have tried to bring it to you in the most practical form possible. However, if you just read this book, it will only be a "read." If you read critically and try to incorporate the presented concepts, insights, and methods into your practice, you will create for yourself new strategic thinking, marketing sophistication, innovative professional services, and effective client relations skills.

Three friends in their younger days. Charles Luckman, Bing Crosby, and Bob Hope

Madison Square Garden and million square foot office building, New York, New York. Cable-suspended roof in Madison Square Garden eliminated all interior columns.

California Federal Savings and Loan Headquarters, Los Angeles, California.

United California Bank, Los Angeles, California (now First Interstate Bank), a 62-story office building.

The Forum, Inglewood, California. The home of the Lakers and the Kings.

Prudential Center, Boston, Massachusetts, a $300 million complex. (Photo Courtesy of Aerial Photos International, Inc.)

NASA Space Center, Cape Canaveral, Florida; lift-off of the "Columbia." (Photo Courtesy of NASA.)

NASA Manned Spacecraft Center, Houston, Texas.

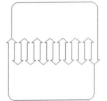

CHAPTER TWO

LEADERSHIP

If you study what our contributors say about leadership, you will find they maintain two primary objectives: find an opportunity and develop a well-considered assessment of the challenge presented by the client. They follow the rule that total client satisfaction can only be achieved if you develop the essential ability to focus attention on the task at hand with a certain degree of freedom from first or obvious conclusions drawn from personal preference or the dynamics of the moment. Open to all possibilities, they experiment with ideas and methods. They act after an experience-based judgement is made between what is critical to an undertaking and what is of lesser consequence.

Unlimited Opportunity Is the Most Promising Vision

The contributors believe that their professional abilities can provide a service of outstanding value to clients. When you believe that what you have to offer is of critical importance, there is no hesitancy in promoting your services. You can forthrightly say that you know something other people don't know, or that you are capable of achieving something that is impossible for others to achieve.

A competitive mind maintains a vision of unlimited opportunities. Everyone who contributed to this book is gifted at sensing and pursuing opportunities and creating a highly competitive organization. Arthur Gensler notes that 85 percent of his work is repeat business. This highly favorable business condition is related to his recognition of the value of offering sophisticated services to clients. Doug Austin, Fred Foote, and Jeffrey Heller find opportunity in providing the highest standard of professional service based on their ability to understand exactly what each client sees as a successful project outcome. As a corporate architect, Judy Rowe finds opportunity in providing her corporation with the means to assure quality achievements in every hospital and medical office building project. The relationship between professional value and knowledge development is clearly shown by Paul Chinowsky's accomplishments. David Gensler creates opportunity by using his insights into the corporate world as the means to attract clients. Jim Brecht finds opportunity as an architect/developer, realizing the many advantages of involving architects at every step of a project. Don Willcox sees a future built on partnerships between owners, architects, and contractors.

Build a High-Performance Practice

The search for opportunity never ends. It is what keeps you in business. Challenged by this search, the executive architect works to develop new capabilities within the firm. Though we have tried to avoid the jargon of management theorists, we make an exception with the term "high-performance practice." It seems that everything management theorists offer turns murky when put into practice, including the concept of high performance. Fortunately, someone steps forward in a confusing situation and turns obscurity into a formula for practical action. That is the executive architect's responsibility. It is the executive architect who must maintain the pace, tempo, and spirit associated with high performance, create utility from advances in technology, and provide opportunity that totally engages the abilities of the firm's associates and staff.

A primary value of a high-performance practice is its significance for clients. When clients recognize a commonality between how they compete and how the architectural firm competes, a sense of shared standards develops. A high-performance practice will encompass every advance in knowledge and technology and emphasize a commitment to continuous improvement. When you increase your intellectual capital, stretching your mind with new ideas, you will never go back to a simple view of practice.

Renew Your Intellectual Capital

You can't buy intellectual capital; it is something you develop. Deciding what to learn is best determined by those who have to do the work. Jim Brecht and Doug Austin believe that management consultants are not particularly helpful. Doug says that he has spent a lot of money on management consultants and now wishes he had gone to someone more knowledgeable about architectural services. Jim recounts his lack of regard for this kind of help. He tells the story about the management consultant who came in, talked to everyone, and proposed a grand scheme, a scheme that appeared mostly to be a positioning for a follow-on contract. What we want to do is create for ourselves the same clean slate we give consultants and the same opportunity for open discussion and critique. We hope you grow to abhor the thought of such things as leadership skills seminars, management by objectives training classes, total quality management retreats, reengineering tutorials, shared-danger executive outings, or ideational brainstorming sessions. There is nothing harmful about these social events unless you consider spur of the moment thinking a danger and lost time and money unacceptable. While each firm has a constant need for renewal, let's be parsimonious by creating retreat agenda that emphasize the following four lessons.

Consider Carefully What People Can Do and What People Are Willing to Do

To help your associates grow professionally you ask, "What can you do? What are you willing to do?" This suggests that leadership begins when you listen to people. Why strive to establish a high-performance firm by telling people what to do and how to do it? You want associates who are active, not passive. You also ask these two questions because human relations show that the poorest return from what you pay in salary and benefits occurs when you use people as a mere means to some end. People need to feel they are necessary to the firm, that their history within the practice will be more than a seemingly random series of events. The owners and principals of the practice must convince associates that their work is not trivial, that what they do cannot be done as well by the next graduate with a B. Arch. degree. Finally, we are always doing more for less, more than what our fees allow, and as a result we are burning people out. When you maintain a practice of hardship, you are the worst of leaders.

Let's consider this lesson in terms of what you can do to motivate people. Your firm employs 25 architects, project managers, and specialists. What are you going to say when you talk one-on-one with the members of the firm? You might create a view of the future that you feel will certainly motivate them to take more responsibility and then, so they know you have heart, ask how they are doing at work and at home and what can you do to help. This is patronization at its worst. The better approach is to lean across the table and ask, "What can you do? What are you willing to do?" These questions tell people you are waiting to hear from them.

Appreciate the Importance of Teamwork as a Pooling of Experience and Expertise

Our contributors know how to lead in a manner that creates a sense of cooperation, collaboration, and shared responsibility throughout their organizations. Don't look for a single figure to dominate; from time to time every one of the firm's principals and associates must assume leadership responsibility. This is the only way to realize the full potential of the firm's professional resources, although there will certainly be prominent figures, such as the firm's founders and owners. Likewise, the principals of the firm must consider themselves executive architects, and be as concerned for the future of the firm as they are for their immediate responsibilities. Further, a recently promoted associate of the firm, being given his or her first major responsibility, must learn how to think and act like an executive architect. People with selected responsibilities, such as those responsible for developing the firm's technological, information, and construction administration assets, have to consider both the world inside the office and the world outside the office. In all these strategically important positions in the firm, leadership is essential and must be developed. The result is that the entire office is one team.

Be Willing to Hustle

A practice that builds in promising directions, seeks a variety of opportunities, and builds expertise and flexibility within the firm so that new directions and opportunities are possible, is a firm on the move. This firm would appreciate one of the more humorous images about opportunity from ancient folklore: a peasant must stand on a hillside with his mouth open for a long time before a roast duck flies in. Not content to wait for that slim chance, every member of such a firm is alert to opportunity. They serve on community boards, join local historical societies and garden clubs, and are active in community fund raising organizations. In other words, each member of the firm must be recognized as a trusted member of the community. Members of the firm must give papers and talks within the building industry and, even more important, in our clients' professional and business conventions and conferences. If we have special knowledge about trends in school design and what these mean for quality education, we must share this with the National Education Association. Special knowledge about high-technology manufacturing facilities must be shared with members of the Society of Manufacturing Engineers. Special knowledge about quality of life in offices and research centers must be shared with chapters of the International Facility Managers Association, the American Management Association, and contract buyers associations. Your responsibility to promote the firm means more than "turning over rocks." It means making a place for yourself in a special market for professional services.

Be Willing to Answer All Questions Related to Cash Flow and Profit Margins

This is the plumb line for all projects. It provides the reference point for all deliberations. The firm's constant battle is with cash flow and profit margins. Several of the professionals interviewed refer to the very different economic climates of the 80's and the 90's, and their effect on the building industry. We are all aware of a variety of difficult business situations related to cash flow and profit margins. How many firms do you know that have had to dissolve the practice because client payment schedules were not adhered to and the standing line of credit at the bank was overdrawn? How many firms have placed themselves in the position where the contracts they signed did not provide the billable hours necessary to do a good job? We have all seen developers close down a project because of an increase in the interest rate or because a construction loan was not available. Sometimes a firm wins a major contract from an institutional client, at the expense of precious overhead monies, and then a new president is appointed who cancels the project. Situations of difficulty arise when a newly elected governing board demands stricter zoning or environmental standards. Perhaps the worst business condition of all occurs when margins and fees are cut below what is professionally ethical, turning the profession into a bazaar

A leader builds assurance in the firm when he or she has the ability to identify profitable innovations, to consider new possibilities. Art Gensler notes that you don't have to accomplish everything in the first tug; you accomplish over a series of stages and steps. The idea is to undertake new activities in a self-funding fashion. Reducing risk by making projects self-funding is a constant element in corporate, business, and institutional organizations. We want to be more modest than is common with management consultants by never starting a strategic undertaking with an investment of funds. First act on a possibility, show some success, and then spend a little.

Insights

M. Arthur Gensler, Jr., F.A.I.A.

Larkspur Landing is a splendid mixed-use development located across the bay from San Francisco in Marin County, on the water's edge. If you take the commuter ferry into San Francisco, it is just a six-block walk up California Street to the office of Gensler and Associates. Larkspur Landing is a perfect setting for combining the life of the City with all the attractions of Marin County and the Northern California coastline. We met Arthur Gensler here for breakfast, as it is only a few minutes from his home.

Arthur devotes a lot of time to fund raising for his alma mater, Cornell, and even more time to encouraging young staff members in their professional development. Of all the people we interviewed and worked with to create the concept of the executive architect, Arthur was the most prepared to contribute to the undertaking. He is a benchmark for the concept. All around us as we had our breakfast and conducted the interview, people were talking about the day ahead and what they might accomplish in the city. Nothing was a distraction for Arthur.

Interview Highlights

Critical reading is a lost art; we all scan. Be sure to pause and consider the implications of Arthur Gensler's thoughts for the professional practice of architecture. Be alert to the following:

- The disturbing thing is that, as a profession, we've walked away from leadership.
- One of the reasons that we're adding additional services is to get profits back up.
- We hire people who do a variety of tasks that were never defined as architecture or interior design or graphic design.
- As for overseas markets, I'm convinced that although we think we sell aesthetics, we're selling knowledge.
- Our role is to help international clients to understand how things really work, from a financial and technological point of view.

- I made a comment a long time ago that you hire and gather around you people who are smarter than you are.
- I team with people I trust and respect, and I build self-respect among all those people, so that the whole is greater than the individual parts.

The Interview

Leadership is a critical topic in our profession right now. I think the profession has sorely lacked leadership in terms of where it's going and what service it provides. I am most concerned right now with finding leaders for our firm. We are growing exponentially: we have fourteen offices and we need to establish more locations. We have clients clamoring for our people to service them. Where do we find the leaders to guide all our projects and teams?

The disturbing thing to me is that architecture as a profession has walked away from leadership. Our firm is starting to offer a variety of services that are different from those offered in the current architectural marketplace. We are basically going back to the point where an architect was the leader of the team. When I entered the profession 35 years ago, architects were the leaders. Unfortunately, over the years they became fearful about liability and as a result they were pushed aside because they did not really understand what was happening. Program managers and construction managers entered the picture, various other people got in, and they all assumed the leadership role while architects were left with the liability. We dropped to a second-tier position, where I am not very comfortable because I can't fully do justice to my client's wishes.

So what our firm is trying to do now, and I think quite successfully, is to go back and take on the leadership responsibilities for a project. That does not mean abdicating design responsibilities or technical knowledge or expertise. But it clearly requires a much broader understanding of the real estate, construction, and financial industries than most architects are prepared to explore. That's what I think is currently lacking in our profession. Architects have pigeonholed themselves into being designers or production specialists or field observers. They have walked away from what I think is the most important role, that of a creative leader. If we don't start out with the right project, we'll never end up with the right project. Often the creative part—what the project ought to be, how it should be put together—is really the issue before any design can even start.

The fact that New York State architectural firms only have principals who are registered architects represents this sort of self-defeating, false protectionism, or cocoonlike thinking. Recently we were talking to a firm about merging their interiors group into our firm. They had formed a separate interiors group, only because the head of this group was a nonarchitect and could never have been part of the regular firm. So they actually had two parallel firms—an interiors firm and an architecture firm—with double books, double everything. When you look at their work, you can literally see a line where the architecture firm stops and the interiors firm starts. What a tragedy for the client, what a silly way to run a business, and what a lack of understanding of the real purpose of architecture.

As architects, we have to change perceptions, we have to change restrictive legislation, we have to go back and change the way architectural school curriculums are set up. It probably even goes back farther than that: we have to attract people into the profession who recognize that a broader scope of expertise is available within the profession than what we have practiced for the last twenty years.

For example I have four sons, two of whom have gone into this business. One is an architect educated at Cornell and one is a businessman educated at Dartmouth and Stanford Business School. Both of them are making incredible contributions to the organization. One son is working on a very sophisticated real estate facilities plan in order to assist with the merger of two financial institutions. We planned and designed the headquarters for one institution, now we'll probably work on the facilities for the merged institutions. But we wouldn't necessarily have gotten that assignment if we didn't have someone who could contribute the creative leadership of understanding finances as well as other aspects of the complex project.

Day after day, we get calls from other major corporations with similar needs. Recently we learned from real estate contacts that Taco Bell needed design and planning input in order to make a decision on where to locate their corporate headquarters. We were brought in as part of the team to add that component. An architectural firm doesn't necessarily have to have all the elements of a team to evaluate real estate decisions. But we certainly ought to be on the initial team, rather than being retained after all the decisions regarding site, costs, budgets, and schedules have been made by people with no design or creative skills, who are only looking at the numbers.

Corporations are poor developers, and someone noted that in the future the developers will all be these real estate investment trusts. Everyone is going to a REIT and it's all driven out of Wall Street, and I know they're going to be poor developers, too. True developers are visionaries; they don't need Excel spreadsheets and long reports to tell them whether a project is going to work out or not. It's a creative, intuitive process, and architects who work with these visionaries have really come up with great results. I'm proud that I've been able to establish a firm that attracts people who have that larger scope and interest. They want to do more than just sit behind a drafting board or a computer screen, coming up with solutions to problems that other people have defined. They want to define and analyze the problem and then create the solution. So that's where our firm is going and where I think the profession needs to go—go back and take over the ground we unfortunately gave up in a very big way over the last twenty years.

My son David works in our Los Angeles office, where he's formed a separate group called "Gensler Information Solutions." David went out and found software that his team uses to help companies manage their facilities, examine strategic issues, and generate solutions. By offering this service, we are clearly stretching the envelope for an "architectural" firm.

Even though we're a private company, every year we publish a regular corporate-style annual report, which contains our final numbers as well as our philosophy, ideas, and activities. The theme of this year's annual report is "Stretch," because I believe the profession has to start stretching instead of building walls around itself and focusing on the protection issue. I compare the process of stretch to a rubber band. The successful project is stretched to a certain point and then you do it. Architects often tend to stretch so far that the rubber band breaks, or the project fails, because they are trying to do too much with a project and they don't really know what they are doing. They are so into building for themselves, rather than for the client, that they fail to realize that they have taken a project too far.

I also believe that when you stretch something, it never goes back to where it originally was, so you move things along. We have clients for whom we are constantly doing additional work—85 percent of our firm's work is repeat business. Each time we work with them we stretch them and they stretch us, and we move along in the process. We achieve results over a series of stages and steps. It's a realistic way of innovating and creating that is really more powerful and wonderful than trying to break all the rules at one time in order to gain notoriety. I think architects often don't have as the end result meeting the budget, adhering to the schedule, or solving the problem. The finished project may look great in a magazine, but God knows who's going to ever use it, and it doesn't solve anything financially. There's a lot of that happening in our profession, and I also think there's a lot of it outside the profession. Every day I deal with close friends and competitors who are providing really quality service. We go out in the marketplace and compete for work, and there are some very fine and knowledgeable competitors out there. There are also others who make me wonder what they're offering.

Another interesting point is that frequently we receive requests for proposals that just say "design it" or "do the documents" or "get it built." We submit our fee, another firm submits its fee, and another does as well. But then we go back to the client and offer to also manage the project, for a program management fee. We just hired five or six program managers for that purpose. So, we are hired to run the project, and we're back to where we were twenty years ago as architects—when we were the agent for the owner, and we really led the project. But the difference is that now we have to divide the project into two fee pieces because the owner wants to compare our fee against the other firm's fee. In order to get a reasonable fee to do what ought to be done anyway, we have to break it into the design fee and the program management fee. It's fine if you want to call it two different things, but it's what architectural service ought to be. So, we're now doing pre-design, design service, and post-design. We are hiring people who perform a variety of tasks that were never defined as architecture or interior design or graphic design. We're doing product design, we're doing all sorts of leadership tasks. Again, that's part of this whole process of stretching, stretching the services that we provide.

I think the most wonderful part of all this is that an architectural education is one of the best trainings for business leadership. It teaches you a wonderful way of thinking, which is not linear, but more spherical. It allows you to think about issues in a multifaceted way without focusing in a linear way. Many people with architectural training have finally come to the conclusion that they really don't want to work for an architectural firm, and many of them have become leaders in other fields. I am proud of that, and it's fun to deal with those people because they have at least a sense of what our firm is doing.

As for overseas markets, I'm convinced that although we think we sell aesthetics, we're really selling knowledge. There are some very talented designers in international markets, but many don't understand how to integrate the functional, the technological, and the team structure into the process. They don't know how to get a project built very well, and the economics have not been fine-tuned or refined. Our role is to help international clients understand how things really work, from a financial, functional, and technological point of view. When you combine that with good design, you have something of real value. When we go out into an international market, our clients look for those qualities.

It's also important to be able to communicate with people who either do not speak your language or have only a rudimentary understanding of it. Clients want people who can communicate with them and feel comfortable doing it. Unfortunately, 99 percent of Americans don't speak a foreign language well enough to be able to communicate, so the client is almost always the one who has to come to us from a language point of view, rather than our going to them. That's a sad statement on architectural education. At Cornell, I had to have three years training in a foreign language, or two years of two languages as a high school graduate. I had three years of Latin in high school, and a lot of good that's done me! I probably would never have graduated from Cornell or anywhere else if there had been a language requirement because I am horrible at foreign languages. But language clearly is an issue for me now that I am working with people around the world. I've learned to work with interpreters, and I've learned to communicate in other ways. As a profession we can't just communicate with drawings, we have to really understand what is going on in a particular country, the social, cultural, and political issues. It's easy to say or do some awfully dumb things without realizing it. So, all of us in the firm read a lot to try to understand social and political issues in the places where we work. When you do that I think you can really add value. Most of us thought that we would build our international practice based on working with U.S. companies going abroad, but once we've gotten there we've been able to add value on a local basis and we enjoy that part of the practice.

I suppose people would ask, "How do you lead a firm that's in fourteen different locations? How do you control it?" And the answer is, I don't control it. I team with people I trust and respect, and I build self-respect among those people so that the whole is greater than the individual parts. These people have a sense of commitment to the firm, not to their own egos. There are really two ways of implementing our profession. One is the "star" system, which is built around an individual or several individuals. As long as they're there, the star rises and the firm does well. When they leave, the embers die and the firm basically dissolves and goes away. I can think of only a very few firms that were built on a star system and then in the second or third generation have been able to come close to what the original star accomplished. On the other hand, there are many remarkable firms that have been built on a team approach, where the firm is the star, not the individual. When a generation passes, the firm just continues to go on in a very successful way. Hopefully, each time the leadership changes, the firm takes a slightly different direction, but it builds on its heritage rather than on the "star" qualities of one or two individuals.

If you have great people working with you, they keep you informed and you communicate. I'm on the phone to almost every Gensler office once or twice a day. We talk all the time. New technology is remarkable, and we are spending a great deal of money networking our firm so that we can communicate by E-mail and direct communication. We can do work in any of our offices for any other office, so the interface of where the work is done for the client is transparent. You need to locate the program and project people near the client, but you don't necessarily need to have production people, or even design people, near the client.

Reading is a critical part of my life. I read three newspapers a day and 50 magazines a month, either weekly, biweekly, or monthly. I read two weekly business newspapers, as well as *The Wall Street Journal*, the San Francisco paper, and the local Marin paper. I also read a lot of novels, a lot of business books, and we constantly pass articles around the firm. I underline or highlight pages in almost every magazine or book I read and my secretary makes copies to distribute. These may be items in which I have no particular interest or no need to know about, but there is someone else in the firm who does need the information. I probably receive two or three articles a day from my associates, and I send five or six a day. Six nights a week I read from 8 to 11, which means I carry a lot of papers around in my briefcase. But to keep in front of this crowd, in this business, that's what I have to do.

How do I ask young associates to grow? I made a comment a long time ago that I hire and gather around me people who are smarter than I am. Most people are afraid to hire bright people because they think that to remain the leader, they need to hire less intelligent people. I think to remain the leader, you hire the smartest people you can find, the smarter the better, and then you give them a chance to grow. You don't put a lot of constraints around them; you encourage them and you prod them.

We've tried to help our people understand that they must expand and grow and take on more. We have reading lists, we have Gensler University where we take them through different programs, we have training sessions, and we just try to expose them to bright people. We invite speakers on various subjects to come in every week. Again, we're stretching our minds, stretching what the profession is all about every day, because our business is changing every day. We have to keep up with it—have to keep in front of it if possible—but we certainly have to keep up with it.

It's frustrating to me that at the moment we're so busy and the margins in our business have gotten so thin, because people in the profession don't value what they provide. They're so eager to provide something that they don't place a value on it. One of the reasons that we're adding services is to get profits back up. I've never thought profits were anything to be embarrassed about. I don't understand why architects who add enormous value to a project should make nothing, while developers and corporations, who are the recipients of our work, gain great value from it. It's ironic that California recently passed a law that every time a piece of artwork is sold, the artist is supposed to get five percent of the appreciated value of the piece. What if architects could charge an initial fee and then every time the building was sold they received a piece of the profits on the increased value of the property? There would be some wealthy architects.

Finally, I'd like to comment on the lack of communication skills in the profession today. In architectural school, I took a public speaking course as a part of freshman English, but I was never a very good writer. Yet I've developed into a fairly competent writer. I try to write quite a bit. I work with a writer—we have two full-time writers on staff to help our people with research and ideas that we want to share. Many architects don't have the ability to communicate their thoughts and ideas very well. Yet the leaders of successful firms—I. M. Pei, Cesar Pelli, Philip Johnson—are very articulate people. They have learned to talk in "non-architecty talk." I find the nonsense that many architects write and speak to be frankly an insult to the profession. When my son first came home from college, he would show us his work and say, "The plane intersects and twists, paralleling the intersecting point of vision, turning and twisting to the . . . ." That's what he was hearing in architectural school, rather than just saying what a particular line or plane does. I read these architectural journals that go on for hours with this drivel and I think it obscures some very good ideas. Architects should be forced to write and rewrite until they communicate clearly what they need to say.

I also believe the profession has put itself in a position where it attracts people who are almost introverts. If you have some talent and you're introverted, become an architect. If you're creative and you're introverted, become an architect. If you're outgoing and effervescent, architecture may not be a good profession for you. We are not attracting the breadth of students into architectural schools that the profession really needs. It seems to be a self-selecting process that's built into "what is an architect," and I think it's a really dangerous concept. I see so many designers coming through our offices who mumble and just want to show you their drawings rather than tell you about the design. I know that the schools are doing a better job of culling the people who apply, but I still think that it's self-selecting.

Most architects have always wanted to be designers. I've wanted to be an architect since about age six, and to this day I can't tell you why. I remember drawing little houses and building models when I was a child, and I just never stopped. Other kids built airplane models, I built house models. I'm not a great sketcher and I'm not a beautiful designer, but I can critique and set a direction and find a concept for a project as well as anyone. That's the value I add—to set the direction. If I had to make a living as an artist and a designer working out all the details, I'd be digging ditches because I would make more money that way. That is not my focus, although certainly I know when the design is right, and I can make damn sure it is right. I read clients and projects better than most, and that's the value I add to the firm.

San Francisco Museum of
Modern Art Bookstore, San
Francisco, California
(Photo: C. McGrath).

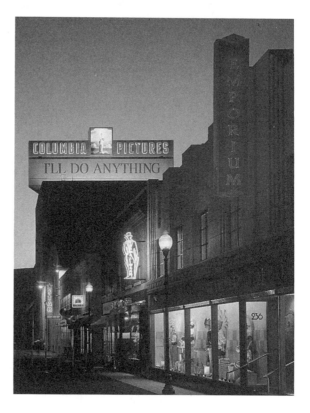

Sony Pictures, Los Angeles, California.
(Photo: M. Lorenzetti).

Delta Airlines Terminal, Los Angeles International Airport, Los Angeles, California. (Photo by N. Merrick)

Gensler and Associates, San Francisco, California. (Photo: C. McGrath.)

Apple Research and Development, Cupertino, California. (Photo: C. McGrath).

Davis, Polk, and Ward, New York, New York. (Photo: N. Merrick)

Jeffrey Heller, F.A.I.A.

The office of Heller • Manus Architects commands a panoramic view of San Francisco Bay and the skylines of Berkeley and Oakland, which is shared by everyone in the office. This setting is particularly dynamic because it is completely open. The whole staff shares busy and challenging days.

A graduate of MIT, Jeffrey is known for his design abilities and a personality that inspires a sense of confidence in every client. Our view is that if we were asked to list the characteristics of an exceptional architect and then rank all the professionals we know, Heller would be right at the top. As we did with Arthur Gensler, we conducted this interview over breakfast. Perhaps, if you are a leader, your only spare time is before the work day begins.

Interview Highlights

Jeffrey Heller is aware of every aspect of competition. Be alert to the following thoughts:

- There are design opportunities everywhere.
- These days I take my own counsel a lot. I don't follow trends. I don't follow the herd.
- Trying to be all things to all people really is not a great thing.
- The only way to develop an association of trust is to do what you're asked to do and do what you say you're going to do and be scrupulously honest about all things.
- We are known for our client loyalty. We are very loyal and partial and give them a lot of service and attention, not only during the job but after the job.
- Too many of the architectural programs in the schools focus on design to the exclusion of the practical side of the profession.

The Interview

You've asked a lot of interesting questions here, and I guess I'll start with the challenge of changing markets.

After 1990, the economy in this country changed drastically. We went from a cyclical real estate process which had sort of moderate ups and downs for the last, say, 30 or 40 years, to a significant sea change. The need for new buildings disappeared overnight for a couple of reasons. One is that the economy went in the tank, the other is that during the 1980's we overbuilt substantially because of the tax laws of the early 1980's. The two of those combined to create a lack of need for buildings that will go on probably until the end of the century. The exceptions to that rule are infrastructure projects, including transit, health care projects, jails, and other institutional projects. In fact, there's been a lot of building in health care. So those are the kinds of projects that are happening, whereas most commercial projects have come to a standstill. There's a little bit of a start-up in that, but it's really just a fraction of what has happened before. Again, there are some exceptions: low cost housing, the remodeling of older shopping centers, and certain international growth areas, such as Asia and a little bit in Russia, where there's still a need for buildings. I have no real prediction for how long that'll last.

So, the marketplace shifted from a fairly steady one of market rate housing and commercial office buildings and retail centers to institutional projects and a chase around the globe for international work. The institutional work is in a little trouble also because, as the economy has slowed down, the budgets of states, cities, and the federal government have also hit certain snags. Jerry Hines gave a talk in Chicago about six or seven years ago now, and he said everything was going to change, that half the people at the conference weren't going to be there in five years, and everybody's office would be half the size it was. Everybody just kind of ignored him—they didn't want to hear it, and things weren't like that. But he was absolutely correct. What that means for the profession is the chase for the institutional or international jobs, fewer jobs, fewer architects, perhaps, more interior type of work, much more aggressive competition for work. It's not a pretty picture, in terms of the professional career track and the ability to make a lot of money. The idea is to turn over every stone to find work and, I think, do the best possible work because this is a quality-driven market. People will tend to hire people who they know will do a good job, or do a good job and do it very cheaply, because they have a lot of choice in whom they pick. Everybody's gotten a lot tougher and selection processes have become a lot harder and meaner. In California and elsewhere, of course, things like racial and ethnic diversity have become issues. So, it's a very beleaguered profession.

In a city like San Francisco, and probably in a lot of places, there's also sort of a mystique about the architect from out of town versus the guy who's there. So when we go out of town, it's something of an advantage. When we're here in the city we have to overcome that in certain sectors. It would be nice if people were more objective about these things but they're not necessarily that way.

The bigger firms generally have an easier time because they're willing to invest the time and dollars to chase the big projects in Asia and so on. They're also willing to invest heavily in the effort to secure institutional work. The application process becomes increasingly difficult and one spends a ton of money and wastes a lot of time going after these things, with no great chance of snagging them. So, huge investments are borne by these large companies, and they're stressed by that but they're better able to afford it. The middle-range companies have a much more difficult time. The small guy operating out of his house—you know, off his desk, doing the occasional kitchen remodeling or the shoe-string job—has an easier time, because he or she doesn't have the burdens of the chase at that scale. He also knows that he's not going to be viable for those projects unless he associates with some bigger firm.

We are basing our strategy on diversity. We've shifted from a firm well-known for large, high-rise urban projects to one that is doing an amphitheater in Sacramento for Bill Graham Presents, a train station in Emeryville for Amtrak, an elderly housing project in the city, and a Costco warehouse. We're chasing some work in Florida and Detroit. We're looking at a project in Mexico and we're doing a project in Moscow. We're going to have to formalize our relations with the locals as the projects go beyond the concept stage, which they're in now. I think for projects overseas, or even for projects across the country, it's important to have a local association. We did that in Florida and we did it in Detroit as well. It helps to have someone who can watch out for local issues and deal with the local conditions, especially while a building's being built. They're there, they're closer. They have to be very carefully picked, however. In both the Detroit and Florida cases our reputation led clients to us. In Florida we were invited into a competition, which we won, and in Detroit the client simply hired us to do the design work. The Russian project evolved from contacts that I developed when I went there after the Armenian earthquake. So, we're all over the place and, in fact, the only way to go is to pursue anything that is pursuable as an opportunity.

There are design opportunities everywhere. I don't think it matters a bit what the program or the dynamics or the politics of the situation are, it always presents a design opportunity. It's the issue of perceiving the opportunity and understanding the opportunity, but there are never not design opportunities. I read everything, I listen to everybody, and I look for ideas wherever I can find them. These days I take my own counsel a lot. I don't follow trends. I don't follow the herd. I don't follow organizational approaches. I'm constantly on the lookout for things and I try to pick them out as I find them. I pursue things, spend a lot of energy doing it. I'm sort of unorthodox about it.

We also do things like "due diligence" reports for clients who are looking at purchasing or rehabbing an older building. The banks have gotten fanatic about knowing all of the factors about these buildings. How is its structure? Does it have asbestos? What is its situation relative to building codes and fire codes? What condition is it in? So one does a comprehensive report on the building. Now these reports are very tricky, because if you miss something significant or if you're wrong, there's a direct financial impact on the purchaser. All of a sudden he might have a million-dollar problem that, when he bought the building, he didn't see. It is a report that must be done with great precision and usually by people with a lot of experience, so you have to put together a team—the architect, the engineer, the mechanical engineer, the electrical guy—and everybody's got to be very careful in analyzing the situation.

As far as offering a complete spectrum of outsourcing services, however, my opinion is that you can't do all things. You have to decide what it is you are. We tend to stay in architecture. Now that may mean a feasibility study or a due diligence report, but that's analyzing the fabric of the building. Lease arrangements— we wouldn't do things like that. Contract buying—things like that are for other people to do. Or, if you have a big firm, you can hire specialists if you can afford it, but for a medium-size firm like ours, or a smaller firm, you have to stay in the realm of what you do well. Just doing what you do well is a pretty big task. So I think trying to be all things to all people really is not a great thing.

One of the things that we think makes us unique is that we combine the basic cornerstone pieces. One is being a very heavily service-oriented firm, which works closely with the client, hands on. This includes the partners. The second thing is a very high focus on design quality in every project, especially low-budget projects, to get the most out of what we work with. The Amtrak station we did is a good example. It only cost $1.1 million and a comparable building being built down the track, which has had a lot of trouble, cost over $6.5 million. Our building just won an international award, actually, the Cope-Brunelle award, so we're pretty excited about that. This is one of only two in the world that have won for that category for that building. Now, the third element of our approach is that we're known for a very good political sense. In California certainly, and increasingly else-where, issues of growth and environment and traffic—the politics of growth—are heavily affecting projects of all kinds. We're known for being very skilled at combining good politics and good design to achieve a good result. I think that we're recognized for those kinds of things uniquely, although we're not the only ones, but that's the thing that's helped us keep a clientele base. I think we're also pretty well known for our client loyalty. If our clients treat us well, we are very loyal and partial and give them a lot of service and attention, not only during the job but after the job.

I think it's important to understand that the private developer has shifted over the last ten years from one who is mostly conscious about going through the approvals process successfully and having an attractive and marketable product, to one who cares about all those things but is desperately driven by the dollar in the private sector. We've had to become much more sensitive to that factor in dealing with our clients. On the institutional side, the client tends to be a larger organization and the individuals working on the project want to appear good to their superiors and the world at large, so they're going to be driven to work with people who they are confident will at least do a good job for them. This often leads to very mediocre work because they want to be safe, but some are driven by a higher level of sensitivity and are looking for something that is both excellent and sound. That's a fairly demanding road to go down.

The only way to develop an association of trust is to do what you're asked to do and do what you say you're going to do and be scrupulously honest about all things. You've got to be trying at all times to serve your client as best as you can and make sure that they have the sense that you're doing that. Clients don't like it when you spring surprises on them, so you have to be very straightforward in your dealings with them, about what you're doing and budgeting issues and so on. Even if you're lodging a complaint about the fee or this or that, it doesn't necessarily have to be a negative conversation. It just becomes a dialogue, and sometimes it gives you the benefit of the doubt. You have to be careful about making your commitments, and once you've made a commitment you have to fulfill the commitment. There are a lot of firms that get into a job and start nickel-and-diming people, by the way, especially institutional clients. The big firms sometimes get away with that and milk the institutional cow, but we've found that that's not helpful for a firm like ours. So, once we've made a commitment, we try to keep it for as long as possible, until there is a significant, not a minor, shift in the program or the scope. Then, when there is, and everybody's real clear that that's happened, it's much more comfortable to ask for an additional fee or more time or a change of the agreement.

Then there's this issue of conflicting views, when a design feature appears too costly. In the 1980's we would argue with the client and try to force him. For one thing, the client didn't care that much; for another, the politics were pushing things, maybe, for better design, or maybe you felt more secure about the work you had. But in the 1990's you have to achieve a finer balance. Again, going back to this train station example, we were on a murderously tight budget and we fought for some things when we had to, but we were always keeping our eye on the budget. There is sufficient design freedom within the limits of what you actually can do, and you can wish for other things, but that can get you into trouble when you try to push the client further than is possible. For example, in the case of that train station, the building is stucco. We accepted the use of stucco: it's not a very large station, it's in California, and stucco's been used on a lot of famous buildings. We could have fought like crazy for a different material but it would have been pointless—there was no money for the thing. It also helped us preserve some other intricate detailing that survived through design. So, at some point, you have to back off.

More that ten years ago now, maybe more like twelve or fourteen years ago, I was working in a larger firm and we were fired because we pushed a client too hard on a design feature. After it happened, in hindsight, I recognized that it was a case of pushing the client too hard and actually that's helped me to know where that line is and not to cross it. A lot of people see the client as an adversary, especially people working in the firm who are not principals, people working in a large firm, working with a large institutional client. You kind of get lost in the sense of it, but ultimately, we are a service industry and you have to be more clever than that. You can't just go at a client or a client representative in a direct confrontation unless you're on really solid ground.

Finally, I want to say that I think architecture is a very practically grounded profession. When you understand that, you actually become a better designer because you know how to take advantage of things in a cost-effective way rather than forcing them. Too many of the architectural programs in the schools focus on design to the exclusion of the practical side of the profession. I would like to see a more well-rounded curriculum in the universities, where a lot more time is spent watching a building get built. Witnessing the construction process is actually very educational, and I think we've lost a little bit of that. Because our society is so litigious, we tend to spend a lot more time drawing than we do going through the building process. Traditionally—a century ago or at the beginning of this century—the architect spent a lot more time in the construction part of the process than in the drawing part of the process. I think we lose something when we don't do that, so if I had my way, I would rather see a bigger component of fee available for the construction administration portion. The client is always trying to save money, so he's trying to say well, we don't need that. I try sometimes to argue that that's where problems get solved, and that's one of the most important things, and it shouldn't be short-cut or under-cut.

St. Francis Medical Office Building, San Francisco, California.

Emeryville Amtrak Station, Emeryville, California.

455 Market Street, San Francisco, California.   *One Second Street, San Francisco, California*

1333 North California Street, Walnut Creek, California.

Orlando City Hall, Orlando, Florida

Method No.1
Critical Thinking

Critical thinking is the foundation for executive leadership. We employ critical thinking to define opportunity, identify promising innovations, and form the concepts needed to direct and market professional services. We use critical thinking to help us avoid the narrow view as we focus on the goal of realizing our potential and mapping the challenges ahead. Critical thinking is something we must expect from ourselves as much as we expect it from scholars and laureates and universities and foundations. The concepts developed in this section are, in part, philosophical inquiries, for that is what critical thinking most often is. When facing complex issues we must, like scholars, conduct a questioning process that seems endless. To do anything less would be unwise. To avoid critical thinking is to permit an illusion of certainty, which is the primary source of every bad decision and the loss of competitive potential.

Let's consider the scholarly tradition of critical thinking. How is it taught? When professors introduce students to critical thinking they guide the discussion toward increasingly complex considerations. They may hold an object before a class and ask what it is. Professor Otto Reibstock from Tubingen would hold a wicker basket before the class. "What is this?" Each answer was followed by the same query. Louis Agassiz (Cooper, 1994) would place before a student an unidentified biological specimen, perhaps a fish. He would tell the student to find out as much as he or she could without going to the reference library. Only after hours of observation would the student's description of the specimen become acceptable to Agassiz. When introducing algebraic topology, Chris Zeeman of Cambridge would pose only two questions for an entire semester's work: "Can you comb a furry bull smooth?" and "Can you comb the whorl out of your hair?" From these two simple questions evolved a mathematical model of great elegance. Paul K. Feyerabend from Berkeley guides a whole semester's work with the single thought: "When you find one hundred crows to be black, you must continue the search for the exception, the white crow." This means we must never stop questioning what we think we know. Kenneth Clark, whose work as a social psychologist was pivotal in the outcome of *Brown* v. *Board of Education of Topeka*, educates students to develop lines of questioning that invalidate preconceptions. Professor John J. Pauson, when applying the Socratic method, would let the student start the query and then drive the student's thinking with question after question.

The intent of each of these professors is to instill in their students a habit of intellectual openness and constant questioning. Professors of architecture might have us experiment with critical thinking by requiring us to walk through a selected building, asking us to describe it, rejecting the first answer as being incomplete or superficial, and then continuing to reject answer after answer until we find the exceptional aspects of the building's purpose and design. We would be asked to do this because every space, building, facility, and planned development is a living laboratory for us, where we can truly learn, but only if we reject the superficial question and incomplete answer.

This demand to keep looking and looking until we find the exception is not idle speculation. The practical consequences of critical thinking are appreciated by corporations facing the same economic and business conditions as we are. When developing a new strategy, some corporate managers require associates to ask "Why?" five times in a row in order to verify the worth of an idea. Development engineers may step through as many as nine levels of increasingly complex questions in order to design a new product or manufacturing process.

Chris Argyris (1994) points to the consequences of not employing critical thinking. He suggests that in the uncritical organization, people avoid asking the necessary questions. The problem is that people protect themselves by avoiding probes into exactly what it is they do rather than what they say they do. As a result, effort and time committed to improving an organization are wasted. Critical thinking is not designed to make friends. It is not about personal satisfaction. It is what it takes to do a good job.

There is a direct relationship between critical thinking and the winning of contracts and jobs. When making this point, Thomas C. Keiser (1988: 217) notes that, while negotiating with a customer, the more options you have to offer, the more flexible your strategy. We take this to mean that business strategy is not developed at the point of sale. It begins with critical thinking, the in-depth questioning that identifies the spectrum of options needed when marketing to clients. Think about all the variables that enter into your preparation for a presentation to a client. You start with a response to an invitation to enter the competition. In the selection process the list gets shorter and shorter, and then you are on the final list of three firms. Recall how every aspect of the project was considered in preparation for the final presentation. This is critical thinking in action.

The Goal of Realizing Our Potential

Critical thinking characterizes the future as you want it to be by means of guiding visions. An instructive example of someone with such a guiding vision may be found in General Electric's CEO, Jack Welch. His vision for competitive revolution is speed, simplicity, and self-confidence. In his vision, speed occurs when people make decisions in minutes, face-to-face, without producing months of staff work or mounds of paper. Welch sees simplicity as an atmosphere in the organization that fosters clarity of purpose from its leaders. Self-confidence, the third aspect of his guiding vision, is needed because complacent people are terrified by speed and hate simplicity. Thus it requires enormous self-confidence to be simple and fast (Slater, 1993: 254–255).

The direction and guidance that result from the critical thinking of executives like Jack Welch will have little significance unless they are derived from and committed to by all those within the firm who have something of importance to contribute. For Akio Morita, founding chairman of Sony, (1988, *en passem*: 153–165), no theory or plan or government policy will make a business a success; that can only be done by people. A company will get nowhere if all the thinking is left to management. To motivate people, you must bring them into the family and treat them like respected members of it. A further word of caution: it is much easier to recognize and accept the value of a guiding vision than it is to execute it successfully. Zabriskie and Huellmantel (1994: 117) note that plans have failed because the strategies in them cannot be implemented profitably. Even the best operational people cannot implement broad, generalized strategies not expressed in competitive terms. It is also important to note something that is well known but surprisingly often overlooked: when only one person has a guiding vision its value is lost. The concept must be pervasive, found in every corner of the organization. On the other hand, Morita will accept controversy, as cooperation and consensus should not be stressed at the risk of failing to utilize aggressive individuals and their ideas. Once you have a staff of prepared, intelligent, and energetic people, the firm will begin to act with enterprise. These objectives can be precisely stated. John Rau (1994), in a review of a McKinsey & Co. study of what traits make companies succeed, includes the following statements in his article. High-performing companies relentlessly pursue a vision; are intense, performance-driven, and demanding; develop simple structures; provide world-class training; value "people skills"; and are entreprenueurial. This is a guiding vision of note from which we can all profit .

It is wise to be somewhat skeptical about the worth of guiding visions, as many people will say that the last thing they need is a vision. Bill Gates, chairman of Microsoft, has said that being a visionary is trivial (Lavin, 1994). Let's consider the concept of "marketing myopia." This critique of corporate management visions was published in 1960 by Theodore Levitt in the *Harvard Business Review* and subsequently presented in a retrospective commentary (Levitt, 1975). This is one of the most seminal articles ever written by a management theorist. Fifteen years after publication the Harvard Business Review office had sold more than 265,000 reprints of the article. In his critique, Levitt notes that when a corporation's growth is threatened, slowed, or stopped the cause is failure at the top, those responsible for broad aims and policies. Railroads stopped growing, not because the passengers weren't there, but because the companies were railroad-oriented instead of transportation-oriented, that is, product-oriented instead of customer-oriented. He notes that the failure of the movie industry to realize the opportunities provided by a new technology, television, occurred because executives thought of themselves as being in the movie business rather than the entertainment business. Enterprises such as electric utilities and oil companies were cautioned to beware of marketing myopia, to recognize that they are in the energy business and not just providers of electricity and petroleum products. Rolex is on the ball. They see themselves not as producers of watches but as purveyors of luxury.

The opposite of corporate myopia is a guiding vision produced by raising difficult questions and challenging conventional assumptions (Lazer, 1994). Henry Mintzberg (1987: 68) supports the importance of a guiding vision. "Strategies need not be deliberate—they can also emerge." This statement provides a practical view of what is involved in developing a guiding vision. Mintzberg wants us to learn from all sources and then synthesize this learning into a vision of the accomplishments our business should pursue. He wants us to invent new facets for our business, not just rearrange old ones, and cautions that the world doesn't stand still while we develop and execute our plan. Furthermore, you cannot be remote from the problem. Mintzberg notes that "innovation has never been institutionalized. Systems have never been able to reproduce the synthesis created by the genius entrepreneur or even the ordinary competent professional" (1994: 110). "Formal systems can process more information, at least hard information. But they could never internalize it, comprehend it, synthesize it" (1994: 111). Akio Morita (1988: 217), when recounting the history of his corporation, provides a set of admonitions designed to help foresee the future direction of the firm. He suggests that it helps to have a special sense, generated by knowledge and experience—a feel for the business that goes beyond the facts and figures. Rather than stressing the putting of one fact together with another, he advises grasping a general idea as a whole and then using this information to make decisions. This is critical thinking at its best. It may not appear radical, yet if fully implemented it often is.

Mapping the Challenges Ahead

When executive architects ask professional associates to develop new information, skills, and knowledge and to live through an exacting and challenging transformation of a practice, which for some could be a threatening experience, they need justification for what they are proposing. Architects know how to think about the work at hand, about commissions, contracts, and projects. The question is whether they know how to think about tomorrow, the future. We need critical thinking to help us identify where things have changed or will change and the dynamics of change involved. When we anticipate these changes, we move ahead of our competitors. Likewise, as we identify where our competitors have experienced decline and stagnation because they were unaware of the changing requirements of clients, we will find gaps in the marketplace into which we can move.

Let's consider an academic discourse that aptly describes the origins of change. Marshall D. Sahlins and Elman R. Service (1960), concerned with the need to anticipate change and to recognize where the potential for change is minimal, anticipated a concept that has become popular today in management theory—the concept of breakpoints (Strebel, 1992). Their analysis of the dynamics of change, freely applied, goes something like this. Progress may be accomplished in one of two ways, each with its own promise and cost. One is the stage-by-stage advance, which is seen, for instance, in corporate enterprise when a major new opportunity for competition develops. The cost for such an advance is the struggle between ideas for domination. This struggle creates opportunity. Consider the strategies of reengineering and downsizing and their implications for what is designed and built. Consider how these ideas may change the manner in which clients view their real estate assets as they look for unrealized profit and sources of funding for new enterprises. If we are alert to our clients' struggle with new ideas, we will find our own ideas about where we should be going. The second aspect of progress, as modeled by Sahlins and Service, is fixed adaptations related to specific situations. In his history of China, John King Fairbank (1992: 3) notes Nathan Sivin's comment, which we will use as an example of what is meant by fixed adaptations, that the Chinese abacus as a calculator was limited to a dozen or so digits in linear array and so was useless for advanced algebra. Sivin suggests that the relative lack of Chinese mathematical innovations from the mid-1300's to the 1600's may have been the price paid for the convenience of the abacus. In this case, successful adaptations went along so smoothly that a culture become satisfied with the status quo. Every company that is losing business or has gone out of business is an example of this. We must identify fixed adaptations so that we can break through and create new services as early as possible.

There is another thought in the work of Sahlins and Service that is important to us. That is the leapfrogging that occurs when one organization surpasses the market leader. Clients and client organizations know how to create potential. They know they have to be open to opportunity, ahead of competitors in their thinking about the future. Likewise, we have to be open to opportunity, ahead of competitors in thinking about the future, and enterprising when developing new services. While we don't know specifically what the future holds, we do know that we must find new opportunities. Strebel (1992), as he develops guidelines for applying the concept of breakpoints, tell us that our future is all about the discovery of openings for change and the opportunity to experiment with new ideas. He advises us to be alert and recognize that change is not linear, with one concept leading to another. Overall progress is irregular and discontinuous rather than a direct line from one advance to another. It is this discontinuity that Strebel is talking about when he advises organizations to be constantly alert to the potential for change.

A Unique Challenge

It is the responsibility of the executive architect to be open to new ideas and services, to create a unique image in the marketplace. Hamel and Prahalad (1993) tell us how to break down complacency within an organization and increase its potential for change. They say we can create this potential by extending our ambitions beyond our resources. Creating this pressure on our practice begins with critical thinking. This idea is normal for architects, who can discover reality as scientists and engineers do and, at the same time, as designers, can be devoted to the creation of a new reality.

CHAPTER 3

STRATEGY

Strategy involves the ability to perceive what it is that leads clients to set a high value on architectural services. The goal is enlightened clients who appreciate that the primary objective of architectural services is an improved quality of life at work, at home, and in the community. Architects are remarkable for their ability to make this the foundation of business enterprise. The interviews often stress that it is essential for architects to adhere to traditional values. Consider how unique this is in the world of business.

There are two notable differences between corporate strategy and the practice-building strategy employed by architects. One has to do with the nature of the architect's market challenge and the second with the level of personal involvement required. In terms of the market situation, a corporation is a highly structured organization developed around specific opportunities toward which all resources are directed. Corporate strategy identifies potential market segments and then determines the cost structure required to beat the competition. Architectural practice, on the other hand, is organized around individuals who direct themselves toward a broad spectrum of professional opportunities. In terms of service to customers and clients, corporate marketing is impersonal, similar to commercial fishermen dragging a trawl or setting a gill net. Architects are like fly fishermen casting to a trophy fish. They are going after specific clients; they know who these individuals are and what they are doing. In terms of the involvement demanded of architects, no executive is more challenged to personally manage his or her work. Detachment may be possible for some, but architects will accept no relationship to their work other than a direct and personal one. When corporate customers remain loyal they become a statistic. An architect's clients are welcomed on a first name basis. It is certain that clients expect this type of relationship.

Architects Are Respected for Their Creativity and Contributions to Quality of Life

The contributing professionals are all highly esteemed by their clients. They derive the energy they need to create and expand their practices from clients who recognize the value of architectural service. High esteem develops in direct relationship to the emphasis we place on values and concerns about society. This may sound naive to those who have been squeezed by clients interested primarily in cost containment. However, thoughtful institutional and corporate clients do demand a regard for human assets. Institutions serve people. Corporations spend more money on their human resources than all other expenditures put together. Communities undertake capital facility projects to benefit individuals and families. Wise clients know that unfavorable environmental conditions may make successful activities and satisfying experiences difficult or impossible.

The Challenge to Strategy Is to Identify Needed Innovations

As shown by the experiences of the contributors, the search for professional opportunity requires you to discover what is important to clients, which forces you to enter the world of clients, investors, and stakeholders. As corporate and institutional clients formulate new organizational, business, and human resource concepts, opportunities are created. New technologies present innovative possibilities for architectural services.

This suggests that you might experiment with thinking like a consultant when developing strategy. A good consulting firm is alert to economic trends likely to transform market requirements, and works to anticipate technological, social, economic, and environmental events that promise opportunity. Competitive innovations are most easily found in blurred markets, changing markets, and unmet client needs. What you see happening outside the office helps you identify needed competencies. This is a step that streamlines your firm. When you create such a focus you can concentrate on your unique identity.

A Competitive Strategy Places a Firm Ahead of Conventional Wisdom

To be attractive to the sophisticated client investing capital in new enterprises, the executive architect must create a competitive strategy that places the firm ahead of conventional wisdom. The contributing professionals share the desire to create and sell the next big idea. For them, strategy means being smarter and better prepared, so one can influence clients in a significant way. Fred Foote suggests that we can create opportunities for ourselves. We can invent a project: find a site, get an option on the site, find a target clientele on which to focus, do the architecture, and perhaps even lease and manage the project. This is what Larry Simons and Jim Brecht are doing. They became developers because they saw this as the means to realize their full potential as architects.

Strategy Does Not Consist of Simple Choices Between Clear-Cut Alternatives

Strategic thinking and planning within the professional practice of architecture lies somewhere between immediate action and deliberative action, between the strategy of the chess board and that of the board room. For a professional practice, strategy takes what we are, where we want to go, looks to the outside for opportunity, plays with the idea of innovations, identifies required resources and skills, and produces action plans. This is more of a personal battle than this logical sequence suggests. Let's apply some current phrases from management theory to ourselves: be aggressive, seize no market you can't hold, fight downhill, and create a dynamic, proactive setting. As specifically noted by Fred Foote, we need confidence-building management methodologies. While methods such as those contained in this book will help us in many ways, they will not make the challenge any less demanding.

Insights

Jim Brecht, A.I.A.

The principals of Simons & Brecht, Inc.—Larry Simons, F.A.I.A., and Jim Brecht, A.I.A., a graduate of Cal Poly—are architect/developers. A visit to their Stony Point corporate park in Santa Rosa will overwhelm you with the quality of life at work they have achieved for their tenants. We recently heard several associates say they wish this team had not become involved in development because it limits the amount of architectural design they do and lessens the opportunity to see more of their exceptionally fine work in our communities.

Jim and Larry Simons are not absentee landlords. Their corporate office, where we conducted the interview, is located in the center of Stony Point. On one hand, this provides easy tenant access to them with all the demands associated with facility management. On the other, it is very satisfying to have an office in the corporate park you designed and developed and in which your community takes great pride.

Interview Highlights

Jim Brecht discusses every aspect of his strategic thinking and planning. Be alert to the following points:

- We've tried to approach all of our projects with the highest ideals as far as the quality and the architecture.
- You need to talk to people, other professionals, but I think my bottom line is that only you can make decisions.
- We found that a lot of projects would get into the architectural phase and wouldn't go further because people didn't understand the entire process, the financing and other elements.
- We found that we were much better at serving the final needs of the customer by being the developer and making those decisions than we were as architects making a very limited range of decisions.

- We are now making decisions on establishing the budget, identifying the location, deciding how the project should be managed after the completion of construction, and relating to the tenants and their business needs.
- Fairly early on we started doing an annual survey of our tenants as to what they felt were the most important things we were doing.
- As an architect, heating, ventilation, and air conditioning are sometimes very low on your priority list, but once you own and manage buildings, they become some of your highest priorities.
- We realized that architects aren't trained for many things that the development industry requires.
- When I was in school, a lot of professors were highly design-oriented and had no management skills.

The Interview

We've always looked at the end user—how buildings are used and what the requirements of the end user are—and designed around that need. I think that varies from the traditional approach to commercial architecture.

Early on we realized that we were doing the building designs and the interiors were being left unfinished. We'd turn the building over and all of a sudden they'd move in folding chairs and things. We'd really feel like it hadn't been a complete project, so we began taking on things like interior design and furnishings along with the building design.

Also, we found that a lot of the projects would get into the architectural phase and wouldn't go further because people didn't understand the entire process, the financing and other elements. We saw that people needed to get a building built but weren't able to go through that process. Larry had done development projects prior to when I came on board, and I think my background gave a human-factors-orientation toward the end user. Design was always very important, but the design was used as the tool to integrate all those other elements and solve the problems. When I joined the firm, I wanted to become a licensed architect so I did traditional projects and project management, but I also tended to assist in the development projects. I worked with the real estate brokers or, once we got to the point where we owned buildings, took the calls to unplug the toilet and those kinds of things. Over time, we had the two different elements in the office: providing traditional architectural services and doing development. In the development arena, our clients were office users. The market was limited; there were few choices as far as the kinds of space available. As we started building space, we were pretty much the quality leader in the market and there was a reasonably strong demand for high quality office space.

The practice, then, included both traditional architecture and speculative office building development. We found that we were much better at serving the final needs of the customer by being the developer and making those decisions than we were as architects making a very limited range of decisions. So we were now making decisions on establishing the budget, identifying the location, deciding how the project would be managed after the completion of construction, and relating to the tenants and their business needs. Fairly early on we started doing an annual survey of our tenants as to what they felt were the most important things that we were doing. Initially there were maybe 50 tenants; there may now be 150. One of the things that we found was that a lot of the things that you're trained to consider as an architect—the critical visual elements of design—are not as important to your final customer/tenant. There are some important things that relate to design, but there are some very basic requirements that they feel are most important. Probably the primary ones are heating, ventilation, and air conditioning. As an architect those are sometimes very low on your priority list, but once you own and manage buildings, they become some of your highest priorities. We also found that there's a difference between how architects rate each other and how the final user of space looks at us.

We finally reached a point in time where we made a decision to no longer do outside services. We had enough critical mass in the development that we were doing, caught up in the boom times of the 80's, and it was the best economic decision. In traditional architectural service, you take on a substantial amount of liability with very minimal financial returns. As our assets began to expand and we started to look at protecting that, we realized that your whole net worth is literally put on the line with the professional liabilities incurred as an architect. You can get errors and omissions insurance, but it generally runs at most a "window" of coverage; in other words, if it's below a certain amount or above a certain amount you're not covered, but if the hat falls within that window, you're covered. So it was kind of a natural thing at that point for us to begin to focus more on development.

At that time we also began doing our own construction, so we were buying the property, designing the building, building the building, leasing it to the tenant, and then owning and operating it. We were very active in the "architect as developer" program promoted by the A.I.A. and we participated in their conferences. Larry was on several panels on the "architect as developer." It was really interesting and exciting. We also realized that architects aren't trained for many things that the development industry requires. Some relate to management issues in that you need to come to it as a broad generalist and be able to look at a wide range of problems and solutions and work it down to some fairly specific directions without having too much of a preconceived architectural approach. Through that process we realized some of our strengths and weaknesses and we felt comfortable in the approach that were taking. We had a relatively small architectural staff and a construction company, and we were designing and building buildings. What you see here—everything in the park—we designed and built. Again, we were doing the surveys and getting involved in the issue of productivity. As we started talking to tenants more and more and asking about their business issues, the recurring theme was, "We're looking at our businesses, trying to enhance the bottom line. What can you do as a developer/architect/facilities person to enhance the bottom line of our business?"

The big challenge in development is that you have to deal with the marketing process as well as the requirements of the end user. You're dealing with brokers, you're dealing with facilities people, and you're dealing with operational people. Sometimes those three groups have three totally different products in mind. We've tried to approach all of our projects with the highest ideals as far as the quality and the architecture, and we find that some people, in the brokerage industry, try to turn the product into a commodity where price is the only issue.

When talking with a client, you can see very clearly that he is coming from one of three different camps. You may have a broker type who's trying to create a commodity, compare it with other building commodities, and our job becomes to do it as cheaply as possible. Or you may have the facilities person, who typically is more facility-oriented. A lot of them have come through the ranks of mechanical and maintenance people and they are more concerned with ongoing maintenance issues. Finally, you get what I would call the most current facilities thinking, which is: "How does this enhance my business position?" That relates to productivity. How can the facility itself be used to improve productivity, to attract quality employees, to retain quality employees, and to further other business goals? We really find it exciting when we work directly with people that are trying to solve those problems.

I think it is a disservice for architects to have to deal only with how inexpensively can we do a building. When I talk to people about buildings, I use an analogy with, say, a computer system. You could purchase a $1,000 computer system that would do very little for your business, and it would not be worth even $1,000. On the other hand, you could buy a computer system that was specifically designed for your industry, one that handled purchasing, accounting functions, and marketing functions, all integrated. That computer system might cost $15,000 but the value to your business would be many times that. The decision would be that it's much better to get the computer that works for the specifics of your business. One of our goals has been to try to teach people about what a building can do for their business and then train them to shop accordingly.

We use a slide presentation to demonstrate our ideas to prospective tenants. We show slides of this park along with such comments as, "An environment that's designed to reduce employee distraction and increase productivity is essential to any company's success." We try to create a sense of a place where people enjoy working. We show the on-site amentities such as the shops, restaurants, and business services, the training and conference facilities, the building design and construction, the tenant improvements and interiors, and the management services. For example, we created a lake within the park in order to attract on-site food service because that is important to tenants. We also talk about the location amenities: this is a central location, it's accessible by public transportation, there are a number of nearby shopping and dining choices, as well as fitness and recreation facilities. There is a city park adjoining the property and a number of child-care options within a one-mile radius, which means that employees can meet their kids for lunch in the park and spend some time with them during the day.

At first we had actual statistics about increased productivity in the slide show, and although factual, the numbers were so unbelievable that we took them out. Basically, we went through some of the Building Owners and Managers Association (BOMA) studies on employee productivity and looked at differences in productivity when poor facilities are compared to quality facilities, based on building design, heating, ventilation, air conditioning, on-site food service, maintenance issues, responsiveness of property management—all these different issues. These studies actually said that you could increase the productivity of an employee by ten to twenty percent if you dealt with all these issues. In other words, if someone was hot and worried about being hot or complaining to the person next to him, or if people were going off-campus for lunch and coming back late, and if people had problems with noise or lighting—we'd take that and work it all the way down from their numbers, which could go as high as twenty percent, and say, well, what if it's just a two percent increase? And you run a two percent increase in productivity. This is really where I think architects have the greatest leverage for the future—to create environments that improve productivity, and to be able to quantify this. Instead of focusing strictly on doing the least expensive building, you need to understand how each of these elements can accomplish gains in productivity and decide how much you want to spend to achieve those gains.

We find a very receptive audience, on one hand, in the business community. We find less receptive audiences in the real estate and brokerage industries, because it makes the project much more complicated to evaluate. It is no longer 5,000 square feet at $1.50 versus 5,000 at $1.45. They have to consider other factors. What kind of HVAC does it have? What kind of acoustical treatments? What kind of on-site amenities? We've been kind of leading this charge, and one of the large developers in San Francisco has now hired somebody to quantify the productivity impact of the amenities in their project. They contacted us to ask where we found this information. We are by no means an expert on it but we've come across some of it out there. BOMA has information. Herman Miller, Westinghouse, and some of the systems furniture people have done studies.

Again, I think by looking at the base of tenants that we have and the kinds of things that they have done over time, we can anticipate what is probably going to occur in the next phase or generation of office buildings. One thing I would say is that in the past people got into very specific designs for interiors, for office space, and a lot of specialty improvements. The idea that I can design something that meets your specific needs, which I think is something that all of us architects felt—we were creating this "custom suit" just for you—I think that is disappearing because the flexibility of the corporate user is critical. Businesses change so quickly that one of the objectives is an environment that suits present needs, but one that can be changed as needs change. As far as office space is concerned, this means fewer permanent walls. You're not going to demolish a whole interior and rebuild it every two or three years because business is changing. Interiors are becoming more flexible, and tenants want more flexibility in the sizes of spaces as well. They don't want to sign a ten-year lease for 5,000 square feet. They want 5,000 square feet with an option to come back in two years and cut back or expand, and they literally cannot project which of these two options they will take. For the architect or the building owner or the space planner, it takes a lot of creativity to be able to be that flexible without just throwing a lot of dollars at the problem.

We are trying to create what we call a fairly classic space with the infrastructure in place—the data cabling, the phone cabling, the HVAC necessary. A 5,000 square foot user can come in with systems furniture and set it up for his or her needs. In a year, the first user may move to a similar space with 10,000 square feet and another user can take the original space. Some of the tenants have suggested things like raised floors, which makes wiring completely flexible. Workstations and cabling can be changed at any time and for any configuration.

Attracting and retaining quality employees has also been a strong concern, although perhaps less critical in this last year or two with the recession. Amenities are important—recreation, daycare, education, meeting space, food service, shopping—all those things that make an employee's life more efficient.

When we try to convince people that our viewpoint is correct, we try not to present it as our viewpoint. We let them answer some questions. "How much time do you think your employees spend doing X? How much time would they save if they had Y?" We take some notes, then become the facilitator and say, "Okay, let's go through the calculations. You've told me how important this is and how much time you'd save, so let's see how much that really costs." This can be a real eye-opener.

I think the other thing about conflicting views is that you have to follow the dollar. In other words, where is the money being spent and why are views the way they are? What is the most efficient way for a broker to present a building? If he or she has to survey the employees and determine the subtle differences between buildings, the job becomes very difficult. People tend to lean in the direction that will make their lives simpler, but that tends to leave a big hole in the middle where nobody is really looking at the big questions and the big issues. I also think that a large segment of the development industry does not want to complicate their lives, either, and would just like to work to the lowest common denominator. Don't confuse things by talking about how productive someone might be within this building; I will just sell you the cheapest building. So a lot of times the developer forces the architect into the lowest cost game. We are trying to take a different approach, but it is by no means common for developers to consider productivity.

We have to understand productivity and how we can be competitive because otherwise we are going to begin to lag behind. I'm active in the Chamber of Commerce here and I chaired the committee on economic development. They're promoting this concept of "industry clusters" for economic development. Instead of advertising and real estate brokerage, we're trying to develop core industries and create intense competition, so that those industries are better in our region than anywhere else in the world. For example, we have the wine industry, for which we're world-renowned. Industries would be attracted to this because of the knowledge and expertise that we have here. This would create a spin off of marketing and manufacturing elements.

In a similar process we elected to set up a software entity called Soft Tech, about six months ago. There were a lot of software people here but they were working in their homes and scattered around the Bay Area. Soft Tech has a membership of 150, with a number of corporate sponsors. These people are coming out of the woodwork, and it's become a conduit for jobs. There are companies that would like to come to Santa Rosa but they didn't know about the engineers and software people. Engineers who wanted to relocate didn't know if there were any jobs available. So now we've created this entity that matches up all these companies and engineers. The same thing has happened in the construction industry. Different industries have to work together, but the concept involves the city, the businesses, and both Sonoma State University and Santa Rosa Junior College. They're all part of the industry cluster. If somebody in the business community needs people trained in C+ programming language, they can ask one of the schools to hire instructors. We'll either contract for an education through the schools or just set it up on a regular term basis. We're developing a solid working relationship within the community; the presidents of both Sonoma State and the Junior College sit on the Chamber's Board. Everyone is working on this concept together, and it's great to see that.

Other than the Chamber of Commerce, we also find that national associations are a good source of business development ideas. I think it's important to have several viewpoints, because each organization has its own agenda. I belong to the National Association of Office and Industrial Parks (the NAOIP), and the Urban Land Institute (or ULI). Those are the major development associations, with the ULI being oriented more toward national education and the NAOIP toward local chapters and networking. They both have good libraries and they publish books on an annual basis, such as current books about real estate. We have gone through some tremendous upheavals in the last few years, with changes in the market and the value of real estate dropping, and they are producing books that address that. Not ahead of the changes, which you would like, but at least at the same time you're going through it. Typically, they also discuss related management issues, which is helpful.

Being active in the community, with the Chamber of Commerce and other groups, means that I am constantly in contact with a broad range of viewpoints. I also listen to our tenants. I try to learn as much as I can about attitudes and opinions toward architects and developers.

At one time our office was geared toward building buildings. About 80 percent of our business was in construction, in architecture. Now, that is maybe 10 percent of our business. We have one architect other than Larry and me, and everyone else lives off the operation of these buildings. I think architects need to think about these cycles of construction—what do architects do in a nonconstruction cycle? If they have broadened their base by doing some facilities management, maybe that can smooth out the peaks and the valleys. The latest development management books deal with this issue: what do you do when there are no buildings to be built? How do you keep staff? The suggestion is that property management and tenant services can keep you going until there's another building cycle. In this latest no-building cycle a lot of architects had no cushion and had to reduce their staff.

About ten years ago, at the height of all the building activity, we brought in a consultant in management. That was an interesting experience. We were overwhelmed by our success and there was more on the table than we could easily digest. The consultant used it as an opportunity to say, "Look at all these problems you have. I need to be here to solve them." He created more work because of our lack of confidence. His suggestion was to put a big structure in place so that we could grow, grow, grow—unlimited. But our feeling at the time was that we were getting too big, that we should probably try to slow it down, consolidate, and focus more on just a few things. That was the reason we consulted him. He went through the office and talked to the staff—we had a lot of bright young people working for us and they said, "Just let us go and we'll take over the world." Well, we let it go for a couple of years and then took a hard look and said, "No, this is not for us." It probably took us several years to undo all that, to rein it back in. About two years into this cycle, I read a book by Eric Flamholtz, *How to make the Transition from an Entrepreneurial Business to a Professionally Managed Business* (1986), which pointed out that all these problems were natural phases that businesses go through and were very simple to deal with. I wish I had read that book before we embarked on that whole process!

Again, you need to talk to people, other professionals, but I think my bottom line is that only you can make the decisions. You can bring in professionals on very specific issues, but it is your decision, it is your company, and you need to follow your gut a lot of times. A lot of times there is something in there that's telling you what you should be doing and you need to pay attention to it. Even if the professionals say something opposed to it, you should do a lot of soul searching before you go against your instincts.

Most architectural education programs seem to be very focused on design, at the expense of important related areas. I think that, although we are taught to be very open-minded and objective as designers, we don't carry that through in a lot of other areas. When I was in school, a lot of professors were highly design-oriented and had no management skills. To these people, human factors are not design, business and real estate are not design, and they would say that you're better off taking a pottery class or a painting class than a class in these other areas. I think that's still true. But I think that in the future we're not going to be able to afford architects who practice that way. There will be far fewer of those self-expression, "Here, architect, do your thing" kinds of projects. We saw the last of them in the 80's. If there are still people graduating with those attitudes, they should start changing very quickly. I think it is the responsibility of the educators to train people for more appropriate roles, but often educators themselves are entrenched in their own ideas and not willing to change.

Stony Point Office Park, Santa Rosa, California, Stony Point Lake—Retail.

Stony Point Office Park—Office Complex.

Stony Point Office Park, Stony Point Lake— after-dark illumination.

Stony Point Office Park,
Stony Point Lake—
interior.

Stony Point Office Park, Stony Point Lake—
interior set up for concert.

Real Estate Services Center, Santa Rosa,
California

Method No. 2
Thorough Analysis

Professional practice is all about attracting a client, closing a contract, managing a project, and meeting a payroll. Building design professionals are challenged daily by new clients, new technology, and new situations. Strategic thinking and planning are the bywords of architects as they strive to succeed, develop their businesses, and create and market new services. Whatever the challenge, there is often some confusion about strategy. Is it the thinking about the future that is most important? Is it planning that is the essential activity? Let's simply consider strategy as thorough analysis that directs and justifies our efforts.

In the discussion of critical thinking, we noted that in the scholarly view the question is more important than the answer. In professional practice, however, we have to make both the question and the answer work for us. Thorough analysis is the work we do to find the right questions and provide justified and reasonably complete answers as we devise and evaluate strategies. We will always pair critical thinking with thorough analysis, which forces us to consider opportunity and innovation in concrete terms. Critical thinking considers opportunities, the development of innovations appropriate to an opportunity, and the institution of new or extended professional services. We then need to articulate what we want to accomplish and how we will go about it. We have to meet the challenge to improve bottom-line performance. What we propose has to be understood as a sound investment of time and money.

Suppose that your critical thinking generates an idea for attracting clients, a concept that will differentiate your firm in the eyes of potential clients. It may concern an achievement in quality of life at work, at home, and in the community that clients don't even realize they need. We have to consider the consequences of implementing these concepts and demonstrate that our ideas can be put to work. A word of caution: do not place too much reliance on detailed planning. When people think about strategy they often tend to think in terms of an itinerary, a step-by-step program for change. Thorough analysis should not create a standarized management program; it should promote flexibility and enterprise. Hayes and Pisano (1994: 86) note that in today's world, where nothing is predictable and familiar, competitors emerge from unexpected directions at the worst possible time. They would say that a firm should think of itself as a collection of evolving capabilities that provides the flexibility needed to embark in new directions. Flexibility and enterprise are held in high esteem because we know that strategic generalities can lead to confusion in the firm, and that detailed plans can very quickly be outdated or overcome by events. We recognize that there are no clear-cut alternatives, no simple answers when you attempt to transform a practice. It is always a risk-taking event.

Anchor Points

Thorough analysis is not a prescribed process. It is an open process designed to help us use the resources and assets of our firms and identify where we need to invest in the development of new capabilities. It is not our goal to tell you how to conduct thorough analyses. That is something so closely related to your situation and experience that there can be no forced fit between your customary way of working and methodology. What we want to do here is present five anchor points—benchmarks, action plans, assets, design guidelines, and financial analyses—which, when emphasized in your strategic presentations to professional associates, business partners, investors, and stakeholders, will markedly improve the acceptance of your ideas and strategies.

Anchor points are the times and places in a strategic deliberation or presentation where you want to be the most persuasive. Our business is always about persuasion. Whether we want professional associates, business partners, clients, or investors to accept a point of view, a goal, a course of action, an investment perspective, or a design or land development concept, persuasion is the objective. Anchor points are the places where you combine recommendations and justification into a forceful statement. Conduct your analysis and form your goals in the way that you are most creative and effective. Then, use anchor points as the centerpieces in presentations, as focal points for argument, and to promote and justify what you are proposing.

First Anchor Point: Benchmarks

In his publication *The Baldrige Quality System: The Do-It-Yourself Way to Transform Your Business*, Stephen George defines benchmarking as "the process of understanding your performance, comparing it against the performance of best-in-class companies, learning how they perform better, and using that information to improve" (George, 1992: 75). While discussing the role of benchmarks in the process of transforming a business, George notes that the scrutiny of competitors is an activity as old as business. Enterprising organizations compare what they are involved in with the price, product features, sales approach, and product quality of competitors. "Benchmarking is a power tool because it promotes quantum improvements in processes and because it motivates people. Working the same process day after day, tinkering with improvements suggested by the same team members, it is natural for new ideas to dry up. Xerox describes it as 'building a box around ourselves.' When you benchmark others, you cut windows in the box" (George, 1992: 75).

A benchmark may be the reference point for a short-, mid-, or long-range business development. Benchmark advocates, such as Hayes and Pisano (1994: 78–82), state that the key to long-term success is being able to do certain things better than your competitors. They suggest that using benchmarks to steer a firm in the intended directions will have ramifications for almost every aspect of running a business. Supporting this line of thought, Gross, Pascale, and Athos (1993: 98–108) note that benchmarks involve reinvention, entailing the creation of new possibilities for the future that past experiences and current predictions may even indicate are impossible. If an opportunity is significant, it will most likely mean the firm will have to reinvent itself. Gross, Pascale, and Athos's recommended process includes such ideas as: realizing that innovation is not changing what is, but creating what isn't; managing the present for the future; creating urgency; discussing the undiscussable; harnessing contention; and engineering organizational breakdown. They see us working to identify the assets we wish to build, to get rid of the soft spots in existing capabilities, and to gain projects that, if undertaken, will build new services. Benchmarks are the focal points for this strategy.

Johnson Controls, a company that is not perceived as a design firm, has nevertheless created a benchmark for architectural, engineering, and construction firms. Their *Wall Street Journal* advertisements state that the company's mission is "to create the ideal building environment." They want clients to contract with them for everything from the physical plant to landscaping, including such details as ensuring comfortable temperature and humidity levels, providing the lighting, and maintaining appearance. To determine structural integrity they will undertake vibration analyses and infrared imaging inspection, predicting structural problems before they occur. Their statement is well targeted to the problem areas that are of primary concern to owners—building performance and interior environmental conditions. It is a well-conceived service. It is a benchmark for competitors.

Let's assume that you have a fine practice, a solid reputation, and a network of clients for whom you are a proven business associate. That is, you have professional visibility. Even so, with the increasing competition for contracts, failing to move into new markets is risky. To accomplish such a move, you must learn to apply what you already do well to new market areas. You may identify hospital and medical office building design as a major market opportunity. You may not have experience in this market and see a long struggle to gain contract opportunities. On the other hand, considering your present competencies, a market entry effort appears promising. You can seek medical clinic commissions to establish a presence in the market and begin to develop the expertise needed to pursue larger projects. This is where you would apply the benchmark concept. You would explore the achievements of firms currently in the medical clinic market, their competitive advantages, what their clients seem responsive to, what working relationships they have established with clients, what they are doing to deal with costs and financing, what added value is being derived from innovative design concepts, and how they are handling the technologies associated with medical clinic services. You would synthesize all this information into a benchmark that sizes up your competition and the expectations and requirements of investors in this area.

Sometimes clients provide a benchmark. For instance, the Niagara Gateway Project for Ontario, Canada, placed the following advertisement in a number of publications:

A WORLD-CLASS SITE NEEDS A WORLD-CLASS DEVELOPER.
The Niagara Gateway Project, Niagara Falls, Ontario, Canada.
Niagara Falls. North America's most spectacular wonder. It draws

more than ten million visitors a year from North America, Europe and the Pacific Rim. Now, a 20 acre site, directly overlooking the world renowned Niagara Horseshoe Falls, is being assembled for development. The Government of Ontario is seeking a developer to design, finance, construct and operate a multi-use tourist attraction. Various commercial and retail components could also be included. Total development costs are anticipated to be in the order of $C500 million. With more than 120 million people living within one day's drive of the Niagara Region, this is truly a significant development opportunity. Documentation relating to this project is available to contractors, developers, architects, leisure operators, financial institutions and others who may be interested.

This ad is a standard for success. You would have to ask if your firm could compete in such an arena. How do successful firms meet such client expectations and requirements? How can we exceed what they offer? The answers to these questions form a benchmark, a target for your strategic thinking and planning.

The topic of competitive site selection may be used to illustrate the utility of benchmarks in business development. If you decide that a competitive site selection capability will offer new opportunities for your firm, then you have to look at the best. Fluor Daniel's Siting and Consulting Services recently completed a site selection process for Mercedes-Benz. As reported by B. William Dorsey (1994: 246), the client's objectives were to find a site that offered:

> a highly educated and trainable work force with an excellent work ethic; minimal influence from traditional automotive manufacturing processes; high educational standards and educational systems in the community; a labor force capable of producing a quality product within reasonable costs; a highly supportive and pro-business attitude within state government and the state Legislature, including strong support from local and county governments, local business and industry, and the general population; the ability to have parts and sub-components delivered in a timely and cost-effective manner; close proximity to highway, rail, seaport and airport transporation systems; and other incentives, as long as none of the other criteria were compromised.

In response to this challenge, Dorsey's team defined the search region, maintained flexibility in evaluating alternate locations, defined and ranked potential sites and communities, formed detailed comparative evaluations, compared incentives offered by candidate communities, and identified critical differences between these communities. Final negotiations were conducted with Alamance County, North Carolina, Charleston,

South Carolina, and Tuscaloosa, Alabama. It is interesting to note that selection of Tucaloosa, Alabama, was not based on cost, but rather on the commitment of local and state businesses and officials, which assured a successful project for Mercedes-Benz. Throughout the entire process Fluor Daniel employed effective research, selection, analytic, and decision-making processes, establishing a new benchmark for competitive site selection deliberations.

The question is, how do you top this professional service capability? Allowing for the possibility that the published descriptions of their process may not reveal everything considered by Fluor Daniel, let's suggest what you might add or emphasize in a competitive service. First, you might offer more direct involvement in the client's strategic deliberations, emphasizing capital budgeting, forecasting of facility needs, joint ventures, facility feasibility analysis, and property management. It will be important to have an archive of site selection case studies to help clients understand the challenge and possible problems. To the criteria used for site selection in the Mercedes-Benz project, you might add consideration of area economic growth potential, international considerations, environmental and ecological factors, water and waste systems, security factors, and disaster risks. If your site selection service included consideration of facility design and construction factors when comparing candidate sites, as an architectural firm you could enable clients to envision candidate sites in a fully developed state. This is a demonstration of an asset of your firm: the ability to include architectural factors in the site selection process.

When you establish a benchmark and identify the capabilities needed to compete with accomplished firms with extensive assets and a reputation for excellence, benchmark research will help clarify objectives and identify promising alternatives. You want to identify complex and subtle issues. Even if you consider your challenge unique, you can profit from what others have undertaken in nearly similar situations. You must know what things have worked for others, which have proven unsuccessful, and under what conditions. When attempting to break out of the boundaries of professional practice, we may wish to promote the view that we don't provide buildings—we provide experiences. With this in mind, we have to address the world outside the office. We must take steps that will make us astute about the expectations of our market target. We will want to identify and critique the accomplishments of others. In preparation for this, we will examine the literature and archives that pertain to the subject challenge. We must fully utilize previous information. No one should attempt to develop a benchmark without examining the development of points of view and assumptions across the years. In this way, you can be sure that that your time and resources will produce results with a direct relevance to the task at hand.

Second Anchor Point: Action Plans

Action plans force events to occur in the quickest and most effective way. Certainly, action plans cannot be open-ended. We need to provide a boundary to our undertaking and the scope of our interests. The role of action plans is to create strategy focal points that state intentions and their connection with anticipated outcomes. The necessary follow-up to this is a presentation that describes what you actually will do and what results you anticipate. As action plans unfold, we need to describe progress and results, and identify what remains to be done. At the conclusion of an undertaking, we must show what we have learned from the project and how this accomplishment can be used to enhance our service to clients, and possibly to form the basis for a new service. All of this points to the need for an action plan to be more than a step-by-step scope of work. It must be a thinking plan. Hayes and Pisano (1994: 81–83) note that Japanese corporations do not have an enduring approach to competition. Instead, the form of their attack is flexible and given to innovativeness. The idea of thorough analysis is to avoid starting points and end points. Hayes and Pisano caution that if you think in terms of time periods and framing solutions as specific practices, you will run into two types of problems. The first is equating an improvement in capabilities with a strategy. The second is failing to recognize that new practices build new capabilities that can form the basis of a new strategy—if they are recognized and exploited.

Third Anchor Point: Assets

This anchor point helps us convince others that the resources to fulfill the promise of the action plan are in place. Some of the assets will be yours: that is, professional, technological, and knowledge assets. Some assets will come from the partnerships or alliances you have formed. Stakeholder assets are of particular importance, as we will rely upon those most knowledgeable about the project's antecedents to identity troublesome and subtle issues, strong preferences, and what options and alternatives have already been discussed. It is not enough to review the assets in place and leave clients to infer their relevance to the undertaking. We have to show how assets will be deployed; that is, link assets directly to the action plan. When we evaluate assets we respond to the fact that each project is unique and requires a thoughtful assessment of resource availability. These perspectives are very much like those maintained by science. No scientist will accept data and information as being significant or usable unless the method by which these were derived is specified. In our terms, the elements of the action plan will not be perceived as worthwhile until we demonstrate that we have the means to carry these out.

STAKEHOLDER ASSETS

The assessment of an action plan is based in part on what will be done to obtain the commitment of all the people who will influence and be influenced by the project. How willing these stakeholders are to share their experiences and insights and to contribute to the deliberations of the building design and land development team is a measure of the likelihood that the project outcome will meet all critical success factors.

The primary assets here are those individuals and groups of individuals whose activities will be affected by the space, building, facility, or planned development being considered—stakeholders. The action plan must identify how the potential of the stakeholder resource will be realized. Those evaluating our action plan must be assured that we recognize every individual as a valuable source of information about the things with which he is familiar. To achieve this, we have devoted a major portion of our methodology to this undertaking. Discussions of client assessment strategies, the Knowledge Base System, field studies, research techniques, and decision support systems in the following chapters consider every aspect of deriving design concepts, schemes, forms, and features which reflect the expectations and requirements of stakeholders.

PROFESSIONAL, KNOWLEDGE, AND TECHNOLOGICAL ASSETS

Architecture is a flexible, noncapital-intensive business because the profession relies completely on people for success. Another asset that should be strongly emphasized is knowledge. It would be difficult to persuade a client, investor, partner, or stakeholder that we can do a good job on a project unless we show the data and information that we have documented, analyzed, and evaluated. We will also want to demonstrate the investment the firm has made to keep information resources current. Since technological assets will facilitate project work, we will want to describe our investment in advanced data processing technologies and CAD capabilities.

PARTNERSHIP AND ALLIANCE ASSETS

Let's consider these assets in terms of what many of our contributors have cited as a major opportunity, international work. Arthur Gensler suggested that when working overseas we're really dealing with knowledge. Every country has talented designers who do beautiful work, but they don't understand how to integrate the functional, the technological, and the team structure into the process. We will be working to help design firms to understand how things really work, from a financial point of view, a functional point of view, and a technological point of view. These are particularly complex challenges that are costly to undertake. In addition, these projects incur the burden of understanding foreign laws, politics, culture, work habits, professional ethics, and financial arrangements, and the risks and project management errors that always occur when dealing with the unfamiliar.

Thoughts such as the following enter into our assessment of international partnership and alliance assets. Debra Fleenor (1993) cautions that these undertakings require the very best of alliances. These alliances mean less up-front engagement, provide a competitive combination of resources, and allow for greater flexibility in the long run. While analyzing what is meant by the term "global corporation," she is primarily considering the industrial corporation. However, her insights and those of her commentators are applicable. The barriers she identifies serve as a caution and help us realize the complexity of the challenge. Contributing to Fleenor's analysis, George Yip (1993: 12) suggests that alliance loyalty is always changing as others create better opportunities, and that the competitive advantage of a home-country alliance may rapidly disappear as local business preferences change. Cyrus Freidheim (1993: 13) believes that we should seek the best partners to achieve an objective, instead of settling for who is available and affordable. He notes that it is tough to manage out-of-country alliance structures and assure equitable distribution of returns. These alliances therefore require many different kinds of managerial and leadership skills. No matter how much effort is involved, Sumantra Ghoshal (1993: 13) believes that when we build alliances we will be more competitive because we will have developed the ability to link and leverage our competencies. Stressing alliances as the basis for international work, Fleenor tells us to let others simplify their world view with the concept of "globalization." She argues that this is an outdated strategy; we should concentrate on alliance building. All of these considerations can be redirected to the dynamics of partnerships and alliances in our local and national practices.

Fourth Anchor Point: Design Guidelines

Chapter 5, Working with Clients, deals with this topic at length. At this anchor point, you will show how design guidelines will be customized for the project at hand. The emphasis placed on relating recommended design concepts, schemes, forms, and features to stakeholder expectations and requirements is a most attractive feature of the strategies employed by the executive architect.

Fifth Anchor Point: Financial Analyses

These analyses require detailed study of project costs, financing requirements, and anticipated return on investment. This workup is often accompanied by market evaluations and projections of future performance that assess the relative merit of project options and alternatives. Analyses for office building development projects would address lease rates and durations, lease holder improvements, build-out allowances, and financial obligations of tenants. Certified public accountants, underwriters, development bankers, and mortgage brokers can be helpful in preparing these formulations. Many firms have developed their own worksheets to help them develop initial estimates of the financial picture for a proposed project. They will weigh building features and operational costs against financing burdens and returns. Some worksheets address specific design areas like parking facilities and anticipated revenue from parking fees. The architecture, engineering, and construction industry has hundreds of estimating specialists with fine reputations, either on staff or as an outsourcing service. In other words, project costs, financing requirements, and anticipated return on investment considerations are being thoughtfully addressed in the A/E/C industry, producing reliable estimates.

Let's shift to the human dimensions of financing developments. One of the San Francisco Bay Area's most highly esteemed developers, John Raiser, thoroughly understands the relationship between development financing and the successful outcome of a development. He stresses that the client's profit concerns must be the foremost concern of the architecture, engineering, and construction team. He discusses the A/E/C team and the concept of master builders, people who can control every aspect of a project. This is related to his own professional development, which went from a degree in architecture to a degree in engineering, and on to work within the construction industry. It is hard for him to think in any terms other than that of a team of professionals. He also recognizes that money is a commodity, and sees it in terms of sources of funding and the cost of buying it. Obtaining an option on a promising piece of land may cost 50 percent interest on the money. Creating the plans for the project and conducting the studies that verify the site's suitability for development will incur professional fees and a supporting loan at 30 percent interest. If you obtain a buy-out commitment, an agreement to purchase the project on completion, then the construction loan may cost 2 percent over prime. During these phases, Mr. Raiser works with financing sources, such as an insurance company with a real estate investment department that will place pension funds into the project. Mr. Raiser was willing to answer all kinds of questions: Will you undertake speculation projects? Do you work with banks? What kind of staff do you have to handle the financing picture? He said that what he loves above all else is being on the construction site, managing the daily work. All of this is a characterization of a professional immersed in the world of development and finance and hands-on construction management. It shows us that behind all the spreadsheets and financial projections are professionals who make projects succeed, always with financial risk to themselves. When you take out a loan, you are taking a risk.

Innovation

Research conducted by the Minnesota Innovation Research Program (Van De Ven, 1993: 275) describes the innovation process as an accumulation of the results of numerous events performed by many different people over an extended period of time. Innovation processes begin with critical thinking, followed by a variety of events that set the stage for launching an organizational innovation. If this view is correct, then when we consider the variability of this process—it starts and stops and starts up again—then the utility of anchor points becomes evident. Work the way you wish, let events take place, and then, at critical points, gather your thoughts and present your recommedations anchored to benchmarks, action plans, assests, design guidelines, and financial analyses.

CHAPTER FOUR

CLIENT RELATIONS

A client's favorable perception of your firm is what keeps you in business. Clients must recognize that leadership is exercised in your firm, that you understand strategic thinking and planning as they do, and that you have a sophisticated understanding of client relations and the role of people in the success or failure of a project. What kind of executive action is this? The kind that builds a practice.

Our understanding of client benchmarks and breakpoints is important to our image in the marketplace. We need to stress our knowledge of these patterns and trends, in order to convince clients that our decisions are not trivial or insular. We want to be known for helping clients learn about such things as asset development, capital facility investments, leases, remodeling, occupancy cost control, facility management, land development, competitive site selection, and cost effective prevention of health, safety, security, and environmental problems. Clients have learned to regard shifting markets as an opportunity. Likewise, we must demonstrate our willingness to work within conditions of uncertainty. As we share a client's dilemmas, an association of trust develops. This is particularly true when we use our experience to help clients anticipate the future and identify promising possibilities.

Focus on Your Client's Risks and Critical Success Factors

When clients finance new corporate centers or manufacturing facilities, dedicating precious capital resources, they are always taking risks. If you can demonstrate an understanding of these risks, clients will become committed to your success. More than any other selection criteria, clients award contracts to firms who are willing to work in their interest and invest time and effort to fully understand their risks. As a safeguard, many clients will ask you to work with their corporate architects and facility managers. These co-professionals will demand the best. Once you have proven yourself by exemplary service, more and more of their in-house work will be outsourced to you. Take a thoughtful role in dialogues, analyses, and arguments. Conduct yourself as Jack Welch, CEO of General Electric, would: in a simple, fast, and self-confident manner. Soon people will recognize that you are more than a professional under contract—you are a partner.

Respond to Your Client's Evolving Needs

The executive architect is prepared to meet the expectations and requirements of clients and client organizations, not only as a designer but also as a business associate. Many of our contributors stress that the search for professional opportunity means that you must discover what is important to clients. For example, Fred Foote observes that time and money have become critical elements of the building design process because, in the current economic climate, client organizations are more likely to be run by people with a "bean-counter mentality" than they once were. You should not, however, perceive this as a problem; in reality it presents an opportunity. You should be a champion of time and money management; this front-to-end husbanding of resources should be a part of your service to clients (Apgar, 1993).

In addition, you can teach clients a great deal. Consider the comments of Don Willcox, Executive Facilities Manager of the Eisenhower Medical Center, which appear in the following interview. Don observes that an owner, or client, won't necessarily tell you that a particular mechanical detail or efficiency is necessary because the client doesn't know that it is necessary. The client expects you to educate him or her. Fred Foote suggests that clients often ignore or are unaware of the fundamentals of good project management. He recalls the moment when a new player appeared in the Yerba Buena project with a new set of requirements, which meant reworking the entire design. When questioned about this type of occurrence, Jeff Heller advises that you should keep working on the challenge until it is totally evident to the client that a major revision and additional fees are necessary.

Remain Alert to Changing Goals by Working with Clients as "Insiders"

There will always be new influences throughout client organizations. While clients will invest in facilities to provide new capabilities, their view of what these capabilities should be are subject to instantaneous revision. Recognize that much of the downsizing, restructuring, and reengineering of institutions and corporations that we see today is dedicated to simplicity and directness. This is still such a new management process that every client organization is learning catch-as-catch-can. Overnight, there will be changes of which you must be immediately aware. Quite often you serve your client well when you say, "Stop; let's talk this over."

Insights

Don Willcox, Corporate Executive

The Eisenhower Medical Center in Rancho Mirage, California, serves the entire Coachella Valley and, through the Betty Ford Clinic, people from all over the country. It is a complex of fine buildings and facilities, landscaped with speciality plantings. Don Willcox is the Executive Facilities Manager for the center, responsible for all development, remodeling, and tenant improvements.

It is difficult to enter Don's office and even more difficult to find space for two interviewers. It is wallpapered with construction drawings and specifications. Don personifies the ideal client. His emphasis on conceptual estimating as the first step in every project sets a clear direction for all project participants. Don is the type of professional who knows how to use methods to achieve an end, rather than let methods be an end in themselves. He learned his craft on the construction site and in deliberations with balky architects. He is a major asset to the valley community.

Interview Highlights

This interview offers more lessons than any other. You should take particular note of the following thoughts:

- The architect has to be able to find out, early on, what the needs of the client are, and address those needs.
- It's the architect's responsibility to act as the owner's main consultant on all issues related to design and construction, including coordination of consultants and taking care of the owner's money.
- The architect should take the lead in directing the disciplines when it comes to energy conservation and consumption, and right now that's not being done.
- The biggest challenge of working with the architect is the communication process—getting from a two-dimensional piece of paper to the feel of how the space is actually going to function for the staff.

- Charettes work well for us and we are very comfortable with that process.
- This idea of "partnering" is a real challenge.
- Trust is everything. Usually, that's how an architect gets the job.
- As far as education programs are concerned, my experience has been in construction management, and I think that the education isn't practical enough.

The Interview

From the standpoint of an owner, or client, I've seen the quality of the product from architectural firms go down in recent years, so this is a chance to get some things off my chest. I think part of the reason is that it's become so competitive and the fees are getting so skinny that there are fewer hours going into the design process. When the architect is concerned with the number of billable hours to a client, the owner ends up sacrificing some mechanical efficiencies, or something like that. Then the architect in turn tries to squeak down the consultants and I see this really affecting the quality of the product. You'll get a set of drawings, maybe on a $40 million project in the pre-construction phase, and you'll have a package of questions that's a mess because there are so many holes in the documents, because of a lack of coordination between the disciplines. Architects should be taking a stronger position with the owners and taking a stronger role in leading the team. For instance, in the medical field, which is where I am right now, there should be coordination with the equipment planners and the life cycle analysis of the building components from an operational standpoint. I don't see a lot of that happening and I think the reason is that there are no dollars in the fee to really do that. I'm not advocating increased fees, but that's the response I get when I say, "Why haven't you guys thought about this? Why don't we have variable speed drives on the air handlers? Why don't we have variable volume pumping?" Because the payback on that stuff is quick—it's a couple of years, maybe, when you look at energy consumption. And the architects will say, "Well, we don't have enough money in our fee to get into that kind of an analysis." To me, that's not the right answer. I think that the architect should take the lead in directing the disciplines when it comes to energy conservation and consumption, and right now that's not being done.

I think it's the architect's responsibility to act as the owner's main consultant on all issues related to design and construction, including coordination of consultants and taking care of the owner's money. The architect has to be able to find out, early on, what the needs of the client are, and address those needs. For example, you might be working for a developer who's just trying to make a quick buck. He wants to meet the minimum Title 24 energy requirements and he's not concerned with the operating expense of the building, because he's going to unload it. Even though it may not be the most conscientious thing to do, the architect should provide the services that he was hired to provide, and if that's to whip this thing out for the owner to unload it, then that's what it is. In my case, I have to live with the building, or the facility has to live with the building, so the life cycle cost of that building is very important. The architect has to know that, up front, going in. And if that means he has to build a little more into his fee, to pay a little extra for a mechanical consultant, I think it's real important that he do that.

An owner, especially an unsophisticated owner, won't say that he wants a Pace air handler with a variable speed drive on it, because he doesn't know that. He's expecting the architect to say that, to take it a step further. Since the architect has the constraint of the budget, he may have to educate the owner. He may need to say, "Okay, if you want this energy efficient building, you need an energy management system, or you need a high performance exterior wall glazing system, and it's going to cost you more for it." Otherwise, the architect is not doing the job he's hired to do. He may be doing the service he thinks he was hired to do, which is to build the building within budget, but architects have an implied role, a larger role, because they're managing the team as well.

What I mean to say is that if you build me a building, in this climate, where the temperature is 120 degrees, with a two-story lobby and no air lock on the doors, what is that going to do to my operating expenses? Now I have this lobby with huge double doors that people are going in and out of, and it's the same temperature inside as it is outside. Why did you do that? I hired you to build this thing within budget and not to cost me an arm and a leg to operate, and I shouldn't have to say specifically that this design is wrong. You should be telling me, "No, if you want this, here is the price you're going to pay. You'll have this nice lobby, but no one's going to sit in it because it'll be 120 degrees in there."

I've been working on this great system that I developed for the conceptual phase of a building. For example, I've got this piece of land—this is an actual site. I know the building is going to be 55,000 square feet, and we kind of know what the bay depths are, based on the usage. So I can come up with a conceptual building, even though we haven't designed it yet. Maybe when it's done, it will look a little different, but we're in the conceptual phase now and we're trying to do a budget. Now, I can tell you the tons of steel, I can count the anchor bolts, based on assumptions. I can tell you quantities of excavation, because we have a soils report. I can tell you the cubic yards of concrete. I can tell you the area of the exterior skin, and we can make an assumption early on, that if we do a conventional plaster skin, it's going to cost so much a square foot. If we use an exterior insulation and finish system it's going to cost more. Even though the building's not designed, we can come up with this information. This is a take-off for this building before it was ever designed. You can see the level of detail that I've got in here. This is a conceptual budget. You have a bottom line—now you move into the schematic budget. Now, the architect's role at that phase should be to say, "Okay, we can make real cost-effective decisions here." On this building, we made an assumption that the exterior wall had a sandstone wainscot four feet high, all the way around, at so much a square foot. It's more money than stucco. The architect can use this tool to control the cost, and not just to control the initial cost, but the life cycle cost. There are assumptions in here on the mechanical systems as well.

Now you work with the architect, and in each of the phases, you look at the line-item cost of the decisions that are being made. I think the architect should be doing this, not me, but there's a hole in the industry and I'm trying to fill it. Most owners aren't coming to architects with this level of detail, in terms of life cycle costing. It even gets down to doing a present worth analysis on the cost of the money, spending it today or spending it on the usable life of the building component. I think architects should be selling that service. The mechanical engineers have the expertise to do this but they don't have the time in their fees, and they're not providing that service. So the architect is doing his schematic design, going to design development, turning the base sheets over to the mechanical guy, and nobody's thinking about this. On the other hand, I'm thinking about types of air handlers and their drives and controls early on, when we're making decisions on the elevator cabs, because we only have so much money. Should we spend the money on fancy elevator cabs or should we spend it on an energy management system? And what's the trade-off in making that decision? You might want to use a ten-year planning range, or you may want to use a payback—if it doesn't pay back in five years, maybe it's not worth it. From my standpoint, we have to operate the facility and we're responsible for providing health care at a reasonable price, and this has an impact on how much it costs to provide health care.

There are construction managers out there that are trying to sell something like this. In my opinion, it's not this good, it's not this detailed. Why are construction managers trying to sell this service? Why aren't the architects taking more of a leadership role as the owner's primary consultant, and doing this? I don't understand it, because it seems to me they're the ones with the consultants under contract, they're the ones with the expertise, they're the ones that are drawing it, they're the ones that are putting the components together, so they're the ones that have all the information and they're the ones that should be leading this whole effort in controlling the owner's cost. It's not just health care. If you're fabricating something, you have all this money tied up in capital. If you can control the cost of that, it all gets worked out on a discounted cash flow analysis as far as the cost of the end product, whether it's health care or whatever it is. It's all based on the cost to operate and the cost to build, and I think that architects should be saying this to the owners when they're selling their services.

In my role here, I'm primarily responsible for the budget and the schedule. From the conceptual phase, I have to come up with the budget before anything's on paper, and the budget has to include furniture, design fees, any entitlements, land purchase, medical equipment, consulting fees, and so on. It's also my responsibility to make sure that the space is functional after it's completed.

I think the biggest challenge of working with the architect is the communication process—getting from a two-dimensional piece of paper to the feel of how the space is actually going to function for the staff. In design meetings, you'll sit down with the users—which in my industry are typically physicians, nurses, and nursing directors—and they'll be looking at a schematic layout. They'll say, "This looks great," but to a certain extent they don't have a clue what they're looking at. My role is to help make sure that nobody leaves the room until the architect and the staff understand how that space is going to function. That ends up with me asking questions about staffing, and how they actually operate. "Where do you need the results from the computer in the lab printed out? Do you really need them in the lab or do you need them at the nurse's station? Are you going to have to walk from the nurse's station to the lab to get the results and then walk back again?" Questions like that—and some architects are better than others at getting that information out of the staff. While some architects may know, if they're medical planners, a lot about laying out the space and how it functions, they don't know it at the same level of detail, obviously, as the staff. So the challenge is to get that information from the staff and make sure the staff understands what they're doing, so that when they're sitting in that space afterwards and I walk by, they don't say, "Hey, who designed this? This doesn't work!"

The problem is that the staff needs to start rethinking the way they're actually going to operate the unit. They usually have something in their minds and they start out by thinking of how they function now. They build this false constraint and they put themselves in this little box of how they function now. You'll ask them a question and they'll answer it based on that. But the whole idea is that they're not in that box anymore. We have to get them to rethink the way the space functions, so that they can maybe cut down on full-time employees, and improve patient care, which is the goal. If you can reduce the number of full-time employees, if you can be more efficient, if you can be careful of how you spend money on medical equipment, so you don't have duplication and unnecessary redundancies, you're reducing the cost of health care and making a real difference in the health care delivery system, which is very timely right now. I think that the architects and the designers and the staff can have a real impact on that, so the biggest challenge is achieving that with the team.

I did a job out here recently—the architect is actually a friend of mine. I wanted to bring him back, take him through the space, and have the nurses talk to him, so he could see what happens after his job is finished. What typically happens is that I'll walk in there, as I said, and they'll start saying, "You know, this doesn't work. Who did this?" And the funny part about it is that I try to make sure they have input on the design. It's like, "Well, you did this—it's not the architect." But the problem is, they didn't realize what they were doing when they were directing the architect to do this or that. So I brought this guy back, and the staff were all over him—he was heading for the door. But I wanted him to realize that his poor communication with the staff caused problems later on. I wanted him to see how important it is to achieve that communication in the schematic phase and in the design development phase.

Charettes work well for us and we are very comfortable with that process. I think the one that we did with the Austin Design Group was especially good because we decided to go with that building very quickly and we really didn't have a defined program. The program developed as the layout developed during the charette process. We sat in a room with the executive-level people and the director-level people and their staffs, and we actually talked about what services we were going to deliver to the community and what kind of an image we wanted to have in the community. We developed a program in the front end of the charette, which was very good for us because typically when we try to develop a program, people aren't in the same room. People are making assumptions and it's real difficult and time-consuming to make decisions on exactly what services are going to be offered and things like that. But when everybody was in the room together and we looked at how it impacted the size of the space, the decisions were made very quickly. We said okay, this is what we want to do, this is what we want to be to the community—we want to have a real presence in the community and we want to contribute to the overall health of the community—all those things came out during the charette process. And the process was managed very efficiently by the architects—better than we could have done it, I think—as far as asking the right questions and setting overall goals.

We spent three full days on that charette. It was interesting, because when I sent out the memos for everybody to come, nobody wanted to commit three days to the process. I got a call from one of the directors who said, "So when does this charade start?" They went in with a real cynical attitude, but after dealing with Austin Design Group, particularly on this one, they changed their attitude real fast. They really felt empowered, as to controlling the whole process, not just the layout of the building, but our whole image in the community and how we were going to contribute as a community outreach center. They saw that we're going to do something good and we're not just going to be hammering them on costs.

Usually when we go into these design things the staff starts out with visions of big offices and big spaces because it's their home, it's their little playground. Then my role is to squeak the spaces down so that they're functional and efficient use of space. I try to warn the architects before they meet with the user groups. I'll tell them, "You sit with the doctors and the staff and the space is going to double. I can't let that happen, but we have to make it functional, so you're going to have to help lead the group." It's like: this is where I am, this is where they are, and the architect has to get us to what the real size of the space is. It's difficult for the architect because he doesn't have the clinical expertise to make evaluations on what is really needed, but you can't rely on the staff alone because it just grows.

It's the same thing with medical equipment. You sit down with the doctors and they talk about what type of equipment they want and you see what kind of equipment they really need. Then the manufacturer's representative comes in and flies them to Minnesota in his private jet to look at his product, which is three times more expensive than anything else. The Medical Director now wants a $23,000 bed for the birthing center, whereas I've budgeted for a $10,000 bed, which I thought was extravagant. The architect is part of this process, in that as we start to lay out the equipment, he's there in the room helping me control the costs.

We share information with other hospital groups and we're trying to standardize certain things, such as how many square feet a director's office should have, and how much the furniture should cost. I'm trying to standardize and say, this is the setup for a director, this is the setup for a manager, this is the setup for a supervisor, in terms of how big the space should be and what it should have in it.

Other challenges? Let me think. I'd have to say that this idea of "partnering" is a real challenge. You have the architect, you have the owner, and you have the contractor or the construction manager, and it's a partnering concept, supposedly. What happens is, more of the liability gets shifted to the owner when you do that, and it seems like you can't control the process unless you have more restrictive contracts. In a way, this defeats the partnering concept, but what I've found is that if it's not their money, they don't control their spending. You need to negotiate a contract that says the architect has to redesign it if he's over budget;

otherwise you're paying an added service fee to come back within budget. The whole partnering thing sounds real great, but there has to be a financial implication on all of the team members, not just the owner, who has the ultimate liability anyway. I don't like that, but that's the way it is, it seems, no matter who the architect is and no matter who the construction manager is.

Trust is everything. Usually, that's how an architect gets the job, so there's some trust established going in. I mean, you select an architect based on his fee and his experience, but the cost of a mistake is way more than any difference in the fees, so you walk in by trusting the architect. Then, once you get to the construction phase, it's real hard for the contractor not to point a finger at the architect, because that has a lot to do with him getting his change orders approved. It's impossible to build something 100 percent on paper and not have changes, but the owner will say, "Why do I have this change order?" The first thing out of the contractor's mouth is, "It's the architect. Look at the drawings." And he'll show you a hole in the drawings or something that's not coordinated. That kind of eats away at the credibility of the design team, and some contractors feed on that. That's one of the ways that the trust gets eaten away, and you don't get it back by pointing fingers at the contractor in turn and saying, "Well, that was implied in the drawings. There shouldn't be a change order for this." The contractor has real costs associated with subs or suppliers to put that work in place, and if there are real holes in the drawings that weren't bid by the contractor, it's going to cost him more money to do the work.

I think the key to keeping the trust and keeping the partnering concept going is for the architect to tell the owner up front, going in, that there will be change orders. And when there's a change order because of a mistake in the drawings, I think the architect has to belly up the bar. You can't say you're a partner and then start pointing fingers. You have to be able to explain to the owner, to say that when you do the constructability review and when you actually lay out the work, there are things that have to be tweaked to make it fit.

The architect runs the risk of an owner like me saying, "Okay, the cost of the change order should come out of your fee." This is just a business thing I do to control the cost of a project. In the long run, you end up paying the architect anyway—I mean you don't hold it out of his fee in most cases because you would have had to pay for the work anyway, had it been shown correctly on the drawings. The only problem is that you're not getting the advantage of the competitive bid process for that piece of work, because you're negotiating with a contractor who's already on board. So I try to get the architect to contribute a little bit, which I think is fair. I don't do it on every job—if there's a little bit of it and it's minor, you forget about it because it's part of the nature of the business. Like I said, you can't build something on paper that's going to fall in place 100% in the field—it's impossible. But if it gets excessive, that's when you start talking to the architect about holding back some of his fee to make up for the cost.

For instance, I did a job somewhere where we had two air handlers on the roof. We had all this ductwork and, say, six shafts being fed by one air handler. Then we had another air handler that was feeding, say, eight shafts. After all the ductwork was in place on the roof, we realized that the second air handler didn't have enough capacity. We had to move some of the ductwork from the second air handler to the first. To make the schedule that had to be done on premium time. We had to rework ductwork that had already been put in place, and also the roof looked like a mess—we had ductwork going everywhere! The cost of expediting that work, the premium portion of that work, was something that I legitimately held out of the architect's fee, and I know he didn't get it all from the mechanical engineer.

The other way to build trust is to really take care of the owner's money, as I said earlier. I think architects have a hard time building within a budget unless they have a lot of help as far as breaking down the budget to the actual cost of individual components. Once they do that, or bring somebody in if they don't have the expertise to do that, then the owner can see that the architect is really trying to design within a budget. But if I get a change order for vibration isolation for pumps on the roof and I look through and there's a hole in the drawings or specifications on that, and the architect tries to say, even once, that it's not his fault, that it was really in there, that the contractor doesn't know what he's talking about, then the trust is gone as far as I'm concerned. You can't go back to where you were when you signed the contract because now you have to check everything that he did. I just think accountability is very important—you know, nobody's perfect, but you have to be up front about problems and not try to blame somebody else.

One of my worst experiences was on a $40 million project before I came here. It involved two towers, a parking structure, and a restaurant. I was working for the construction manager, and the drawings were not coordinated at all. We had also issued separate bid packages to expedite the job, which was the owner's fault—he was pushing the architect to expedite the project. One of the worst problems was that we ended up, as a change order, putting a restaurant on the post tension deck of the parking structure—after it was in place. That involved a lot of coring, and sectioning off a piece of the parking structure.

We also had a major problem on that job with the precast panels—trying to get the shop drawings completed so we could hang the panels, and finalize the configuration of the panels. The joining of the panels from an aesthetic standpoint made a big difference in the weight of the panels. We couldn't have the joints where they needed to be from a load standpoint, because it didn't work aesthetically, so the panels became too heavy for the structure to support. On a job like that, precast becomes a deferred approval, because it can't be engineered until the shop drawings are done. We decided to put a tower crane inside the building to erect the steel and the precast panels, which was supposed to come down early, but we couldn't hang the panels because we had to beef up the structure. It was a nightmare—trying to make the schedule and expedite the other trades, and trying to get the precast approved so that we could move the crane out of the way to complete the rest of the structure.

There was also a lot of embedded travertine and Italian marble to be inset in the panels, which we couldn't ship from Italy because we didn't know the size of the panels. The shop drawings for the precast were supposed to be coordinated with the shop drawings for the stone, so that the stone could be cut and honed and polished in Italy and then be shipped here and set in the panels. We ended up having to ship the stone uncut before the shop drawings were approved and paying the precaster to cut the stone.

Dealing with the architect through this whole process was a nightmare for a lot of reasons. We had to get everybody together many times to try to get these problems resolved, and the architect would say the same thing every time. He'd say, "I don't have any more money in this job," and it ended up being a finger-pointing thing. The architect was trying to blame the precast guy, and they were trying to blame the company I was working for, and it got pretty nasty. I remember getting so upset that I threw a drawing at the architect—no, it was the budget for that cafeteria, that change order.

To be honest with you though, it wasn't the architect's fault. Part of it was the owner trying to expedite the project and making unrealistic demands on the design team to get the drawings out. This meant issuing bid packages before all the disciplines had completed their work, so the drawings obviously weren't coordinated. It was tough for us to negotiate all the change orders, to try and find all the holes in the drawings and do a constructability review, when we were getting it in pieces. That was an awful experience.

As far as education programs are concerned, my experience has been in construction management, and I think that the education isn't practical enough. The construction law classes and contract law classes are very good, but they don't teach you how to actually run a job, because the people teaching construction management classes don't have enough field experience or they don't bring in enough people from the industry. They should have somebody who can come in and teach them project management control systems. They should spend more time on actually running a job and putting the work in place: what it takes to do a constructability review; what it takes to set up a site logistics plan; what it takes to control the owner, architect, and contractor and get their questions answered; what it takes to be a team leader in the construction phase of a project when you're asking the questions and trying to get them answered. Even things like the coordination of the submittals—I've had guys working for me right out of school and they don't know, for example, that the guy that's doing the shop drawings for the HVAC needs to look at the shop drawings from the electrical guy, because you only have so much interstitial space. That's something they have to learn when they get out of school and I think that's where the programs are lacking.

On the architectural side, I don't know so much about the education, but to be honest with you, I do notice a difference between the young guys right out of school and the ones who have been in business for a long time. I've worked with a lot of design firms where you have older guys with these great resumés, but it seems like they've lost their enthusiasm. It seems like they're looking for the first workable right answer that they can find, and then they're going to move on to the next project because they're only got so many hours in there. But then you get younger guys who'll come up with an answer—it may be the right answer, but they want to look at it one more time and try to come up with another answer that'll work. It seems like they're not looking at their watches so much. One of the problems is that when you interview a design team, the guys with the enthusiasm don't have the experience and, especially in the health care field, you need some experience. You don't want them making all their mistakes on your job. I think if you could take the enthusiasm of the guys coming out of school, who really want to be proud of the building when they drive by, and couple that with the experience of the older guys, who really want to control the number of hours they put into a project—if you could take that enthusiasm and that experience and put it in the same guy, then you'd have a real valuable architect.

Eisenhower Medical Center, Rancho Mirage, California.

James W. West, M.D. Training Center at the Betty Ford Center, Rancho Mirage, California.

James W. West, M.D. Training Center—Lecture Hall.

Lakeview Building, Desert Orthopedic Center at the Eisenhower Medical Center.

Birthing Center, Eisenhower Medical Center—typical labor, delivery, recovery, postpartum room.

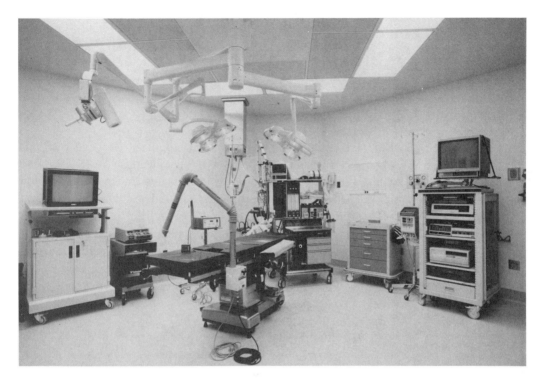

Operating Room, Lakeview Building at the Eisenhower Medical Center

4 . CLIENT RELATIONS | 105

Method No. 3
Client Assessment Strategy

Effective client assessment strategies require that we learn about clients and learn from clients. We must be at the head of the line when we compete for contracts; that is, we want clients to come to us first. You will be the first one called if your reputation is that of a professional firm that first learns from clients and then considers the physical setting and planned environments that provide solutions to problems or the necessary facility support for the client's expanding or new enterprise. During your first meeting with the client you must demonstrate that you already know a great deal about your client's business and the challenges facing those in that business.

Let's illustrate how penetrating your understanding of a client's endeavors should be. Suppose that your client is a high-performance company involved in a demanding enterprise and you are trying to figure out how to sell your services to what is obviously a sophisticated management team, including two M.B.A.s from Harvard and U.C. Berkeley. What do you say? What do they want to hear? Above all else they want assurance that you understand every aspect of their endeavors, critical success factors, and risks. This is what Figure 4.1 helps you achieve. It is derived from the 1995 Malcolm Baldrige Award examination criteria. (Individual copies of this government document can be obtained free of charge from the National Institute of Standards and Technology, telephone number 301-975-2036.) We recommend this as a basic characterization of the world of clients because it is thorough, it is updated annually to reflect the current thinking of what constitutes a successful enterprise, it is generally applicable from one client situation to another, and it provides insights into what is important to client organizations. If you are not familiar with this national award program, let Figure 4.1, which identifies the core values and concepts of the program, be your introduction. Companies and organizations competing for the award were judged in 1995 within these examination categories. Both the examination categories and the associated point

```
┌────────────────────────────────────────────────────────┐
│ EXAMINATION CATEGORIES ................  POINT VALUES    │
│                                                          │
│ 1.0  Leadership........................................ 90 │
│      1.1  Senior Executive Leadership ........................ 45 │
│      1.2  Leadership System and Organization ................. 25 │
│      1.3  Public Responsibility and Corporate Citizenship........ 20 │
│                                                          │
│ 2.0  Information and Analysis ......................... 75 │
│      2.1  Management of Information and Data................ 20 │
│      2.2  Competitive Comparisons and Benchmarking .......... 15 │
│      2.3  Analysis and Use of Company-Level Data ............. 40 │
│                                                          │
│ 3.0  Strategic Planning ............................... 55 │
│      3.1 Strategy Development ............................. 35 │
│      3.2 Strategy Deployment ............................. 20 │
│                                                          │
│ 4.0  Human Resource Development and Management....... 140 │
│      4.1  Human Resource Planning and Evaluation............. 20 │
│      4.2  High Performance Work Systems..................... 45 │
│      4.3  Employee Education, Training, and Development ....... 50 │
│      4.4  Employee Well-Being and Satisfaction ............... 25 │
│                                                          │
│ 5.0  Process Management ............................. 140 │
│      5.1  Design and Introduction of Products and Services ....... 40 │
│      5.2  Process Management: Product and Service            │
│           Production and Delivery .......................... 40 │
│      5.3  Process Management: Support Services .............. 30 │
│      5.4  Management of Supplier Performance................ 30 │
│                                                          │
│ 6.0  Business Results ................................ 250 │
│      6.1  Product and Service Quality Results................. 75 │
│      6.2  Company Operational and Financial Results .......... 130 │
│      6.3  Supplier Performance Results....................... 45 │
│                                                          │
│ 7.0  Customer Focus and Satisfaction .................... 250 │
│      7.1  Customer and Market Knowldge..................... 30 │
│      7.2  Customer Relations Management.................... 30 │
│      7.3  Customer Satisfaction Determination................ 30 │
│      7.4  Customer Satisfaction Results...................... 100 │
│      7.5  Customer Satisfaction Comparison................... 60 │
│                                                          │
│ TOTAL POINTS .................................... 1000   │
└────────────────────────────────────────────────────────┘
```

Figure 4.1. 1995 Baldrige Award examination criteria.

values are instructive for our purposes. The examination categories identify the client organization factors we must fully understand. In this scheme emphasis is placed on leadership, long-range views of the future, management by fact, partnership development, results orientation, continuous improvement and learning, employee participation and development, fast market responsiveness, design quality, problem and waste prevention, and corporate responsibility and citizenship. Finally, the criteria demonstrate that customer satisfaction and preference are key focuses of a company's management system.

Opportunities for Client Engagement and Professional Service

As we were working on this section, we received a call from Nick Watry, A.I.A., P.E., owner and principal of the Watry Design Group. He wanted to share a recent instance in which a prospective client complained of the work of another firm that had never attempted to precisely identify his company's requirements and expectations. As a result, the current project was a complete disaster. The client requested that the Watry Design Group, known for thorough research, exacting design guidelines, and meeting the informational requirements of jurisdictional agencies and local review boards, examine their situation and propose some solutions to alleviate the problems. The important point here is that this client went to the Watry Design Group with a sense of confidence, knowing that they wouldn't take a step without identifying the client's critical success factors.

Let's return to the Malcolm Baldrige National Quality Award 1995 criteria. Figure 4.2 (U.S. Department of Commerce, 1995: *en passem*, 6–14) suggests many possibilities for client engagement and service. As you read each statement, consider what you can offer in direct support of the client's endeavors and activities. Be innovative—think as a consultant with a wealth of experience in achieving quality of life at work. Another way of putting this scheme to work is to use it as a line of discovery for your initial study of the client organization or as a list of topics for inclusion in a response to a corporate client's RFP. Finally, what is depicted in Figure 4.2 is the vocabulary used by executives when describing their activities and responsibilities.

The study of the Malcolm Baldrige program and its international surrogate, O.S.I. 9000, provides an essential view of the increasing sophistication of client organizations. The perceived value and utility of the Baldrige program increases when you become aware that it now encompasses education and health care organizations, Recognizing the importance of this program, scholars such as Robin Goodman, School of Civil and Environmental

1.0 Leadership

- Discover how the client's senior executives set strategic directions and build and maintain a leadership system conducive to high performance, individual development, and organizational learning.
- Discover how the client's organization, management, and work processes support its customer and performance objectives and how the company's values, expectations, and directions are "made real" throughout the company via effective communications.
- Discover how the client organization integrates its public responsibilities and corporate citizenship into its business planning and performance improvement practices.

2.0 Information and Analysis

- Determine how the client selects and manages information and data to support overall business goals with primary emphasis on supporting process management and performance improvement.
- Determine how the client forms competitive comparisons and benchmarking information and uses these to help drive improvement of overall company performance, where this information provides impetus for significant breakthrough and alerts companies to competitive threats and new practices.
- Determine how the client uses analyses and company-level data to guide the company's process management toward business results. This action will establish an understanding of the cause/effect connection among processes and between processes and business results, providing a sound analytic basis for decisions.

3.0 Strategic Planning

- Identify how the client organization develops its view of the future, sets strategic directions, and translates these directions into usable key business drivers, including customer satisfaction and market leadership requirements.
- Identify key performance requirements, alignment of work unit, supplier, and/or partner plans, how productivity, cycle time, and waste reduction are addressed, and the principal resources committed to the accomplishment of plans.

4.0 Human Resource Development and Management

- Identify the direct linkage between human resource planning and the client's strategic directions, addressing the entire work force and the needs of a high performance workplace.
- Identify where job design and work organizations are called for that enable employees to exercise more discretion and decision making, leading to greater flexibility and more rapid response to the changing requirements of the marketplace.
- Identify how education and training are designed, delivered, reinforced, and evaluated with special emphasis upon on-the-job application of knowledge and skills.
- Identify the work environment, the work climate, and how they are tailored to foster the well-being, satisfaction, and development of all employees, including information regarding safe and healthful work environments, to determine how the company includes such factors in its planning and improvement activities.

Figure 4.2. A process of discovery. (Continued on the following page.)

5.0 Process Management

- Evaluate how the client designs and introduces products and services. A major focus is how production and delivery systems are integrated early in the design phase and how this integration is intended to minimize downstream problems for customers and/or eliminate the need for design changes that might be costly to the company.
- Evaluate how processes and services are improved to achieve better performance. Better performance means not only better quality from the customers' perspective but also better operational performance—such as productivity—from the client's perspective.
- Evaluate how the company designs, improves, and maintains the performance of the key support service processes.
- Evaluate how the company manages performance of external providers of goods and services. Such management might be built around longer-term partnering relationships, particularly with key suppliers.

6.0 Business Results

- Study current levels and trends in product and service quality using key measures and/or indicators that matter to the customer and the marketplace. These features are derived from customer-related "listening posts," which may reveal emerging or changing market segments, changing importance of requirements, or even potential obsolescence of products and/or services.
- Study the company's operational and financial results factors in terms of generic factors—common to all companies including financial indicators, cycle time, and productivity and human resource indicators such as safety, absenteeism, and turnover. Also study business- or company-specific effectiveness indicators including rates of invention, environmental quality, export levels, new markets, percent of sales from recently introduced products or services, and shifts toward new segments.
- Study external providers of materials and services, "upstream" and/or "downstream" from the company. The focus should be on the most critical requirements from the point of view of the company—the buyer of the products and services.

7.0 Customer Focus and Satisfaction

- Become familiar with how the company determines current and emerging customer requirements and expectations. The thrust of the effort is that many factors may affect customer preferences and customer loyalty, making it necessary to listen and learn on a continuous basis.
- Become familiar with how the client evaluates and improves its customer response management. Examples include improving service standards, such as complaint resolution time and resolution effectiveness, and improving the use of customer feedback to improve production/delivery processes, training, and hiring.
- Become familiar with how the company evaluates and improves its processes and measurement scales for determining customer satisfaction and satisfaction relative to competitors.
- Become familiar with the client's customer satisfaction and dissatisfaction information as these usually provide different perspectives. The main approach involves viewing increasing satisfaction and decreasing dissatisfaction as a means, not an end. The end is customer retention and positive referral.

Figure 4.2 (continued).
A process of discovery.

Engineering, Georgia Institute of Technology, are studying application possibilities for the architecture/engineering/construction (A/E/C) industry. Goodman's research provides a means for building industry executives to assess their competitiveness in terms of their critical success factors, organizational competencies, and human resources.

Entering a New Market

What can we learn about potential clients? Just about everything we need to impress a client with our preparation to do a good job on their behalf. How is this achieved? Quickly and cheaply. Every member of a firm is a stakeholder, because the success of the firm has an impact on everyone's future. In a sound firm people are as committed to future success as they are to doing a good job on the contract at hand. Let's put this commitment to work.

For example, let's suppose that we want to enter a new market in a region with which we are unfamiliar. The border communities joining Mexico and America constitute, in a sense, separate communities with unique characteristics. San Diego and Tijuana, El Paso and Ciudad Juarez, and even Miami and South and Central America have unique market and business dynamics and customs. How do we prepare to enter these markets? First, we make sure that several members of the firm are fluent in Spanish. If we do not have this resource, it will be necessary to hire it or develop it. A Turkish A/E/C firm with major business opportunities in Germany selected two young associates and required them to become fluent in German within two years or lose their place in the firm. While this may seem harsh, these individuals were given an opportunity to become valuable assets of the firm.

If we choose to pursue international work, we might select science city developments as a new market area. We will immediately select an associate of the firm to become expert in this type of development. The charge is to become acquainted with every aspect of this opportunity, using professional journals devoted to international economic dynamics and developments, trade publications such as those published by the Urban Land Institute, periodic publications stressing economic development such as the *Economist*, and selected business newspapers such as *The Wall Street Journal*, *The Asian Wall Street Journal*, and *The Nikkei Weekly*. This person will soon learn that the term "science city" is used globally to identify a land development that commonly includes corporate centers, marketing, business and financial offices, research and development facilities, and distribution and pilot plant operations. He or she will discover that most science cities develop in association with university research and academic centers, that they commonly include conference, convention, training, education, recreation, athletic and cultural facilities, and often have residential communities and developments mirroring city life with markets, restaurants, retail stores, hotels, and business and professional services. Your associate will see that many terms are used to describe science city developments, such as "technopolis," "enterprise zone," "techno-garden," "academic town," and "science park." Benchmark projects in Japan, such as Tsukuba Science City, Kansai Science City, Kazusa Akademic Park, and Miyazaki Academy Town, will be identified. In America, he or she will take note of such developments as Research Triangle Park, Lansdowne, and Interlocken. There are many exemplary developments, examples of investment in the future by a nation, a region, or a community.

The associate conducting this research may reach the conclusion that corporate centers are the heart of science city developments, and then find benchmarks in this area. An astute associate will discover that the force for change from an emphasis on style to one on image and performance developed outside professional design offices. It came from clients, investors, and stakeholders. The articles of value he or she identifies might include "Distribution center shuns industrial image" (Wright, 1989); and "Michigan National's headquarters reflects firm's philosophy toward its staff" (Umlauf, 1991). One benchmark might be the Corporate Development Center at Steelcase, Inc. (Cooper, 1989), which is a successful response to the need to quicken product development processes by achieving the ultimate environment for the creative process. Another possibility is the $900 million Chrysler Technology Center in Auburn Hills (Olson, 1992), which responds to the requirements of global business by integrating people and process. The Cray Research Park (Wright, 1991), a site where people spend their day realizing the potential of supercomputers for clients around the world, is yet another example of sophisticated client demand for exceptional building performance. In this case, the emphasis was on perfecting facility spaces and features for "knowledge workers," the corporation's principal resource. Each of these performance-oriented facilities is also an achievement in image. Throughout every architectural space, the visual surround demonstrates the care the building design and land development team has taken to create an image of quality.

The products of such research and the learning of a host country's language form the foundation for your entry into new markets. What is done once can be repeated for other new business ventures. A word of caution: during archival research a common error is to simply collect information. To be successful, archival research must combine information with a commentary on the significance of this information for the project at hand. When studying your archives, it is also important to keep in mind that professional architectural renderers and photographers are hired to make buildings and developments look as attractive as possible. A photograph may depict a condominium whose design is praised by architects, but which is not a good home for families; if you were to visit this building, walk up and down the stairs and visit the apartments, you would see how difficult it would be to live there. Home designs that appear attractive but in which it is impossible to live can be found worldwide. Never trust a drawing or photograph that does not depict life within the building, and look for problems as much as you look for good ideas. This judicious skepticism is a necessary safeguard.

Learning from Clients

If we are to become leaders in the marketplace we must recognize that clients have a great deal to teach us. This strategy calls upon us to learn from clients and not merely study the client organization. To learn from clients you must look beyond the immediate design challenge and project yourself into the daily life of the client's organization. You must go beyond the superficial to discover the insider's point of view. Listen to what clients say; note how they act. Look for regularities, variations, and significant events, regardless of how seldom they occur.

Spradly (1972, 1979) calls the idea of learning from clients "strategic research." From this perspective you must become a skilled observer and listener. You will certainly theorize about the client's situation and formulate critical questions and analyze in a complete and systematic way. However, you must strive not to distort or misinterpret the situation as found. A singularly valuable aspect of strategic research is that it asks you to look at people. When physical settings and planned environments fail to meet expectations and requirements, it is because designers maintained a remote professionalism from the facility users. For instance, a recent field study undertaken on behalf of the University of California, Davis, focused on the new Social Sciences & Humanities building designed by Antoine Predock (Giovannini, 1995). In this case, a preeminent American architect has achieved an attractive building image and realized a great deal of the potential for this $25 million investment. Unfortunately, the highly talented people within the client organization, who worked so hard and thoughtfully on the project, now must deal with nearly overwhelming post-occupancy problems. As noted in campus discussions, following the opening of the Social Sciences & Humanities building in the fall of 1994, a number of concerns regarding safety, security, accessibility, and convenience were expressed by various occupants of the building as well as the campus community at large. Additional issues of concern had to do with signage, outdoor lighting and seating, curb cuts, emergency telephones, the large number of exterior doors needed to accommodate the fourteen different departments and programs housed within the building, and elevator access after hours. This case is a perfect example of what happens when professionals and clients fail to bring life to a building before there is a building. Somewhere, at some time, those responsible for project success lost the "faces" of those who look to the building to support their activities and facilitate their endeavors as students, staff, and faculty.

From this case and so many others, we find that learning from clients requires a twofold perspective: the individual factor and the organization factor. The individual factor is a reference to the personal, or what people say they expect and require. The emphasis given to the individual factor reflects the view held by many that potential facility users know what is needed better than anyone else. Members of the client organization, with their reservoir of experience and knowledge, must become a principal source of information. Likewise, there is no deliberation that cannot be made more effective by learning as much as you can about the client's organization. Keep in mind that the search for this understanding never ends. It continues to evolve. How do we know that we have learned all that is possible from our clients? Wolcott (1975) suggests that a deceptively simple test is to ask whether we can behave appropriately within the client organization, or, more effectively, whether we can anticipate and interpret what occurs in the organization as accurately as can its own members.

When learning from clients there should be a concern for making them active thinkers, as opposed to passive participants who offer little that goes beyond the specific question. The goal will always be to take the individual into the realm of judgement, to encourage the feeling that a personal view is valuable and should not be held back. Be patient when listening to what clients say. You must certainly be direct and outspoken when it is required; however, you are not paid to lose clients. As we listen to clients, we must be alert to the management philosophies that underlie their statements and behavior. Such philosophies will differ from client to client. Some will stress efficiency and productivity, while others will emphasize individual satisfaction and performance. In some organizations, daily activities will be highly structured, while in others activities will be flexible and vary in the way individual responsibilities are fulfilled. Some client organizations have a permanent structure, with no desire to change the way things are accomplished. Others are in a constant state of change. When attempting to gain insights into a client's management philosophy, remember that what clients say may be very superficial, merely expressing intentions in a currently acceptable fashion. In any situation, you must determine how people are actually being guided, and not just how people would like things to be.

International Enterprises

When you become a partner in an international enterprise, your client assessment strategy must include careful attention to norms, customs, traditions, and lifestyles. Nuances and subtleties exist in every culture and are always tangible. Violate a norm, denigrate a custom, ignore a tradition, or fail to identify emerging lifestyles, and you have the worst possible event in a foreign business relationship. International work comes to us when we are known for our thorough attention to cultural dynamics and lifestyles. When this capability is combined with our information resources and analytic skills, and the internationally esteemed reputation of American firms, we have the opportunity to surpass what is normally offered by indigenous building industry firms.

Let's say that you want to develop a reputation for professional services in Japan. Many Japanese corporations employ American architects, particularly when they have a reputation for learning from and about clients and the ability to develop correct cultural insights and, of course, when there is a favorable monetary exchange rate. Four projects sponsored by Japanese corporations are described in the following sections.

Honoring a Tradition

Client assessment strategy requires awareness of what is important to the community. In spite of pictures that highlight Asian architectural achievements, and the inference that what is important is what is new, much recent development is challenged by those who feel that national traditions should be honored. In Japan this is illustrated by the comments of Hiroyuki Nishimura (1992). "When it comes to shaping the physical structure of communities in Japan, government authorities and private developers almost always call the shots. That's slowly changing now, and the implications for grass roots democracy here could be profound. Local autonomous bodies and enterprises are becoming increasingly active in encouraging citizens' groups to help design, mold and modify their communities, much as Americans have been doing for decades." This challenge is quite apparent when projects are located in communities particularly proud of their cultural traditions. Writing about Kyoto, with its 1000-year-old tone and atmosphere, the location of the world-renowned Kinkakuji and Ryoanji temples and the Kyoto Buddhist Association, Yoshiaki Itoh (1992) reports that a proposed skyscraper riles custodians of temples, and a showdown over the development of a 16-story hotel in the inner city has divided Kyoto's 1.5 million residents into pro- and antidevelopment groups. Making matters worse is the design for the new central train station, which to many citizens is an abomination in terms of the architectural traditions of Kyoto.

With this as a background, consider a project in the city of Fukuoka, the government center of the southern island of Kyushu. The site is sandwiched between a major teaching hospital and one of the most renowned monastaries in Japan, which is historically important as one of the earliest centers of Buddhist thought. The developer's goal is to create an apartment compex for hospital staff members that will contribute significantly to their quality of life. At the same time, he wishes to honor tradition and demonstrate respect for the monastery community next door. This firm has previously hired such internationally known designers as Stanley Tigerman and Michael Graves (Nesmith, 1990) to symbolize the high quality of life that is possible in the Prefecture and City of Fukuoka. The developer wishes this project to be a comparable undertaking.

Work on the Fukuoka project began with a day spent visiting with the abbot and touring the monastery grounds as well as the adjacent hospital. We toured the neighborhoods around the monastery and hospital block by block, taking note of services and social and recreational opportunities that would be available to apartment dwellers, as well as amenity preferences. It became evident that the developer's image of the project was too grand; in fact, it bore little relationship to either the requirements or lifestyles of the hospital staff.

To gain further insight, a number of related situations were considered. For example, Japanese corporations provide apartments to employees living away from home. When a family lives in Tokyo and the husband is transferred, only the father relocates, so that family life and the educational activities of children are not disrupted. Visits were made to executive apartments owned by corporations and investment groups, which ranged from stark accommodations to stylish complexes with extensive amenities. We also visited apartments for college students. Most student housing in Japan is offered by private companies that have no connection with the colleges. Students from as many as ten or twelve colleges live in the same complex, selected on the basis of amenities, cost, and availability of public transporation. Almost every student accommodation has a private room for each resident, containing a small refrigerator and one-burner stove, a modular bathroom, hanging closet, built-in bed and dresser, desk, cable outlet, and balcony. All these observations were included in design deliberations, resulting in a concept that was markedly more modest than the developer's original scheme.

The emphasis in this study was on facts, while the developer's original staff work was simply speculation about possible styles and lavish amenities that, when analyzed, proved to be of little value to the residents and economically unfeasible in terms of land and development costs. Insights were shared and the presentations to the developer were orchestrated to assure that findings were accurately and completely given. As is almost always the case, a disciplined approach to a cultural challenge delivers design solutions that are equally acceptable to clients and to those who wish their traditions honored.

While the value of developing cultural assessment skills is evident, it must be remembered that a client's initial concept is often absolutely correct. For example, there is a remarkable building in Kyoto, which is the sole product of the owner's creativity. His firm manufactures clothing and specializes in women's fashions. Considering every limitation placed on professional women in Japan, the owner designed an appropriate facility. The ground floor has display rooms and space for fashion shows, the top floor contains company offices, and on the middle floor is a private club for professional women and their guests, which is the most unique feature. When you have a creative and enterprising client, it is best to reinforce his or her concept by verifying that the details are correct.

Contributing to a New Enterprise

Here we consider the case of a development concept that includes an outdoor life retail complex located in Tokyo, catalogue stores throughout the nation, a rural destination resort, and a monthly magazine to increase interest in outdoor activities. This project is an investment enterprise that capitalizes on a major breakpoint— the anticipated significant increase in leisure time in Japan. In this case, America became the focal point. A trip was made to Freeport, Maine, to visit the L. L. Bean company and learn how a small downeast township became an international destination. Recreational industry expositions in America and Japan were also attended. Examination of sales records of mail order firms indicated a great deal of interest in American recreational products. In one instance, 2,000 Japanese were found to be mail order customers of an American firm. Advertising copy and recreational articles in national magazines were studied. A further refinement was the decision to add to the retail complex an education center for various interest groups wishing to promote their activities, as well as a social center with lounges and restaurants. The Japanese consumer is experimental, always on the lookout for a good place to make friends and take up a new interest. The profitable Tokyo-based Sports Connection, for example, offers nineteen forms of recreation and study, ranging from canoeing and equestrian training to English language courses (Nihon Keizai Shimbun, 1992).

The publication of an outdoor life magazine is an example of sound enterprise because, in Japan, there is a magazine for every possible subgrouping of society (*Nikkei Marketing Journal*, 1991). The developers of this project recognized the important premise that once a recreational interest is established it becomes all-consuming. The battle is to use existing information to create interest and entice individuals and families to consider a new activity. With this as a starting point, archival research has a firm target.

Perfecting a Design Center

This project concerns the development of design concepts, schemes, forms, and features for a home design center in Osaka. This city is a center of intense economic activity, which provides an opportunity for the marketing of high-quality products and professional services. What can an American firm contribute to such a project? Open-mindedness. Due to the emphasis placed on the study of architectural history, there is a little bit of anthropologist in each of us. We understand well that the tempo and concerns that guide everyday activities must become part of our comprehensive understanding of what constitutes a perfect building. One essential activity is to visit sites that have facilities and activities as similar as possible to the current project.

In the case of the home design center, similar retail outlets throughout Japan were visited. A one-week itinerary looked like this: Sunday evening, dinner with client; Monday, site visits throughout Tokyo, including the Home Information Center, Matsushita Electronic Company showroom, Tokyo Department Store, Takashimaya Department Store, Mitsukoshi Department Store, and Bath and Sanitaryware Showroom; Tuesday, similar site visits in Hiroshima and Fukuoka; Wednesday and Thursday, additional site visits in Tokyo and Yokohama; and Friday and Saturday, a review of findings. Although the pace was hectic while traveling, once a site was reached it became deliberate. Attention to people, customers, and staff requires a snail's pace. This is when you notice opportunities or innovations that escape the local professionals, particularly if you pay the closest possible attention to what people are doing, their tasks and objectives. Another important aspect of this experience is that foreign clients want to get to know you as a person, with a family, social interests, and professional associates. An invitation to have your Japanese colleagues, for instance, come and work with you at your home office is always accepted.

Quality of Life at Work, at Home, and in the Community

The last project used to illustrate the dynamics of cultural assessment is a proposed science city development of 400 hectares located in Japan, between Tokyo and the Nikko National Forest. The developers estimate a working population of 4,500 people and 9,000 permanent residents. The objective is to blend the best of city and country life to make the development attractive to corporations and the families of employees. The guiding vision here is to concentrate human, social, educational, cultural, business, and engineering and scientific resources in a locale perfectly designed to support energetic and creative enterprises. The developers believe that this concept creates the impetus for investment and development.

An examination of Tsukuba Science City was the starting point for this project. This is the first science city in Japan, founded in 1963, with a budget of $5 billion in public funds. Tsukuba was selected because of the number of problems reported. Rogers and Chen note that this development is not yet livable by Japanese standards. In support of their view, they cite the existence of the:

> Tsukuba syndrome, a medical phenomenon consisting of skin rash, diarrhea, and other health problems that reflect individuals' maladjustment to the lifestyle of this new city. Tsukuba has an unusually high suicide rate. The technopolis, with a total population of 150,000, lacks an adequate number of bars, restaurants, and other services that the Japanese consider essential to urban life. Many residents of Tsukuba City still maintain a residence in Tokyo, spend the weekends there, or even commute every day (Rogers and Chen, 1990: 26).

During the site visit in 1990, the city's first community event was being held, with dancing, food stalls, folk art, and all the amusements common to events planned to draw individuals and families together. The lack of quality of life became a red flag, highlighting the need to consider the social and cultural fabric of a science city development.

Site visits in America provided examples of science city master plans that support the lifestyles of people and the achievement of quality of life at work, at home, and in the community, such as the University Research Park in Charlotte, North Carolina, Woodlands in Houston, Texas, and the Gateway in south Florida. The examples most relevant to the proposed development were found in Lansdowne, Virginia, and Interlocken, Boulder County, Colorado. These science parks are successful because they are responsive to the strategic thinking of corporations and alert to the needs of individuals and families. Corporations recognize these developments as places in which they can bring together their research and development, marketing, and business staffs. These developments provide highly desirable facilities, the needed technical and business services, and outstanding family life and community features.

The report to the client suggested that it is not enough to present a "pretty picture" of life in a science city. Young scientists and engineers must have opportunities for evening social activities, and children need to be able to participate in group activities and sporting events. The exact nature of these needs, such as tutorials for children studying for university entrance examinations and enriching educational experiences for young mothers, must be identified. Quality of life concepts must be responsive to a wide spectrum of personal needs and desires. Young children, high school students, young adults, older people, and retired people will all be affected by life in the science city development. A thorough cultural assessment will ensure that such concerns are addressed.

Safeguards

The cultural challenge, in cases such as the four presented, is always paradoxical. For instance, when we work to be concise and clear, complete and correct in everything we say and write, we will find that what is considered concise and clear, complete and correct varies from culture to culture. The challenge is not insurmountable. One solution is to avoid words and use visual images to characterize findings and recommendations. The utility of perceptual meaning is the great advantage the building industry has over other businesses. The sketches, drawings, and models we create are informative across cultures. The findings and numerical analyses for the home design center project were accompanied by sketches depicting the source of concepts and recommendations. When we reduce reliance on words, we avoid the nuances and subtleties of language. If nothing more, we reduce the time delays and expense associated with translations, which no matter how well done, will always fail to convey exact meaning or intent.

One final thought—international practice is extremely competitive. Michael J. Crosbie (1994) makes this clear when he describes the practice of Tai Soo Kim, an architect with a practice in America and in Korea. The most remarkable aspect is that this is a 24-hour practice. At the close of each day, materials are faxed to Korea and by the next morning the assignment is returned to New York. Although he competes with the largest American and Japanese firms, Kim's presence in Korea, backed by the resources in his American office, makes him a winner again and again. This is a benchmark practice that demonstrates how to compete effectively in Asia.

Shoulder to Shoulder

There is no culture in which remoteness is acceptable. When hearts and minds are joined in an enterprise, the results are trust and confidence. In the four cases described, we relied on Taeko Matsuda, Chairman, Japan Housing Organization, Ministry of Construction, and Kozue Honda, now Director of the Human Factors Advisory Service, Daiwa House. Matsuda and Honda are known throughout Japan for their understanding of enterprise and innovative services to the building industry. The relationship between us always focused on the projects, and yet the real drama was the development of trust and confidence. This relationship allowed us to learn from one another and critique recommendations with ease. What surprised us was that this relationship bore little resemblance to the common advice about how to behave in Japan. This suggests that we should not rely on hearsay, but work directly and daily with our associates. You can validate this by reading *On Track with the Japanese* by Patricia Gercik (1992), Managing Director of the M.I.T.–Japan Program. This account of personal experiences has been reviewed as the finest book available about the vital human element of the Japanese, and is seen as the "golden key" to making cross-cultural communincations work. One favorite insight is: "In the early stages of a relationship, Japanese are conscious of sincerity and believe that choice is the best indicator of character. Often a newcomer to a situation will be offered several choices in order to test his dedication and his sensitivity to nuance" (Gercik, 1992: 197). In one case, it was suggested that a newcomer to Japan take the rest of the day off to recover from jet lag. By rejecting the offer and continuing to work, commitment was shown. There is little question that in this culture you will be tested for years.

Information Resources

You must be ready to profit from the information and knowledge resources that are more readily available in America than in any other nation in the world. In the case of the science city development, prior experience with Japanese professionals, families, and communities was sufficient to understand what is meant by quality of life at work, at home, and in the community. With this background it was possible to review the archives for similar situations and associated design concepts, schemes, forms, and features. Consider how easy it is for us to follow events in Asia as compared to the difficulties faced by the Asian people themselves. To overcome this, for instance, a major Japanese construction corporation maintains a staff of five in Cambridge, Massachusetts, with one assignment: read everything and attend everything. This is a necessary investment because Japanese archives pertaining to the building industry are meager and spotty. Even the National Diet Library has very limited resources for those wishing to follow architectural, engineering, and construction innovations and opportunities. Also, American firms freely exchange new concepts, whereas Japanese corporate innovations are not widely reported because they are considered to be proprietary assets.

You don't have to leave the country to find situations in which norms, customs, traditions, and lifestyles require the closest possible scrutiny. Norms, customs, and traditions are as important to individuals, families, and communities in America as anywhere in the world. Suggestions for dealing with foreign clients may be applied in your immediate area of practice. Consider, for example, the matter of competitive site selection. Earlier, it was noted that the commitment of local and state businesses and officials led to the selection of Tuscaloosa, Alabama, as the site for the new Mercedes-Benz manufacturing center. "Commitment" is a reference to the work ethic of the community and its willingness to contribute to the success of resident corporations. This community used its cultural heritage to promote its selection. In the case of a speciality food corporation selecting sites for new stores, lifestyles will be of particular concern because of the direct relationship between these and product preferences. A great deal of what you need to know is at your fingertips when you consider the considerable work of cultural anthropologists, the thorough work of historians, the archives maintained by community museum curators, and the willingness of local cultural associations to share their experiences with you.

CHAPTER FIVE

WORKING WITH CLIENTS

The consideration of leadership, strategy, and client relations and the associated methods of critical thinking, thorough analysis, and client assessment strategy brings us to this point in the characterization of the work of the executive architect. Here the focus is on managing the efforts associated with the attainment of quality of life at work, at home, and in the community. The executive architect must be a performance leader in this management effort. The executive architect must form building design and land development professionals and clients into a team, help the team focus on objectives related to quality of life, and assure that every decision is open to evaluation and critique. The strategy recommended by the contributors is to do everything you can to make your client representatives feel that they are members of the project team and as responsible for success as you are. This kind of partnership can be achieved if the following lessons are put to use.

Make Client Representatives Feel Essential

Clients are much more likely to contribute to project success when they are asked to work on a problem rather than just serving as a source of information. If you allow client representatives to become mere spectators, you forfeit the benefit of their knowledge, experience, and skills. Though individuals and groups of individuals have much in common, distinct viewpoints always exist. The goal of your collaboration with client representatives will always be to take the individual into the realm of judgment, to encourage the feeling that a personal view is valuable and should not be held back.

Provide Time for Give and Take

Always provide time for considerable give and take. If you don't, you will never hear that unique question that creates a valuable opportunity. Measure your relations with communication audits. Who has talked to whom, how often, and what information was exchanged? This is one instance where measured performance is essential.

Detect Barriers to Project Success

There are difficult clients, those with whom, as soon as one need is satisfied, another immediately appears. In the worst of cases this process is unending, continuing from project beginning to facility occupancy. It is the architect who allows this situation to occur, not the client. Discussions with client representatives will minimize these difficulties if you are alert to attitudes and pressures that lead people to maintain untenable positions.

You Can Easily Change the "Why"—
The Challenge Is to Change the "How"

This lesson is offered by Eric Richert, Director of Real Estate and the Workplace, Sun Microsystems Computer Corporation. He observes that while people will readily accept the reason why we are doing something new, it is far more difficult to convince them to change how they work to achieve the newly prescribed objectives. When working with client representatives, never take that nod of agreement as meaning too much. It may mean the acceptance of why things have to be changed, but doesn't necessarily mean that people will change the way they work.

Insights

Fred L. Foote, F.A.I.A.

Fred Foote, a graduate of the University of Pennsylvania, and his partner, Lauren Mallas, A.I.A., practice in San Francisco. Their office is in a Victorian residence on Pacific Street, near the Golden Gate Bridge and Chinatown. Nice location, dim sum for lunch. Their investment in computer technology and advanced software makes this office as productive as any in the city.

Fred is seen on campuses around the country, as he serves on accreditation teams. You will meet few brighter people in the profession. If your practice depended on dealings at the highest levels of major corporations, Fred is a person who naturally fits into that scene.

Interview Highlights

Working with clients demands attention to every project management challenge in a way that satisfies all parties. The wisdom needed would tax even Solomon.

+ There are still visionary clients around, but they're not as prevalent as they once were and they're not in the same level of control.

+ The client's priorities and concerns are the issues that need to be better understood and more aggressively understood.

+ Very often one gets the feeling that architects, ourselves included, tend to see clients as a means to an end as opposed to an end in itself, where they provide us the opportunity to do what we want to do.

+ Architects are better trained to deal with design issues because addressing these things has to be overlaid with values, priorities, concerns for user needs, and all those things that the architect does feel comfortable with.

+ In some areas like programming, cost control, time scheduling, and so on, architects seem to be either unfocused or inherently weak, and this allows the intrusion of construction managers, engineering people, and others who are not in fact more knowl-edgeable about these matters of time and money.

- Architects are very slow to come to the realization that being involved in programming means they don't have to redo it when they start the project because it is "goofed up" or out of date, both of which are very high possibilities.

- The lesson you have to learn over and over is that whenever constraints come in on a project, you've got to find a way to make the project better and stronger.

- We're looking for both inventing the kind of projects that we want to work on, and reinventing ourselves in the process.

The Interview

I think there's no question that the profession is changing. Society is changing; its needs are changing. Certainly it seems as though there is very much a perception of changing client needs, and I think architects have lost a good deal of credibility with client groups. When I say client groups, I mean particularly the institutional clients and universities, as well as corporate clients. I think a lot of it has to do with businesses maturing over the years, from being new businesses to sophisticated and more competitive ones. In recent years, business has grown more by consolidation than growth of markets, shall we say, although the international market has certainly grown. As architects look for new clients, there's a new awareness of some of the concerns that clients have, concerns that we may not have focused on as much as we might have in the past.

Since I've been in architecture, there have been two major "boom" periods. There was the period, both in terms of work and the recognition of what architects were doing, in the 60's and early 70's. This was followed by a recessionary period in the 70's, and then there was the boom period of the 80's, when it seemed like every office building that could have been built was built, whether there were people to sit in those offices or not (and it turned out there weren't, in many areas). So the 25- or 30-year period from the beginning of the 60's to the early 90's was a growth period. Even during the recessionary period of the 70's, which didn't last as long as the current one, there was the feeling on the part of the architectural profession that this was only a temporary swoon and it was only a matter of moments before there would be another boom period.

I think there's a different feeling settling in now. Client organizations are downsizing, universities and other one-time major clients are not building the way they once were. The idea of new communities and new towns—all those things are getting rethought, in the context of the fact that they've discovered in many areas, particularly in California, that there's no "there" there after all. People are seeking different kinds of things. All that is over-layered with the skepticism that's developed, just by the very nature of the economy and society's needs. There seems to be little expectation that most areas that are accessible to architectural practice in general are going to be stable for quite a long time. Anybody who doesn't think that is misguided, in my view. Although there are growth areas, such as health care and so on, they're limited to more specialized practices and very hard to break into.

At the same time as clients become more and more scarce, skepticism about the performance of architects in two areas—time and money—has become more crucial, to some extent as a result of the general "tightening of the belts." I'm not talking now about some of the more high-profile spending that's taking place in the Far East and Asia. A very small percentage of architects practice outside the U.S., and 85 or 90 percent of the firms practicing in the U.S. are small. In any case, organizations are getting more scrutiny from their stockholders, more scrutiny from their management, and one could even say that more organizations are now being operated by lawyers and accountants, and other people with a "bean-counter mentality," than they once were.

At one time, some major organizations—Volvo comes to mind, because that was a client of ours back East—were run by a single, powerful, visionary person, and that person set the tone for everything. If an architect ever got access to a person like that, as our partner did, then you were really speaking to Moses right there on the mountain and not to a committee of people. The whole process was driven by a visionary. There are still visionaries around, but they're not as prevalent as they once were and they're not in the same level of control.

Architects have, over the centuries I suppose, been very project-oriented and supported by the sponsorship of what used to be princes and kings, or the "captains of industry." In a sense, with that sort of simple client contact as a prototype, the focus has always been on the project itself. Very often one gets the feeling that architects, ourselves included, tend to see the clients as a means to an end as opposed to an end in itself, where they provide us the opportunity to do what we want to do, which is make buildings or make environments and design things. Sometimes the client is seen—often in fact, the client is seen—as a barrier to doing that properly, of having the freedom to do that, and very often these barriers tend to be financially oriented.

Also, there has been a change in the types of clients. For instance, developers came to be perceived as the master builders of our time. These were the people that were doing the great monuments and so on. Well, they were building monuments to themselves is what they were doing. Sometimes the architect got to ride on that ego trip as well, but I think the fact is that developers hired architects primarily for their aesthetic contribution, not so much for their management abilities. Those things were put in other people's hands because the developer was a client who, for the first time, didn't have an elastic budget.

I mean, historically, universities and other types of clients, particularly if they were supported by a donor, would come to you and say, "We want to do this project." You said, "That's very well and good, but what you really need is this." In fact most of the time that was the case; their needs were beyond what they thought they wanted. For instance, we did a project in Philadelphia for the University of Pennsylvania. It was an addition and alteration to the Annenberg Center, which had been funded by Walter and Lenore Annenberg. If the client in this case saw, through the studies that the architect was doing, something that they felt would be good to have but it didn't quite fit, they had a source. They could go back and say, "Look, this would really be great, if we had another 3 million bucks," and more often than not, that would happen. The same thing happened with the Princeton Art Museum. It started out to be a simple remodeling and it turned into a very major, big multi-million dollar project because of that very same thing. The director said, "I want to do this; I'll go find the money."

Developers have a certain limitation on that–on a scale of 1 to 100, a private enterprise with a lot of money might be 100, a developer may be 2 on that scale, and a university might be somewhere in between. Developers don't have the flexibility of saying, "Oh, that would be great, let's do that." If the formula doesn't work out with the payback and all that, there's no place else to go to enhance the thing.

In some of these areas, like programming, cost control, time scheduling, and so on, architects seem to be either unfocused or inherently weak, and this allows the intrusion of construction managers, engineering people, and others who are not in fact more knowledgeable about these matters of time and money but are recognized to be more so. This is notwithstanding the fact that architects still remain very high in the respect category for their creativity and their contribution to society. These are the things, I think, that make architects different from engineers and different from accountants and other people, as valuable as their contributions might be. I think that's where the credibility problem started: the architect felt that if you came up with the right project, the right design, the right amount of this or that, it was incumbent upon the client to find the money for it, and approve it, and go ahead.

That really is the point I was leading up to—that by focusing on the project, you begin to lose touch with the client. Architects need to regain credibility in some of these areas and discover new areas of influence where, by being smarter, being better prepared, one can influence the process in a more significant way and not end up being relegated to picking the colors. It's very ironic that during the late 80's when Helmut Jahn was on the cover of the United Airlines flight magazine, and architects were being both recognized and exploited for their design profile, shall we say—I don't know whether it was their building design or their physical profile in this case—but at the same time, there was kind of a snide lack of confidence in their overall abilities to deal with the complexities and these heart of the matter issues that can make or break a project.

A number of years ago, I was involved with the Wharton School for a period of time. I had some discussions with a graduate architect who was working there and had kind of bridged over into contacts with some organization development people. The most interesting discussions were about the broader realm of what architecture is, and what it means from an organizational standpoint. It was very much of a holistic approach, which identified stakeholders who were in the process already—the actual client and the actual users—with a broader realm of stakeholders relating to the urban context—the public at large, society at large, and all of these things, which broadened the continuum of what the built environment is about. In other words, what would be the greatest thing, and what has happened on occasion, is that at the moment when ideas are coming together about what some particular organization needs—organization used in its broadest context—that assessment of long-term needs and strategies, architects are in a position at that particular time to interact in the process. That then puts them in a position to be involved in two already codified areas of expertise—one is programming and the other is site selection and site evaluation. Historically, the opposite is the case. A company like Smith-Kline, with its own structure of businessmen, technicians, lawyers, accountants, and so on, would process this information virtually forever and come to a conclusion on both of those subjects before ever thinking of an architect. This is a lost opportunity, because I think that a contribution can be made in those two areas by the architect.

Architects are very slow to come to the realization that being involved in programming means they don't have to redo it when they start the project because it is "goofed up" or out of date, both of which are very high possibilities, and also that they are involved in all the decisions. But the fact is that programming, and to a lesser extent site selection, is just a matter of being willing to be somewhat more rigorous in terms of methodologies. In other words, programming methodologies are not well regarded or widely used in the practice of architecture because this is not what architects are used to doing. Again, they're project-oriented and programming tends to be more people-oriented, with interviews and surveys and all those things that architects frankly hate. But it's something that puts them in a position, if they're involved early on, for the follow-through, which then leads to a commission for a building or not, depending on the assessment of needs. And then at the back end of a project there's post-construction evaluation, maintenance and operations, replanning to meet future needs, and so on, for which the architect has all the information. But very often the interest is not there and the relationship has deteriorated over time because the project is over budget and late. This is not necessarily the fault of the architect, but I can tell you that the client or the construction manager, both of whom report to the higher-ups in the organization, are not going to blame themselves. So who's going to be blamed? Well, the architect— he's always right there saying, "Who me?" and is usually too naive to defend himself very successfully.

I think the key is to be more concerned about the client's priorities and less concerned about some abstract set of priorities that you come up with. The client's priorities and concerns are the issues that need to be better understood and more aggressively addressed—what does the client want to do, how does he want to do it, and how much money does he want to spend doing it? Internally, I think architects are better trained to deal with these issues than contractors, construction managers, engineers, or anybody else, because addressing those things has to be overlaid with values, priorities, concerns for user needs, and all those things that the architect does feel comfortable with. But there's a lack of confidence that comes from not having at their disposal the rigorous techniques or methodologies to deal with things like life cycle costing and other "pay me now or pay me later" kinds of concerns. All this sort of management is intended to make the design of a project better and more effective.

I have an old theory that any management technique or anything in the process that makes your work harder ought to be rethought. The test of any management exercise is: does it make your architecture easier—or, not necessarily easier, but better? Or, what are those elements of the management process that make your job more difficult in terms of producing a quality project? So some of these techniques would be more work, and some will be just a matter of saying let's do it a different way, let's design a process to deal foremost with the client.

There's a follow-on to that—if you find those ways of relating to clients, of having them do all the things that you know to try to do as the decision-making process goes on, they are buying into the process, so that they are on the hook too. If you can get people to buy into your strategy, to buy into your approach to the project, to buy into your design, then they will tend to support it, particularly if they believe that they were engaged in the process. If they want to take credit for it, that's all to the better, because then they will defend it under attack from inside or outside and support it as it goes through the crucial approval processes. That's a critical thing and that happens at all levels; each of the players at each of the levels has a role to play. I think the fact is that you tend to say that some of the people that you work with on a day-to-day basis in the client group don't matter, but they matter a great deal, because their support is important and not having opposition from all these levels of people is extremely important. People can very quickly get the feeling that they're being excluded from the process, that this is all going on without their involvement. Ninety-nine percent of the time they couldn't care less about the way it's going, it's just that if people are left out, then the way it's going is not going to suit them—or where it gets to, not the way it's going—where it gets to will not suit them, and therefore they will not be supportive in the long run.

In our practice, we have been involved with an extraordinary number of public clients. This is not something we set out to do—I mean, if you set out a long-term strategy for your firm, you'd never rely almost entirely on public clients—but it just sort of happened. Our former firm in the East had done similar projects—a courthouse in one case, and a project for the State Department—and they did a lot of university work, which is somewhere in between private and public. We did the extension and renovation of the Art Museum at Princeton. Princeton's a private university, but that tended to be a public type of project. We did the Museum at the University of North Carolina also, and we did an extension years before that at the University of Pennsylvania Museum. That firm had gotten the job for the San Jose Convention Center, and that's what brought us out here. I was partner in charge of that project, which turned out to be a $100 million public project. That led, in certain ways, to successfully getting the Yerba Buena Gardens project here in San Francisco.

We had to really learn a new way of dealing with these clients because there were players and plays that were unique to the public sector. The Volvo client was an industrial "king," if you will, who was able to wave his wand and have things happen. That was fantastic, but it was a dying breed, shall we say. We went from that to trying to do business in San Francisco, where you have a public entity with all sorts of local responsibilities. It has an ever-changing Board of Commissioners, it has changing mayors (we've been through three mayors on the Yerba Buena project), and community groups that are very, very active and empowered by the process. Whether they're intrinsically powerful or not doesn't really matter—their power over the process is accepted by the people who listen to them. Those people do tend to be more stable and more consistent over time than public officials, because public officials come and go. This creates a need for a very different view of the decision-making process by a client or an owner. Since there's no single point of responsibility, it tends to be much more complicated when you've got so many players in the game. Even if you feel you've gotten approval of something, you can't believe it until all of the votes are in. And some of the players show up at a late date. They have no history in the deal, but all of a sudden they are somehow brought in or empowered, and you have to work through that.

This means that the process is different, and also that the time frame is very different. In other words, many projects can be pushed and can be aggressively scheduled to get from here to there in a specific amount of time. In many public projects it's not over till it's over. The process has to go through a certain number of steps, and there's no way of cramming it through. This is a very different kind of a management hurdle, if you will. With private projects, there is a certain power structure—if you can you convince the power structure, they make the rest of it happen. As soon as you get into the public realm, those abilities are very, very different. You find contractors and construction managers pulling their hair out and wringing their hands because a decision cannot be made. They say, "We have to have this decision by next Thursday," and the potential is not even close. It might happen a month or two months after that. You have to have a realistic attitude and not allow the process to be a constant source of chagrin. Otherwise you end up feeling that nothing's being accomplished, that you can't get anything done, when in fact it's just knowing which decisions are not possible except under a certain structural reality and a certain time reality.

I'll give you an anecdote about the Yerba Buena Gardens project, just to give you an idea of how that bureaucratic process can affect your work. Because it was a city project, it was tied into other redevelopment plans—the Moscone expansion, other plans for Yerba Buena, and different things on different blocks. The Moscone expansion was in the same footprint and ended up being underneath Yerba Buena Gardens. We did several design schemes to explore the overall realm of the project and try to pull all these elements together, none of which had anything to do with the project at hand, *per se*. We tried to find something that was a broad-based combination of function and urban design. Then we were working away on what seemed to be our project, finally, and it was fairly complicated. At one time, it had restaurants and book shops, it had a conservatory and it had this and that. It had all these things in some measure because, as a public project, it needed to meet the needs of different community groups, different interest groups, different power groups, different political groups—God knows what. There were even some ingredients that seemed to be discussed in the context of trading off for concessions that didn't have anything to do with the project—the most insidious kind of problem to deal with, where other agendas are being leveraged by, "Well, I'll support this if you get me this over here." These issues seem to be sometimes the hardest to accept and deal with, but they are realities of a project. In any case, we had done a schematic design that everybody seemed pretty much happy with, except for a couple of substantial people who thought there was one element in the project that they couldn't relate to. They didn't think it was necessary—they thought it cost too much, or there was some other problem with it. In any case, this particular element of the design came in for a lot of discussion, a lot of questioning, and in the end, they said to us, in an official way, "Okay, we'll approve the schematic design on this project, but without that element." We said "Well, okay, that's interesting." It was the first time they'd ever approved anything on the project, I think.

This whole process took about two and one-half years, starting back in 1986 and going to at least '88, or something like that, maybe '89. Over this time we had done several different designs for the project, and we got to that point. There were a few other things that we felt had been kind of chipped away, but that was the major one. We said, "That's great, we got approval of the schematics. Now let's go back and figure out what to do with this major location in the project." Well, we worked for, I don't know, four to six weeks, and we came to the realization that we couldn't do the project as designed, without that element, and without being able to find a replacement element that wouldn't come under the same criticism. We finally went back to the client and said, "We hate to tell you this, but we think we really have to start over. We've wrung this out as much as we can, and there are too many things that were designed in context with this missing ingredient. We feel that the rest of it is now in question and we can't really deal with that." They said, "Fine," and we basically started over. Now you never really start over on a project because you have so many things in hand that it comes back fairly quickly. But the result was a dramatically different design all the way around, and we hope that it turned out as well or better than the other one would have. That design was on the verge of being finally approved when the retail developer came in and said, "We want to do something over here on this side that's totally different." This led to another major redesign, but it was clearly a big advancement for the retail and fortunately, we feel those alterations made the project stronger.

So, I think the lesson you have to learn over and over is that whenever these constraints come in on a project, you've got to find a way to make the project better and stronger, even if you have to start over. And you have to learn what can be accommodated and when accommodation crosses over into something that is not as worth doing, or not what you think the client wants or deserves. I guess to make everything fit is a matter of being clear and focusing, to some extent at least, on what the client's priorities are, what makes his clock tick, what motivates him—what motivates him in a positive sense and on the other side, what things will turn him off and erode his support of his own project. It's always sort of a tug of war on priorities because there's only so much quality that can be sacrificed.

Where are we headed? What do we see as the future? I think the tragedy of organizational development in architectural firms is that architects with talent, vision, design character, and so on end up as principal of an office—a small office, or sometimes a big office—either way, they end up doing far too much management and don't do architecture any more. We decided that we wanted to get back to doing architecture, as opposed to having our employees do all the architecture, less well than we could probably do it, having to argue with them in the process, and not having any fun at all. That's not to say we didn't enjoy and do a lot of business development and office management stuff. I was managing partner of the firm in Philadelphia for years and years, and my partner, Lauren Mallas, was very much involved in management, even though each of the partners insisted on maintaining project activities. We felt good if we could spend 60 percent of our time on projects and 40 percent on management, or even 50–50, we felt we were doing well. But half the time we felt we were being torn, and also, until you invest the time to educate yourself in areas that you didn't learn anything about in architectural school, you just don't feel equipped to deal with a complex organism and a large project.

We had organizational consultants in a number of years ago, when we grew from a small six-person firm to a firm with twenty or thirty people and two offices, one in Philadelphia and one in New York. We did the best we could—we bought as many of the prayer books on business development as we could find and went to all the seminars. But the fact is that even though we felt that there is a potential for large firms to restructure themselves, the traditional way that one has advanced in the profession has been through growth of the firm. The prototypical large firm, Skidmore Owings & Merrill, and other famous ones, grew from being a small group of partners to thousands of employees. Well, now they're back down to hundreds of employees and trying to figure out what to do next. I'm sure there are techniques of managing a large firm in a stable economy, which we're going to be facing for a very long time. People are not going to be promoted, either within a firm or going from one firm to another, on this explosive tidal wave of work that we had in the 60's and again in the 80's. That won't happen in the 90's and may not happen in the millennium. Years ago, someone predicted that the profession was heading toward a healthy environment for both small and large firms, but that medium-sized firms were going to be in trouble. Being part of a medium-sized firm at the time, I of course rejected that argument altogether, but I think to some extent it's coming to pass. I think the reality of the profession has always been that 80 percent of the employees in the U.S. are in large firms, but 85 or 90 percent of all the firms are small firms of ten or less.

So, we have begun to address that reality personally, as well as wanting to get back to doing things ourselves. Lauren was already way beyond computer-literate when we moved out here, in terms of word processing and bookkeeping and, more importantly, CAD drafting programs. Since then I have learned CAD myself. We recognized that the biggest impact on the architecture profession right now, other than the state of the economy, has been made by computers. Computer programs allow us to do everything without any in-house assistance, and with an extraordinarily small amount of outside bookkeeping help. Lauren does the bookkeeping—she spends maybe three or four days a month on it—and the outside accountant comes in once a quarter, and that's it. That just wouldn't have been possible even ten years ago.

I think our business development ideas right now are mainly looking for ways to find or create work, with a focus on the latter. As a new firm, going after work in the traditional way is difficult because there's less work and it's more competitive. The opportunities are different now and we're also looking to do things differently. We still have some of our own projects, although none of the ones we've been involved in since we've been out here have gone ahead. It's pretty frustrating to get a client and then have nothing happen, but that happens more often than not. We have a big development project in the East Bay that we hope will go ahead, but the original developer went bankrupt. We have a proposal in for a construction management subcontracting role on a job at Yerba Buena, as part of a larger team. That grew out of the role that we provided on Yerba Buena as the local architect for the Philadelphia firm, which was a lot of site trouble-shooting, problem-solving, and quality control. So, you sort of go where there's some opportunity, but our major effort is to pursue work that we're interested in.

Out here, some of the nicest work that's historically been done, in the Bay Area and Northern California, is in housing, both market-rate and affordable housing. When we first started talking about coming out here, that was something that we wanted to do because we had done nothing except some isolated work on single family houses, fairly elaborate houses for clients on the East Coast. The traditional marketing idea is to talk to nonprofit organizations. Well, the ones that everybody knows have hundreds of architects after them, and all these other people have housing experience that we didn't have. So we have written a strategy to develop a nonprofit corporation of our own to develop affordable subsidized housing on a small scale. After looking around and researching the market, if that's the right word, we felt that most of the active projects tend to be larger projects, because larger projects involve tax credits and all these complicated things. We felt that both from the standpoint of our interest and the stage of our careers we'd look for smaller projects, somewhere between ten and fifteen units, where we could then begin to expand our involvement.

For instance, we would sort of invent the project, find the site, get an option on the site, and find a target clientele that we can focus on—either affiliate with organizationally or focus on them as a clientele to be housed. Then we can do all the architectural work and possibly even manage it. In the process of working on another development project that I was trying to invent, which was for-profit housing but low-end, I began to see that I wanted to participate in selling the units, helping people put together packages to renovate warehouse loft units. So I got my real estate sales license and expect to ultimately get my broker's license. A broker can provide management services because this would be rental housing. We have developed a liaison with a major contractor in the city, and basically it will be a kind of "do-it-yourself" design/build. It's not design/build *per se* because we're the client—we don't have to put together a package where there's an architect and a contractor providing design/build services to an administrative client. We're providing those services ourselves, and we'll be working together from the very beginning. So, in a sense, we're looking for both inventing the kind of projects that we want to work on, and reinventing ourselves in the process.

At the same time, we're trying to find a way to take advantage of what we know and what our experience is, because between us we have almost 55 years of experience in the architectural profession. We also want to be able to complete projects. I mean, these big projects are wonderful and have a big impact on the environment and so on, but they take so long. We've worked on Yerba Buena for eight years and it's still not over. We're still doing some miscellaneous consulting with the owners and fortunately came out on good terms with them. I think it was partially because, being separate from our former firm, they took all the end of the project heat, and we were perceived as pitching in to help out and trying to be useful to the client.

Earlier I made note of the fact that many of the largest firms have drastically reduced the number of their employees. Well, a lot of these people are out on the street right now, of course. We hear numbers like more than 40 percent unemployment in architecture in California, 60 percent in Boston, 50 percent in Philadelphia. But the interesting thing is that this may turn out to be the best thing that's happened to architecture in a long time, because these people are going into more peripheral things.

Some graduating students and others in all stages of their careers are changing careers, saying, "I've had it." We were just on the phone with someone from Philadelphia who's working on affordable housing there and hates it. She seems to hate the project, hate the office, hate what she's doing. She's thinking of changing careers. But many people are taking jobs in related fields. Some of them are working for contractors. One extremely high-profile architect that graduated recently went to work for an environmental firm. Many of them are going into the client side, working for clients in both public and private sectors. A former classmate of mine, who had her own practice in Philadelphia, married a man who was teaching at U. VA. She went down there and now she's working in their facilities planning department.

Well, the great thing about all that is that those people are on the client side. That has a plus and a minus to it, because sometimes there's nothing worse than having an architect for a client, but this becomes a sort of economically forced infiltration scheme into society at large. Now, that's a relatively new phenomenon. In other countries, it's more common—Peru and Mexico have had architects as presidents, but you can't imagine that in the U.S., right? I don't have anything but good feelings about all this, because I think an architect's education and experience in practice makes him very suitable for these decision-making jobs that require, again, a set of values, a set of priorities, a set of concerns about society.

In the last ten years, the A.I.A. has changed from being focused almost entirely on practicing architects, to a much broader realm of involvement, and one of the most active committees is Architects in Industry. This means architects who are working in the industrial client side, not architects who do industrial work. These are all high-powered people. The U.C. system has architects as assistant chancellors in a couple of the universities, and Michael Bocchicchio, a former State Architect, is now assistant vice president of the U.C. system. These are architects in powerful positions. Interestingly enough, they are quickest to hop on the weaknesses that architects bring to the program. In other words, they're the worst skeptics, particularly in these areas of time and money, because they know the mind-set of architects.

Yerba Buena Gardens, San Francisco, California. Mallas and Foote Architects with MGA Partners.

Yerba Buena Gardens.

Yerba Buena Gardens.

Yerba Buena Gardens.

*San Jose Convention
Center, San Jose,
California. Mallas and
Foote Architects with
MGA Partners.*

*San Jose Hilton and Towers,
San Jose, California. Mallas
and Foote Architects with
MGA Partners.*

Method No. 4
Knowledge Base System

Critical thinking gives us the big idea, thorough analysis the way to go, and client assessment strategy the first steps toward establishing a sense of cooperation, collaboration, and shared responsibility with stakeholders. This is the foundation for success. Now consider all the people who will become involved in the project, a combination of interests drawn from the following: client and client representatives, investors, lenders, underwriters, facility user representatives, architects, interior designers, building system consultants, facility managers, landscape architects, land planners, structural, civil, and transportation engineers, construction managers, trades and crafts workers, equipment and product manufacturers, institutional investors, marketing personnel, real estate executives, attorneys, business partners, and jurisdictional and government offices. The question facing the executive architect is, how do we remain focused on the needs of the client? It was this challenge that led to the development of the Knowledge Base System as a management tool.

"Bring life to a building before there is a building" is the goal of a Knowledge Base System application; that is, develop an encompassing image of what a successful project outcome is. This suggests that the work of building design and land development teams should be a response to nothing less than a thorough study of what people need and want. Clients, investors, and stakeholders are concerned with life at work, at home, and in the community. Quality of life means everything to these groups. To clients it means attainment of important building performance and building image features, to investors it means increased value and greater return on investment, and to facility users it is the demand for building professionals to recognize that the built environment has an impact on their life every day.

The client success and market development implications of the Knowledge Base System are notable. Only a methodology based on a responsiveness to quality of life concerns will keep building design and land development professionals in business.

Whether building design and land development should be transcendent, seeking to enhance quality of life, or mundane, seeking only to satisfy, is answered in the context of intellectual openness. You cannot provide good results for sophisticated clients developing complex facilities if your client service philosophy adheres to the traditional process: assess the potential of the site, develop a program, identify acceptable building features, create a fashionable design image, control construction costs, and construct the building in a reasonable time. In this management scheme, success is measured by what goes on inside the office. What should be of primary importance is the world outside the office.

Basic Strategy

Figure 5.1 presents in graphic form the basic strategy for applying the Knowledge Base System. It symbolizes the continual flow of information between research and design, showing that research and design are one process. This process is a means for accumulating ideas and sharpening perceptions, for combining design speculation and rigorous analysis. This open process strategy means that every time a new fact or finding about facility users' requirements or expectations is identified, its implications are

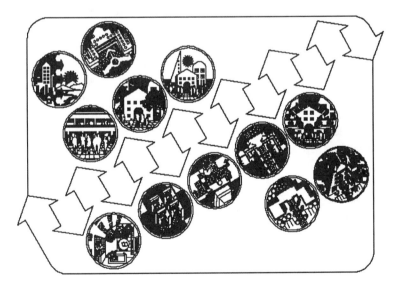

Figure 5.1. Basic Strategy

immediately investigated. Every time a design possibility comes to mind, its potential for meeting facility users' expectations and requirements is assessed. Throughout the entire application of the Knowledge Base System, this is the way to work. Though many speculations, insights, and candidate design features will evolve, no confusion exists because the Knowledge Base System fosters a team effort, makes the process visible, and provides a format for critique.

Although the Knowledge Base System is an open process, it is not the least bit chaotic. The Knowledge Base System provides the "road map" that assures that the building design and land development team will realize its full potential in an organized fashion. There is a special place for every insight and analysis. In fact, the 12 sections of the Knowledge Base System and the 54 question items are mutually exclusive information categories that become unique "addresses" within the process of strategic thinking and decision making. As an open process, the question items are continually reconsidered during the entire application. The goal is to produce design concepts, schemes, forms, and features that are justified in terms of derived knowledge about expectations and requirements related to quality of life. This derived knowledge is the most valuable result of the system. While data and information are factual, knowledge implies interpretation. Specifically, knowledge develops when data and information are reviewed and an experience-based judgment attaches relevance to data and information.

Within this open process, there are several areas of concern. How is the Knowledge Base System applied? What are the activities of the building design and land development team? What are the milestone achievements? What is the end result? The Knowledge Base System is essentially a twelve-step process. The first step, 1.0 Quality of Life Challenge, produces a framework that specifies project concepts. This step takes into account the existing situation, anticipated project outcomes, and the archives of design, planning, and construction and engineering. The next three steps of the Knowledge Base System, 2.0 Facility Life Characteristics, 3.0 Family Life Characteristics, and 4.0 Community Life Characteristics lead to a full and accurate characterization of the expectations and requirements of facility users. Here the activities of facility users are anticipated and significant customs, lifestyles, and traditions identified. The concluding work specifies which facility user characteristics should be emphasized in design. The fifth step, 5.0 Critical Circulation Patterns, begins with a study of facility user movements and equipment and material transport. It concludes with the specification of recommended facility circulation patterns.

The sixth step, 6.0 Interior Architectural Spaces, begins the development of the facility schemes, forms, and features needed to support facility user activities. In the seventh element, 7.0 Workstations, the goal is to identify specialized activities that require customized furnishing, fixtures, equipment, and space features. The eighth step, 8.0 Communication and Information Systems, is an increasingly important design consideration. Facility design features must support communication system requirements and information development and processing activities.

When the ninth step, 9.0 Facility Space Arrangements, is reached, sufficient information exists to create floor plan schemes, options, and alternatives, and associated facility management guidelines. The tenth step, 10.0 Facility Design Image, provides standards that serve to guide the development of exterior and interior design image features. The eleventh step, 11.0 Facility Site Plan, guides the achievement of compatibility between facility and site in terms of anticipated activities. The twelfth step, 12.0 Community Master Plan, considers how the area under development can be planned in order to meet quality of life objectives and neighborhood and community expectations and requirements.

A notable feature of the Knowledge Base System is that each item in the system is written as a question, rather than in the form of a task description. This was done for a distinct reason. When individuals are assigned information development tasks, work becomes formalized and often inflexible. However, when asked a question, an individual begins to contribute immediately, putting what he or she knows to work. The question items in the Knowledge Base System have been specifically written to be useful and understandable by building design and land development professionals, clients, and people in general. Each question item is numerically indexed, which allows for the precise ordering and storing of data and information. Each question item is generic. The question items can be used as is, modified to meet special needs, or supplemented with new items.

Each section of the Knowledge Base System reminds us that questions have always guided the work of building design and land development teams. As simple as any question might be, however, the resulting answers can be lengthy and complex. In quality of life research, it is essential to deal with the full complexity of people's expectations and requirements, raising the possibility that questions asked might complicate a project, rather than making it better understood. In response to this possibility, each question item in the Knowledge Base System has a selective focus that aids research organization and precisely directs inquires into the client's situation. The result is a division of research activities into basic areas of inquiry.

The Knowledge Base System Logos

Each of the twelve sections of the Knowledge Base System has a corresponding logo. These are more than artistic highlights. These logos were thoughtfully created by Larry Wolff, A.I.A., to reflect the intent of each section in a manner that immediately conveys to clients how thoroughly their situation is being addressed.

Knowledge Base System

1.0 QUALITY OF LIFE CHALLENGE

1.1 PROJECT CONCEPTS. Taking into account the existing situation and anticipated project outcomes, what are the project concepts?

1.2 QUALITY OF LIFE OBJECTIVES. Within the context of the stated project concepts, what are the quality of life objectives?

1.3 DESIGN ARCHIVES. Within the archives of architecture, interior design, and facility management, what concepts and designs are significant for the specified quality of life objectives?

1.4 PLANNING ARCHIVES. Within the archives of planning, what concepts and site and master plans are significant for the specified quality of life objectives?

1.5 CONSTRUCTION AND ENGINEERING ARCHIVES. Within the archives of construction and engineering, what theories, standards, and specifications are significant for the specified quality of life objectives?

2.0 FACILITY LIFE CHARACTERISTICS

2.1 **FACILITY USER CATEGORIES.** Who will be active within the facility? How may these individuals be grouped by responsibilities and intentions? How many individuals does each category include?

2.2 **ORGANIZATION STRUCTURE.** What are the common and exceptional relationships between groups and organizations that use the facility and contribute to activities within the facility?

2.3 **FACILITY ACTIVITY DESCRIPTIONS.** What are the anticipated activities of facility users? What is known about the extent, time of occurrence, and duration of anticipated activities?

2.4 **FACILITY LIFE CUSTOMS.** What are the philosophies and values of the organizations and groups that will use the facility? What are the significant customs, lifestyles, norms, and traditions of facility users? Are these characteristics stable or likely to change?

2.5 **FACILITY DESIGN OBJECTIVES.** Responding to identified expectations and requirements, which facility user characteristics should be emphasized in design?

3.0 FAMILY LIFE CHARACTERISTICS

3.1 FAMILY LIFE GROUPS. Who will be living in the residences? How may these individuals be grouped by family life expectations and requirements? How many individuals does each category include?

3.2 FAMILY STRUCTURE. What are the common and exceptional relationships within and between family elements?

3.3 FAMILY ACTIVITY DESCRIPTIONS. What are the characteristic activities of individuals and families while at home and in their neighborhoods? What is known about the extent, time of occurrence, and duration of anticipated activities?

3.4 FAMILY LIFE CUSTOMS. What are the perceived roles of the family in individual and community life? What are the customs, lifestyles, norms, and traditions of individuals and families? Are these characteristics stable or likely to change?

3.5 HOUSING AND NEIGHBORHOOD DESIGN AND PLANNING OBJECTIVES. Responding to identified expectations and requirements, what family life characteristics should be emphasized in housing design and neighborhood planning?

4.0 COMMUNITY LIFE CHARACTERISTICS

4.1 COMMUNITY LIFE GROUPS. Who visits and lives and works in the community? How may these people be grouped by community life expectations and requirements? How many individuals does each category include?

4.2 COMMUNITY STRUCTURE. What are the common and exceptional relationships between groups and organizations that make up the community and influence community life?

4.3 COMMUNITY ACTIVITIES. What are the activities of those who visit and live and work in the community? What is known about the extent and time of occurrence of anticipated activities?

4.4 COMMUNITY LIFE CUSTOMS. What is the perceived role of the community in individual and family life? What are the customs, lifestyles, norms, and traditions of those participating in community life? Are these characteristics stable or likely to change?

4.5 COMMUNITY PLANNING OBJECTIVES. Responding to identified expectations and requirements, what community life characteristics should be emphasized in community master plans and associated facility designs?

5.0 CRITICAL CIRCULATION PATTERNS

5.1 USER FLOW. How many people will be entering, leaving, and moving about within the facility, for what purposes, and how frequently?

5.2 EQUIPMENT AND MATERIAL TRANSPORT. What are the characteristics of the equipment and material that must be transported to and within the facility? How will these items be transported, and what is the frequency of such movements?

5.3 RECOMMENDED CIRCULATION PATTERNS. What are the recommended circulation patterns for user and equipment and material flow? In what way is this proposal a response to concerns for efficiency, convenience, safety, and security?

6.0 INTERIOR ARCHITECTURAL SPACES

6.1 SPACES. What spaces are needed to support facility users' activities?

6.2 FURNISHING, FIXTURES, AND EQUIPMENT ALLOCATIONS. What furnishing, fixtures, and equipment, fixed or mobile, does each facility space require?

6.3 CONVENIENCE, SAFETY, AND SECURITY. Will any facility user group or activity require special fixtures, furnishing, space layouts, information displays, or surface treatments? In anticipation of undesirable events, what special safety and security measures are necessary?

6.4 AMBIENT ENVIRONMENTAL CRITERIA. What provisions should be made for the effect on facility users of temperature, humidity, air quality, air movement, illumination, noise, distractions, annoyances, hazards, and climatic conditions?

6.5 INFORMATION DISPLAYS. What are the required information displays?

6.6 DURABILITY AND MAINTAINABILITY. Where do spaces require special attention to durability and maintainability of surfaces?

6.7 SPACE PLANS. What space plans best correspond to facility users' expectations and requirements?

7.0 WORKSTATIONS

7.1 WORKSTATION FACILITIES. Where are workstations required?

7.2 WORKSTATION ACTIVITIES. What are the specific workstation activities? What task sequences and timelines characterize the activities assigned to the workstation?

7.3 WORKSTATION FEATURES. What are the furnishing, equipment, fixture, tool, and material requirements of the subject workstation?

7.4 WORKSTATION LAYOUT. Since each workstation has unique activities and support requirements, how should each workstation be arranged?

8.0 COMMUNICATION AND INFORMATION SYSTEMS

8.1 COMMUNICATION AND INFORMATION SYSTEM FACILITIES. Where are communication and information system facilities required?

8.2 COMMUNICATION AND INFORMATION SYSTEM ACTIVITIES. What is the relative complexity or uniqueness of the information development and processing activities? What task sequences and timelines characterize the noted activities?

8.3 COMMUNICATION AND INFORMATION SYSTEM FEATURES. What are the furnishing, equipment, fixture, and software requirements of the subject communication or information system?

9.0 FACILITY SPACE ARRANGEMENTS

9.1 PROPOSED FLOOR PLAN SCHEMES. Considering all research findings and developed design concepts, what are the best schemes for achieving project concept and quality of life objectives? In terms of facility user expectations and requirements, what is the benefit and problem resolution potential of each suggested scheme?

9.2 SPACE REQUIREMENTS. How many square meters are estimated to be required for each facility space and support area?

9.3 FACILITY MANAGEMENT SCHEME. What are the necessary guidelines and manuals that show people how to use facility operational features?

9.4 ALTERATION EXPECTANCIES. How soon might it be necessary to modify or expand the facility? What events would most probably

10.0 FACILITY DESIGN IMAGE

10.1 FORM AND STRUCTURE. What are the proposed facility form and structure design concepts?

10.2 EXTERIOR DESIGN IMAGES. What are the proposals for exterior facility design images, details, and accents?

10.3 INTERIOR DESIGN IMAGES. What are the proposals for interior spatial forms, design images, and surface colors, textures and patterns?

10.4 CONCEPT JUSTIFICATION. What are the possible effects on facility users of each design image recommendation?

11.0 FACILITY SITE PLAN

11.1 SITE REQUIREMENTS. What are the site requirements and to what needs and wants do these correspond?

11.2 AREA IMPACT. What are the activities surrounding the site? What will be the impact of facility activities on the surrounding neighborhoods?

11.3 SERVICES IMPACT. What will be the impact of facility-based activities and operations on existing public and private services? Will existing services need to be improved or expanded?

11.4 SITE PLANS. How should the site be planned in order to achieve quality of life objectives, respond to the needs of those occupying nearby sites, and meet requirements for outdoor space in terms of amenities and landscape development?

12.0 COMMUNITY MASTER PLAN

12.1 COMMUNITY SERVICES. What public and private services are needed?

12.2 COMMUNITY FACILITIES. What facilities and planned environments are needed to support community life?

12.3 CHANGING COMMUNITY REQUIREMENTS. How soon might it be necessary to modify or expand community facilities and services? What events would lead to this requirement?

12.4 OUTDOOR SPACE. What are the requirements for outdoor space in terms of amenities, landscape development and preservation, and enhancement of existing natural features?

12.5 MASTER PLAN RECOMMENDATIONS. How should the community be planned in order to meet the full range of identified community life expectations and requirements?

Design Guidelines

Knowledge Base System application results are formed as design guidelines. It is essential to note that these guidelines are only a visible record of the team's progress in developing justified design concepts, schemes, forms, and features. A design guideline should not be considered as a goal in itself, or as a document to be developed. The function of design guidelines is to bring findings and ideas to some point of synthesis. The goal is to provide a focus for discussion in which those knowledgeable about the project can employ their insights and expertise with confidence. This strategy encourages experimentation and debate. These critical evaluations achieve something very essential. No design concept, scheme, form, or feature stands alone; it is always accompanied by a statement of justification. Therefore, every formal design guideline statement must have two parts: the recommendation and the justification for that recommendation.

Programming Has Too Many Shortcomings

Let's address the view that design without a program and programming outside of the context of design are both problem situations. When, as is common in programming undertakings, research and design are not a single process we fail to benefit from professional experience and expertise at the inception of the project. This expertise and experience must not wait in the wings for a program or brief. Put the entire building design and land development team to work from the first moment of project deliberations. Of even greater concern is the false sense of confidence fostered by having a program. All too often we rely on simplification of a complex situation. There is a tendency to make assumptions about facility users' needs and wants, and to believe that these assumptions are recognized and shared by all project participants. In reality, the expectations and requirements of individuals and groups are never that evident. As a result, many decisions are based upon erroneous impressions. Without design as part of the effort there is no critical process that remedies this problem. Design possibilities remain undiscovered because the effort required has been downgraded by a too simplistic view of the value of thoughtful design (Argyris, 1970: 89).

We must make design an integral part of every project deliberation by placing significant findings immediately before the entire building design and land development team. When programming is the first step in a building design project, we forfeit the dialogue, argument, critique, and evaluation that are central to the Knowledge Base System application strategy. Consider the controversy that developed in San Diego, California, regarding plans for a new $90 million, 393,700 square foot central library. As reported in the *San Diego Union* (Oct. 6, 1991), the library programming study was directed to space needs and efficiency, foreshadowing a building concept not unlike the uninspired box the new library was to replace. The potential of the proposed waterfront site and the opportunity to design a unique and appropriate building form were in danger of being overlooked. In fact, the mayor commented that if the programmer's version of the library were actually built, the world's best architects would be relegated to decorating a box of predetermined size and shape. This is a classic example of the results of programming outside of design: a failure to make research and design one process.

Programming is the least productive activity in the office when it perpetuates a linear progression from program to design. The programmer's goal is to tell the design team what the outcome of its work should be. This seems absurd when you consider that one budget modification, the discovery of an additional site constraint, a client modification, an overlooked facility user expectation, a community rejection, discovery of a new technology or product, or an entirely new and better concept for the project, will make the program worthless. The fallacy of making programming an end in itself deserves lengthy criticism (Harrigan, 1987: 160–209). It is nevertheless true that many people, particularly governmental facility development staff, support the use of programming as the first step in building design. CRSS, one of America's finest architectural firms, is adamant that the programming mindset is different from the designing mindset, that programming is problem seeking and design is problem solving, and that the two must be segregated (Peters, 1992: 401–402). The basic strategy for the Knowledge Base System concept suggests something quite different. It makes design and research one process. It involves the entire building design and land development team from the first moment to the last. Project deliberations never end. There is always an opportunity to make a final adjustment that makes the project outcome just a little bit better.

The Emphasis on Fad and Fashion

When an architect shuns the achievement of a high quality of life at work, at home, and in the community, we have the worst possible outcome. Unfortunately, too many people view our work with skepticism. Too many people see building design as dominated by stylistic fads and fashions and see the work of land developers as arrogant clairvoyance (Ashihara,1989). It may well be that people recognize the quality of life importance of physical settings and planned environments more readily than building design and land development professionals. We counter these possibilities through our application of the Knowledge Base System.

Commentaries

The commentaries that follow provide application insights and strategies for each section of the Knowledge Base System.

1.0 QUALITY OF LIFE CHALLENGE

The five question items in this section of the Knowledge Base System help create the boundaries of the project. A bounded problem is essential; without this framework there is no direction or limit to the work of the building design and land development team. You cannot promote a project that is more speculative than strategic, or more assumptive than knowledgeable. The initial project description must be precise, thorough, and comprehensive.

Responding to the first question item, 1.1 Project Concepts, an image of the future is created. The second question item, 1.2 Quality of Life Objectives, establishes the emphasis that will be placed on the achievement of quality of life objectives. In question items 1.3 Design Archives, 1.4 Planning Archives, and 1.5 Construction and Engineering Archives, we learn from the experiences and accomplishments of others and apply this knowledge to the project at hand. This is the first design deliberation in the Knowledge Base System application. The goal is to identify candidate design options and alternatives, based on what others have achieved in projects similar to the one being undertaken.

1.1 PROJECT CONCEPTS. Taking into account the existing situation and anticipated project outcomes, what are the project concepts?

This question item establishes a reference point for all the work that follows. In some situations, project concepts are fully and clearly specified by the client. Sometimes, the degree of preparation will be incomplete. In either instance, the building design and land development team must achieve mutual agreement and understanding of project concepts and their relative importance.

This question item, as well as the ones that follow, provides an opportunity for debate and argument. No project is free of uncertainty and controversy, particularly when emphasis is placed on achieving quality of life objectives. Therefore, successful application of question item 1.1 begins to resolve aspects of the project that are complex, troublesome, unique, subtle, or unresolved. The building design and land development team continually reviews the statement of objectives, confirming or disconfirming the proposed objectives, or stating an opposing view if it exists. In every step of the Knowledge Base System process, critique and evaluation of what has been achieved or recommended is always sought. When people are given an opportunity to state their views, they become committed to the success of a project and provide insights based on their experience, identifying objectives that may have been overlooked by others.

1.2 QUALITY OF LIFE OBJECTIVES. Within the context of the stated project concepts, what are the quality of life objectives?

In the initial response to this question, it is sufficient to convey intent; that is, to identify areas within the project where the quality of life is of particular concern. As you go further into the process and more information becomes available, necessary revisions may become apparent. This is true for every Knowledge Base System application. The most recent information is always used to help refine previously developed information.

There is a direct relationship between question item 1.2 and the question items contained in sections 2.0 Facility Life Characteristics, 3.0 Family Life Characteristics, and 4.0 Community Life Characteristics. As noted before, it is common to return to a question item after additional information is developed. What we learn in the process of answering the question items in sections

2.0, 3.0, and 4.0 will always lead to a revision of the answer to question item 1.2.

1.3 DESIGN ARCHIVES. Within the archives of architecture, interior design, and facility management, what concepts and designs are significant for the specified quality of life objectives?

1.4 PLANNING ARCHIVES. Within the archives of planning, what concepts and site and master plans are significant for the specified quality of life objectives?

1.5 CONSTRUCTION AND ENGINEERING ARCHIVES. Within the archives of construction and engineering, what theories, standards, and specifications are significant for the specified quality of life objectives?

The search for quality of life objectives continues with question items 1.3, 1.4, and 1.5. No one should attempt to conduct a Knowledge Base System application without examining the history of relevant building situations across the years, as well as reviewing current achievements. Even if project objectives are unique, a study of related projects is valuable. We consider the archives of planning because it is important to know which land development features have worked and which have proven unsuccessful, and under what conditions. The archives of construction and engineering are of particular importance. Failure to incorporate this data and information into design guidelines is a serious omission on the part of building design and land development teams.

2.0 FACILITY LIFE CHARACTERISTICS

More building design and land development possibilities originate from this section of the Knowledge Base System than any other.

2.1 FACILITY USER CATEGORIES. Who will be active within the facility? How may these individuals be grouped by responsibilities and intentions? How many individuals does each category include?

This is the most important question item in the entire Knowledge Base System. Although people may be easily distinguished from one another, initial views of which people will use a building are often inaccurate. Too many people are omitted from consideration and those who will use the building are superficially characterized. The problem lies in the extensive variety of users in every type of building design and land development situation.

The first step in this question item is to distinguish one facility user category from another. To this end, question item 2.1 is first addressed by asking the client to provide the names of individuals who are most knowledgeable about each program and activity element in the client's organization. As you work together to develop a comprehensive listing of anticipated facility user groups, the close association established with these individuals will always be beneficial. A collaborative activity like this becomes an insightful experience when client's representatives reveal informally what is important to them and what their concerns are.

2.2 **ORGANIZATION STRUCTURE.** What are the common and exceptional relationships between groups and organizations that use the facility and contribute to activities within the facility?

When we answer this question, more is needed than a reading of existing organization charts. People must be given the opportunity to describe things as they experience them. Successful research will identify the organizational activities that are particularly important and unique to the client. From these results the building design and land development team can compose descriptions of the client's programs and activities in a manner that makes the participants feel as though they have been fairly and accurately represented.

First, people are asked to describe the principal components of the organization, identifying areas of activity and the resulting outcomes. This description is developed by those involved in the identified area of responsibility and activity. Individuals need to talk about the history of their area of responsibility, its special aspects, and their expectations for the planned facility.

2.3 **FACILITY ACTIVITY DESCRIPTIONS.** What are the anticipated activities of facility users? What is known about the extent, time of occurrence, and duration of anticipated activities?

As the building design and land development team works on the development of activity descriptions, they are working to keep the design effort on target and to identify the activity patterns to which a specific response must be formulated. Every facility must support a wide range of daily activities. Therefore, every square meter, each fixture, furnishing and equipment item, as well as the funds expended thereon, will eventually have to be justified in terms of the activities being supported.

People are willing to describe their activities. They want the building design and land development team to understand their day and weigh the importance of their activities as they do. Decisions about the extent of inquiry should be made on an individual basis. More important, complex, unique, or troublesome facility user groups require additional activity information.

2.4 FACILITY LIFE CUSTOMS. What are the philosophies and values of the organizations and groups that will use the facility? What are the significant customs, lifestyles, norms, and traditions of facility users? Are these characteristics stable or likely to change?

The first three question items of this section of the Knowledge Base System deal with objective descriptions of people's responsibilities and activities. This question is concerned with the ways in which people see themselves. If we are concerned with how people are seen, demographic and observationally derived distinctions can be used. On the other hand, if we are concerned with how people see themselves—the state of mind of the facility user—subjective distinctions are needed.

People with common lifestyles, traditions, norms, and customs are identified here and formed into supplementary facility user categories and become part of the answer to question items 2.1. These distinctions are critical. The American Institute of Architects (1972) recognized this when they claimed that an understanding of differences in human needs and lifestyles is a critical first step toward understanding the circumstances surrounding professional practice. This goal poses many problems. People are suspicious about questions that delve into what they consider a highly personal domain. They will have no trouble answering question items 2.1, 2.2, and 2.3, as they believe it is appropriate to identify themselves, state where they fit into the organization, and describe what they do. In question item 2.4, they are being asked a great deal more.

Application of question item 2.4 will distinguish individuals and groups from one another in terms of lifestyle-based activities and preferences. This search for understanding begins with a careful review of the answers to questions items 2.1 and 2.2. This established spectrum of facility user groups tells us which individuals and groups are especially important. From this beginning, we begin to develop not interesting distinctions, but significant differences. This is always part of Knowledge Base System research: we need to know what is significant, not just what is interesting. The need for this strategy is evident. When designs fail, it is usually because some aspect of people's expectations did not occur to building design and land development teams, or was misunderstood. Many of the distinctions between lifestyles are difficult to understand or are so complex or subtle that they are difficult to respond to in design. Nevertheless, if an insightful level of understanding is not achieved, even the most likely opportunities for responding to people's lifestyles will be lost.

2.5 FACILITY DESIGN OBJECTIVES. Responding to identified expectations and requirements, which facility user characteristics should be emphasized in design?

This question item calls for a synthesis of the findings to this point. If this synthesis reveals remaining areas of concern, previously asked questions should be restated, to clarify and refine this information.

3.0 FAMILY LIFE CHARACTERISTICS

The application strategies developed in the preceding section are used here, with the additional consideration that objectives for the quality of life at home are a response to a variety of individual and family life expectations. These expectations are related to local, regional, and national traditions, customs, and norms. Requirements are related to land and capital availability, to family income, cost of living, and family size consideration, and, often, to government housing policies and subsidies. The answers to the following question items are developed in this context.

3.1 FAMILY LIFE GROUPS. Who will be living in the residences? How may these individuals be grouped by family life expectations and requirements? How many individuals does each category include?

3.2 FAMILY STRUCTURE. What are the common and exceptional relationships within and between family elements?

3.3 FAMILY ACTIVITY DESCRIPTIONS. What are the characteristic activities of individuals and families while at home and in their neighborhood? What is known about the extent, time of occurrence, and duration of anticipated activities?

3.4 FAMILY LIFE CUSTOMS. What are the perceived roles of the family in individual and community life? What are the customs, lifestyles, norms, and traditions of individuals and families? Are these characteristics stable or likely to change?

3.5 HOUSING AND NEIGHBORHOOD DESIGN and PLANNING OBJECTIVES. Responding to identified expectations and requirements, what family life characteristics should be emphasized in housing design and neighborhood planning?

Attention must be paid to specific family lifestyles when establishing housing design guidelines. How does the family spend its day together? What are the child rearing practices? How important is privacy? Concern for the quality of life at home for single people, the elderly living alone, and for those with physical limitations that require special design attention extends the complexity of the problem of establishing objectives for a specific project.

4.0 COMMUNITY LIFE CHARACTERISTICS

These question items are a safeguard against the tendency of building design and land development professionals to reduce the complexity of how people live so as to fit them into what has been designed. Simplification of complex situations creates an illusion of certainty, which is a primary source of poor design and planning decisions (Boulding, 1974: 8). Proshansky (1972: 453), recognizing this fact, cautioned that the study of physical settings and planned environments must be done in a way that maintains the integrity of these settings, the people contained in them, and the activities occurring in them. In other words, a concern with the physical environment in all its complexity must be matched by a concern with individuals and groups of individuals in all their complexity.

4.1 COMMUNITY LIFE GROUPS. Who visits and lives and works in the community? How may these people be grouped by community life expectations and requirements? How many individuals does each category include?

4.2 COMMUNITY STRUCTURE. What are the common and exceptional relationships between groups and organizations that make up the community and influence community life?

4.3 COMMUNITY ACTIVITIES. What are the activities of those who visit and live and work in the community? What is known about the extent and time of occurrence of anticipated activities?

4.4 COMMUNITY LIFE CUSTOMS. What is the perceived role of the community in individual and family life? What are the customs, lifestyles, norms, and traditions of those participating in community life? Are these characteristics stable or likely to change?

4.5 COMMUNITY PLANNING OBJECTIVES. Responding to identified expectations and requirements, what community life characteristics should be emphasized in community master plans and associated facility designs?

These question items caution that it is impossible to dictate a way of life to a community. What is needed is some idea as to the extent and variety of expectations: where do people want to experiment with lifestyles, and where do they want the comfort of the traditional? When building design and land development professionals fail to assess the sociocultural context of their projects, recognize people's preferences for one environmental scheme or feature over another, and fail to give full weight to the traditions and customs that permeate daily life, their theories and assumptions distort the reality of life in their projects.

5.0 CRITICAL CIRCULATION PATTERNS

For many building designers, information that describes the circulation patterns of facility users and the movement patterns of equipment and material comprises the essential insight for an appropriate facility design scheme. If facility circulation patterns are perfected, the likelihood of a successful project is markedly increased. The three question items in this section of the Knowledge Base System provide the informational basis for perfecting facility circulation, that is, the movement and flow of people and equipment and material. Like all question items in the Knowledge Base System, these are applied simultaneously. The objective is to determine what people do, their intentions, the importance of their actions, and how their actions vary by time and event.

5.1 USER FLOW. How many people will be entering, leaving, and moving about within the facility, for what purposes, and how frequently?

This question item is really an extension of question items 2.3, 3.3, and 4.3. Again, we need more than data; we have to discover the intentions of the facility users. In the design of a convention center, for instance, the importance of this consideration is evident. This concern for discovering intentions applies equally to hospitals, where efficient movement of visitors is one concern and what benefits can be provided for staff and patients is another. Certainly, in religious facilities, houses of state, and houses of legislature, facility user flow involves traditional ritual movement as well as the simple movement of people. Schools, student unions, government and community centers, corporate offices, housing complexes, and transporation facilities also have this two-fold aspect. This means that information should be collected along two streams: the descriptive and the interpretative.

5.2 EQUIPMENT AND MATERIAL TRANSPORT. What are the characteristics of the equipment and material that must be transported to and within the facility? How will these items be transported, and what is the frequency of such movements?

Detailed information regarding equipment and material flow is valuable. It is important to question with persistence. Certainly, hotels, hospitals, industrial centers, supermarkets, department stores, and convention centers move equipment and material on a daily basis, both for normal operations and to accommodate shifts in activities. Descriptions of objectives, destinations, times of occurrence, frequency, and means of movement are the indicies for determining the significance of equipment and material flow.

Emergency situations require additional considerations. Descriptions of the possible emergency situations, required equipment and material, means of handling, and advance preparation are the additional information objectives.

5.3 RECOMMENDED CIRCULATION PATTERNS. What are the recommended circulation patterns for user and equipment and material flow? In what way is this proposal a response to concerns for efficiency, convenience, safety, and security?

As with every question item in the Knowledge Base System, the answer to this question should be developed step-by-step. All the preceding information gathered from the application of the Knowledge Base System should be used to identify critical circulation patterns. After this information has been summarized, essential adjacencies are modeled into patterns of circulation, clearly indicating the nature of user and equipment and material flow.

Facility user and equipment and material flow is an hour by hour, day by day, and week by week event. A carefully arranged summary of findings, highlighting critical activities, events, periods of time, and design objectives, is essential. Final summary statements of research findings must be cleverly cast, providing both research results and a basis for formulation of insights. When design decisions are being made quickly, and new alternatives and options are being posed rapidly, there is no time to return to data summaries and begin a new evaluation. The design team must have an unequivocal view of what is needed, and a clear justification for each particular design recommendation.

6.0 INTERIOR ARCHITECTURAL SPACES

In the first five sections of the Knowledge Base System, clients and facility users work to reveal their expectations and requirements. Now it is the turn of the building design and land development professionals to take the lead, working to organize and evaluate information, select design elements, and formulate final recommendations. The role of clients and facility users at this stage is to critique proposed design features, offer suggestions, and provide additional information that will speed things along and make any design more representative of individual needs and wants.

This section of the Knowledge Base System is a response to the potential of interior architectural spaces for helping individuals achieve a high standard of performance and experience a personal sense of satisfaction. Conversely, inappropriate interior features can interfere with actions, fail to support important activities, and be incompatible with people's preferred ways of doing things. Further, the responsibilities of building design and land development teams may force them to confront diverse and often conflicting expectations and requirements for interior architectural spaces.

The value of a detailed critique is apparent as building design and land development teams deal with complex facilities and sophisticated clients. Proposed design guidelines can be adequately critiqued only if you visualize facility users as unable to move easily through the facility because allowed space restricts movement; as failing to develop a sense of orientation and direction because the visual surround is confusing and information displays are inadequate; as experiencing fatigue, stress, and frustration because the environment does not support specific activities; as attempting to adapt to light and sound levels that are intolerable; or as being exposed to an environment likely to produce accidents because of the failure to meet facility user safety needs. You must give life to your preliminary formulations by envisioning what the space means to the user. This is the sure way to avoid problems that would otherwise need to be corrected later—a burden the client certainly does not want.

6.1 SPACES. What spaces are needed to support facility users' activities?

The answer to this question provides a framework for the development of interior architectural spaces. The objective is to form a listing of facility spaces that reflects anticipated facility life characteristics as well as the building design and land development team's experience and interpretation of project and quality of life objectives. The listing of candidate spaces should be as extensive as possible, with a broad spectrum of possibilities originating, in part, from the archival research. The initial effort is concluded when the listing created seems to encompass the principal spaces appropriate to the situation. As new information is developed this listing will be reappraised, leading to revisions, additions, and deletions.

During an application of the Knowledge Base System, when do we begin to work on question item 6.1? The answer is that we do this at the same time we begin to work on question item 2.1. Question item 2.1 asks: Who will be active within the facility? How may these individuals be grouped by responsibilities and intentions? How many individuals does each category include? Question item 6.1 asks: What spaces are needed to support facility users' activities? When formed as a matrix these two listings provide a framework for the work of the building design and land development team. The function of this matrix is to keep spaces and people before the team at all times.

6.2 FURNISHING, FIXTURES, AND EQUIPMENT ALLOCATIONS. What furnishing, fixtures, and equipment, fixed or mobile, does each facility space require?

The contents of each space is as much a determinant of facility design as any other building system component, such as structures, building materials, and site features. This is no place for arbitrary thinking and assumptions. Selections must be justified by what have been identified as facility user expectations and requirements. Those who will occupy each space must review the design formulations as well as the rationale for recommendations.

6.3 CONVENIENCE, SAFETY, AND SECURITY. Will any facility user group or activity require special fixtures, furnishing, space layouts, information displays, or surface treatments? In anticipation of undesirable events, what special safety and security measures are necessary?

These three topics are often complex, and should be given special study. The research should be guided by applying the questions in the Knowledge Base System to the case at hand.

Security is a concern requiring a complete design strategy that takes into account what must be secure and the associated threat. Threats to individual security must be described in detail; a mitigating design should then be developed. What is recommended must recognize every detail of facility users' activities. For example, if the building design and land development team anticipates a lot of movement around a site where personal security is a concern, a wide field of view is required in order to monitor movement. If individuals are located in assigned areas, limits to access and control points can be established. Patterns of anticipated behavior may lead to emphasizing exterior lighting, individually controlled locking devices, sensors and triggering mechanisms, or even the establishment of a building or neighborhood watch or escort program. The facility management strategies and design features recommended, and the associated additional cost, if this is to be approved, require crafting a justification statement that portrays the full implications of not responding to the recommendation, as well as the likelihood that the design features will work.

Accidents, fires, earthquakes, and other threats to individual safety certainly require a design response. The two elements of safety design, prevention and lessening of effects, require attention to both design details and the management of people. Detailed analyses with a special concern for safety are always warranted. Even where codes and regulations serve as standards, more study is needed, not only because of the generality of these guidelines but because they do not realize the potential that is in every specific situation for making some very thoughtful, well-directed, and effective contributions to safety. Establishing escape strategies for fires illustrates this point. The location of signs is one thing, the design of multi-modality information displays that work effectively in smoke occluded spaces and when people are panicked is another. By establishing ahead of time the best possible means of providing directions and warnings, and by supporting this effort with design features, the full potential of facility design and emergency event management is realized.

There are many aspects of convenience, some related to specific expectations and requirements, and some to general preferences. This part of question item 6.3 recognizes that convenience is a major topic for design consideration and should be promoted by the results of careful analysis of daily activities. Facility user activity descriptions and circulation information should be scrutinized for opportunities to include convenience features. How significant the contribution will be to individual quality of life and whether it will be recognized and used as such determines whether the recommended design feature becomes part of the final design guidelines.

6.4 **AMBIENT ENVIRONMENTAL CRITERIA.** What provisions should be made for the effect on facility users of temperature, humidity, air quality, air movement, illumination, noise, distractions, annoyances, hazards, and climatic conditions?

Each interior architectural space generates its own microenvironment on the basis of activities, furnishings, and electrical and mechanical equipment, and each requires a selective response. In order to help the building design and land development team justify expenditures for mechanical, electrical, structural, and building materials directed toward environmental control, it is necessary to specify anticipated adverse effects on performance and satisfaction if recommended specifications are not adopted.

6.5 INFORMATION DISPLAYS. What are the required information displays?

The insights needed to determine the characteristics of information displays come from all the other sections of the Knowledge Base System. Ideas should be written down as they come to mind. Toward the end of the research effort the possibilities that were identified can be evaluated and options can be selected. The characteristics of the people using the information displays are of importance. What are the visual and auditory limitations and capabilities of the facility users? Will they be young or old, literate or illiterate, of one language group or several, moving at a leisurely pace or rushed? Usual conditions for the spaces involved, such as illumination and noise levels, and degree of congestion, should also be identified.

The specific proposals for information displays should include the information that will make it easier for individuals to use the facility, under both normal and emergency conditions. The information presentations that guide and direct facility user activities include exterior and interior signs, directories, displays, logos and symbols, illuminated and nonilluminated units, tactile and auditory elements, color coordinated surfaces and accents, and mountings and fixtures. The design features recommended should deal specifically with such detectability factors as location, placement, readability, size, and configuration. The detectability factors for auditory effects are frequency spectrum, loudness, periodicity, and directionality; for tactile effects they are texture, pattern, placement, and durability.

Information displays may also lead people through a sequence of actions. Library information displays are an example of this. From the information desk, to the reference computer terminals, catalogues, and reference room, on to the library's specific holdings, through the library shelving code, and to a document, the library user can be guided by directional aids. A traveler using a transporation facility is guided from the entrance road inwards, to the entrance, to check-in, to the waiting lounge, to boarding, to destination, and through customs. A task sequence in a manufacturing or assembly plant is often guided by displayed information and color-coded surfaces. In a shopping or retail facility the information displays would be in the form of signs, graphics, and surface color-coding and texture.

6.6 DURABILITY AND MAINTAINABILITY. Where do spaces require special attention to durability and maintainability of surfaces?

Whether special attention must be given to walls and ceilings, wall coverings and fixtures, floors and stairs, and doors and windows as interior and exterior building features depends on facility users' activities and regard for their surroundings. Prolonged hard use, movement of awkward material and heavy items, and vandalism are activities that must be anticipated. If there has been a history of disregard and carelessness that is unlikely to change, this should be brought to the attention of the building design and land development team. The team is capable of dealing with this area of concern if they know the likely events and situations. A space by space review by individuals familiar with these issues will identify problem areas; it will also provide valuable suggestions, which would deal with design features and maintenance schedules.

6.7 SPACE PLANS. What space plans best correspond to facility users' expectations and requirements?

What we know about facility life characteristics should be reflected in the work achieved here. The merit of the formulated design guideline is based on the thoroughness of the original research. This sequence of questions will define the main features of the space. With this model as a reference, the building design and land development team must then consider options and alternatives. Certainly, alternative development is a means of critique. As team members review preliminary recommendations, conflicts and omissions will be identified.

7.0 WORKSTATIONS

7.1 WORKSTATION FACILITIES. Where are workstations required?

7.2 WORKSTATION ACTIVITIES. What are the specific workstation activities? What task sequences and timelines characterize the activities assigned to the workstation?

7.3 WORKSTATION FEATURES. What are the furnishing, equipment, fixture, tool, and material requirements of the subject workstation?

7.4 WORKSTATION LAYOUT. Since each workstation has unique activities and support requirements, how should each workstation be arranged?

The term "workstation" is used in a general sense (Harrigan and Chapman, 1991). That is, every individual undertaking prescribed job, home, or community activities is considered to be sited at a workstation. All types of buildings are now equipped with workstations that are designed to support specific task performance. At work, in the classroom, the manufacturing plant, the service center, or convention center; at home, where people run businesses, extend their work day, or utilize distance learning opportunities; and in the community, where people serve others in libraries, adult education programs, or with special opportunities for the disabled or handicapped, workstations are a requirement.

8.0 COMMUNICATION AND INFORMATION SYSTEMS

Complex activities within spaces, buildings, facilities, and planned developments are totally dependent on communication and information system support. The requirements for a specific situation depend on the assigned communication and information monitoring, development, exchange, and application responsibilities. The basic question items provide the framework for this research.

8.1 COMMUNICATION AND INFORMATION SYSTEM FACILITIES. Where are communication and information system facilities required?

8.2 COMMUNICATION AND INFORMATION SYSTEM ACTIVITIES. What is the relative complexity or uniqueness of the information development and processing activities? What task sequences and timelines characterize the noted activities?

8.3 COMMUNICATION AND INFORMATION SYSTEM FEATURES. What are the furnishing, equipment, fixture, and software requirements of the subject communication or information system?

Sections 7.0 and 8.0 demand precise and thorough investigation. Chapter 6, Quality of Life, contains a field study methodology designed to supplement this research (see pp. 232–238).

9.0 FACILITY SPACE ARRANGEMENTS

These question items synthesize all the information heretofore developed to produce the most promising proposals for spatial design. Emphasis is placed on critique and selective modification of proposed design schemes, forms, and features. Research findings and corresponding design recommendations are always placed in the context of such considerations as site constraints, structural systems and materials, construction methods and schedules, and cost analyses. This provides the building design and land development team with a head start on the identification of conflicts and the formulation of compromises.

9.1 PROPOSED FLOOR PLAN SCHEMES. Considering all research findings and developed design concepts, what are the best schemes for achieving project concept and quality of life objectives? In terms of facility user expectations and requirements, what is the benefit and problem resolution potential of each suggested scheme?

9.2 SPACE REQUIREMENTS. How many square meters are estimated to be required for each facility space and support area?

9.3 FACILITY MANAGEMENT SCHEME. What are the necessary guidelines and manuals that show people how to use facility operational features?

9.4 ALTERATION EXPECTANCIES. How soon might it be necessary to modify or expand the facility? What events would most probably lead to this requirement? How do the proposed facility schemes account for this possibility?

In question item 9.1 you will synthesize your findings and provide a summary of the spatial implications for the total design. Your proposed floor plan schemes might take the form of a single-line drawing that brings together information from 6.0 Interior Architectural Spaces and 5.0 Critical Circulation Patterns. Many will consider it premature to become so specific this early in design and may wish to formulate a less binding recommendation. Nevertheless, a drawing conveys more meaning with greater clarity than any other type of information statement. Alternative arrangements can be developed, evaluated, and depicted with ease. It is essential that the design concepts, schemes, forms, and features in a design guideline are presented in terms of options and alternatives. There is always more than one way to meet people's expectations and requirements.

In question item 9.2 Space Requirements, a precise calculation of total square meters for the facility is formulated. Applying a current construction cost index to this calculation provides a reliable initial cost estimate. As the building design and land development team reviews these numbers and attempts to reduce costs, deliberations can be augmented with what is known about the significance of each space. Every square meter is supported by a description of associated client and facility user expectations and requirements.

Question item 9.3 Facility Management Scheme identifies the increasing importance of facility management as a building design and land development concern. Sections 7.0 Workstations and 8.0 Communication and Information Systems illustrate the extent to which this concern is taken.

Question item 9.4 Alteration Expectancies is an attempt to guard against premature obsolescence and to extend the effective life of the facility. Few things should be of greater concern. If this undertaking fails, the client will have to correct, with reorganization, additional staffing, or remodeling, problems that could have been avoided. Wherever new products, advanced technology, new activities, and new facility user groups are likely, these must be identified and the implications determined. Once likely changes in requirements are identified, they have to be evaluated in terms of design significance, relative importance to the client, and likelihood of occurrence.

Building designers often find themselves caught between the benefits of permanent structural elements and the complexity of providing a physical solution for change that is more than showing the on-site footprints of possible facility additions or the provision of a flexible furnishing and partitioning scheme. A progression of steps from the general to the detailed might be valuable here, first identifying sources of change and then evaluating these in terms of likelihood and significance. The design possibilities for both fixed spaces and managed spaces should be sketched out and a judgment made as to what to incorporate as facility features. Whether or not these deliberations are necessary depends on the client. While long-range planning is a characteristic of some organizations, other clients might find it difficult to look ahead because they are constrained by their situation, limited in view, or lacking the necessary information. The following questions need to be answered by the client and anticipated facility users: Considering what lies ahead, which of your current needs are likely to change? How extensive are the changes that you expect? When are these changes likely to occur? Are these anticipated changes part of the organization's plan? Are these changes likely to be generated by factors outside of your organization?

10.0 FACILITY DESIGN IMAGE

10.1 FORM AND STRUCTURE. What are the proposed facility form and structure design concepts?

10.2 EXTERIOR DESIGN IMAGES. What are the proposals for exterior facility design images, details, and accents?

10.3 INTERIOR DESIGN IMAGES. What are the proposals for interior spatial forms, design images, and surface colors, textures, and patterns?

10.4 CONCEPT JUSTIFICATION. What are the possible effects on facility users of each design image recommendation?

Throughout this study of the Knowledge Base System there is always the concern that "design" as the personal contribution of a design professional may seem of secondary importance. That is not the case. Consider the design objective of achieving a building image. The word "image" can be used as an ideal. It can also be used as a pragmatic value. As an ideal, a perfect space symbolizes to the user a regard for his or her needs. Likewise, a perfect space must also be a functional success. Bruno Bettelheim (1974) has stated how symbol and function will always be the two goals of design. Bettelheim suggests that even the smallest detail of a physical setting can make a facility more useful, and at the same time convey symbolic meaning in artistic form. He would not object that design features could be the consequence of a designer's personal preferences, experiences, and convictions about the worth of what it is he or she is attempting to achieve. There are many ways to design a symbolic and functional space for human affairs. What matters is the intention with which something is done—the wish to please and arrange things to make a strong appeal while achieving all functional requirements. Providing users with the best possible physical setting—however different the specific forms and details may be—bespeaks of the care that has been taken to give users the best possible physical and human setting, a message the facility user will seldom fail to receive and appreciate.

Bettelheim's high regard for design is a principal foundation of the Knowledge Base System concept. All that is asked is that the information developed in the first five sections of the Knowledge Base System is always the starting point for design. Don't exclude any building design and land development team member from design endeavors. There is a role for everyone. Design is a process of growth and exploration which can be considered as a potential existing in all members of the team. A child growing and exploring in a classroom, producing demonstrations and presentations for his or her class, is a designer. Likewise, the teacher who is innovating in the direction of providing effective educational settings is a designer. The teacher is, in this instance, neither a scientist nor a technician. He or she is a designer integrating knowledge and intuition, producing finely conceived and directed educational experiences and environments. Thus, although some use the term "designer" professionally, all members of the building design and land development team may share this title.

11.0 FACILITY SITE PLAN

11.1 SITE REQUIREMENTS. What are the site requirements and to what needs and wants do these correspond?

11.2 AREA IMPACT. What are the activities surrounding the site? What will be the impact of facility activities on the surrounding neighborhoods?

11.3 SERVICES IMPACT. What will be the impact of facility-based activities and operations on existing public and private services? Will existing services need to be improved or expanded?

11.4 SITE PLANS. How should the site be planned in order to achieve quality of life objectives, respond to the needs of those occupying nearby sites, and meet requirements for outdoor space in terms of amenities and landscape development?

The sequence of questioning for the Knowledge Base System is organized to develop design concepts, schemes, forms, and features from the "inside out." These question items run parallel with this effort. Preparation for this activity requires consideration of 2.0 Facility Life Characteristics, 3.0 Family Life Characteristics, and 4.0 Community Life Characteristics to identify the expectations and requirements that should be included in the deliberations of the building design and land development team. A thorough application of question items 2.1, 3.1, and 4.1 will identify the people that should be considered during facility site plan deliberations. Too often, facilities do not accommodate those who can benefit from the facility even though they may not be principal facility users. In many cases, insufficient attention is given to those who may threaten or disrupt facility activities. The application strategy for question items 2.1, 3.1, and 4.1 remain the same when applied to the study of site considerations. The particular situation will determine the boundaries of the study, which may extend beyond the site to include the surrounding neighborhood and community.

The client, facility users, and selected individals representing neighborhood and community interests will contribute to the development of site design guidelines. Early in the work of the building design and land development team, these individuals will help identify existing expectations, concerns, and requirements. As site design features are formed, these individuals will critique and help revise preliminary recommendations. These findings must be summarized, indicating source and importance of considerations to various individual and groups. As in every section of the Knowledge Base System, an explanation of the way options and alternatives were developed and evaluated must always accompany final design guideline statements.

12.0 COMMUNITY MASTER PLAN

12.1 COMMUNITY SERVICES. What public and private services are needed?

12.2 COMMUNITY FACILITIES. What facilities and planned environments are needed to support community life?

12.3 CHANGING COMMUNITY REQUIREMENTS. How soon might it be necessary to modify or expand community facilities and services? What events would lead to this requirement?

12.4 OUTDOOR SPACE. What are the requirements for outdoor space in terms of amenities, landscape development and preservation, and enhancement of existing natural features?

12.5 MASTER PLAN RECOMMENDATIONS. How should the community be planned in order to meet the full range of identified community life expectations and requirements?

In the community, quality of life is related on one hand to change, and on the other to tradition. A child wants adventure and yet profits from a stable neighborhood experience. The young adult wants social opportunities as well as the reassurance that comes from being part of a tradition. Parents seek outside opportunities for themselves and their children and yet want the family to be the source of support at all times. The retired person wants the stimulation of new experiences as well as a place where the old is treasured. To this array of contrasting wants is added the tempo of community life, with seasonal and commemorative events and the arrival of new faces. The extent of what is involved in achieving quality of life in the community expands when those who provide work and those who create and manage public services are considered in terms of resource availability and the willingness to contribute capital and effort on behalf of the community. This participation is always evaluated in terms of what the community is willing to do for itself.

The history of community life shows that it is essential that land developers be totally committed to making the experiences of people in the community as satisfying as possible. Facilities must be designed to establish the spirit of the community for all age groups. Those living in a new development must not wait years before developing a sense of community. The first community festival should be planned to occur within the first months of opening. The development must be known from the very beginning as a perfect place to live and visit. Consider the most controversial of projects. A corporation acquires the option to rehabilitate an existing historic landmark resort hotel and develop the surrounding land into single-family dwellings, condominiums, and a marina. This project will have a major impact on the community, increasing the resident population by 30 percent, The land in question is located in a 300-year-old settlement, on an island served by one arterial road connected to the mainland by a causeway on one side and a drawbridge on the other. Although the physical circumscription makes this case extreme, it has a characteristic common to many new developments in existing communities: the project is perceived by some as an investment opportunity and by others as a threat to the quality of life. The developer is seen to have one overriding goal: a profitable venture. No matter what is said to the existing community about responsibility, the allegation exists that it is only a position taken so the process of planning board review and town hearings will be favorable to the developer's proposal. The developer will ask to be allowed to follow the letter of the existing zoning ordinances. The community will want the spirit and intent of the ordinances given full weight.

This scenario could be rewritten for a proposed housing development, shopping center, office building, industrial facility, or science park to be placed within an existing community. The application of the Knowledge Base System concept would also be appropriate for determining the preferred characteristics and location for a new school, hospital, community mental health center, or a halfway house. Projects such as these are probably the most complex of all Knowledge Base System applications because they tend to be highly exploratory. We really do not know the concerns and expectations of community groups until we establish that they exist. A social and behavioral scientist works within a time frame of six months to two years or more; we will have at most a few months to complete the job, and only a limited number of man-hours. To work our way out of these constraints, we again have to rely on our experience. It is possible to deal with controversial situations only if we take the first step—propose to those involved some candidate possibilities. We have to create land development concepts and schemes; this is exactly the procedure followed by the anthropologist when he or she begins a study with a specified hypothesis. Dealing with the values and customs of a community requires some kind of boundary. The Knowledge Base System application process will provide the focus.

CHAPTER SIX

QUALITY OF LIFE

Design is the central aspect of the professional practice of architecture. Design is our competitive edge. It is what distinguishes architectural services from what is offered by others in the building industry. However, while design is an architect's treasured experience, it is the design's effect on individuals and groups of individuals that matters to our clients, the attainment of a high quality of life at work, at home, and in the community.

The phrase "quality of life" is used throughout this book. What does it mean? Is it tangible, something that clients will understand if we talk about it as a necessary consideration? Yes. Experiencing quality of life at work, at home, and in the community is the hope and demand of individuals, families, communities, and clients throughout the world. The idea of quality of life recognizes that a well-designed work place, a comfortable and attractive place in which to do business, a place for learning, a good home, places to rest, relax and get well, good places to entertain our friends, to visit and to shop, a place to park the car and walk, places to get away from it all, and ways to get where we are going are essential aspects of life at work, at home, and in the community. At work, where people are asked to make their best possible contribution to organization success and the organization provides all that is needed to achieve skilled job performance; at home, where family members share quiet and exciting moments and try to make each day pleasant for all; in the community, where individuals and families reach out to others seeking to share experiences and develop all that is needed to foster new customs and protect treasured traditions—physical settings and planned environments must be perfected in terms of people's needs and wants.

We Must Thoroughly Understand What People Need and Want

The most important aspect of creating a high quality of life at work, at home, and in the community is to determine what is important to our clients and the project stakeholders. Talk at length to our contributors and you will find men and women who have made the study of people the core of their practice. This is an undertaking that demands great care because individual needs and wants are highly variable. You can take few things for granted and you must maintain a healthy skepticism about common beliefs. Architects who focus their attention solely on the physical design dictated by their professional concerns may well be maintaining a focus that is overly restricted. Though it may be scrupulously honest and professional, a limited point of view can be intellectually dishonest through this very restriction of focus. The intellectual openness required of every architect means, then, that one must not only consider the first appearance of the client's situation but continually assess what underlies people's expectations and requirements.

We Don't Provide Buildings; We Provide Experiences

This is a most useful thought. There can be no improvement in the quality of life without an understanding of people's patterns of thought and action, particularly the actual processes by which people live, as opposed to what we believe exists. Every step in a building project must be considered in the context of how clients think about the future and how they are going to get there. Certainly, this is not a new criterion of success. It has long been recognized that spaces, buildings, facilities, and planned developments should be responsive to human needs and wants. In the past, it was enough to strive to achieve this, but today those responsible for the development of the built environment must offer guarantees of success.

Verify Every Objective

When working with stakeholders you must create opportunities for experimenting with new outcomes and design features that have the potential to change for the better the way things have always been done. It is always a challenge to find out what the client actually needs and wants, as too many people rely on faulty assumptions and incomplete speculations. For instance, a major corporation recently invested in a new research center crafted to meet the stated needs of the engineering and scientific staff. After the building was occupied, research productivity declined markedly. It was found that the building design encouraged each department to develop an enclave, reducing opportunities for collaboration to a minimum. The client had failed to express the importance of facilitating informal communication throughout the day. This is a classic example of problems created by giving clients exactly what they ask for without further discussion.

Avoid Haphazard Design in Which Everything Is Style and Fad

If building design professionals fail to center their work around quality of life considerations, individuals, families, and communities are vulnerable to haphazard design in which everything is style and fad. Likewise, if land development professionals fail to center their work around what people wish to achieve in their neighborhood and community developments, people are vulnerable to abstract and theoretical thinking. When this occurs, land development is more an effort of site geometry, spatial symmetry, and form massing than one focused on individual, family, and community life. There are, of course, many traditions within the building design and land development professions that specify quality of life-related design criteria. Such traditions provide useful background information and insights. However, building design and land development professionals, when working on the quality of life challenge, should never assume that any building design perspective or land development standard is universally applicable. They must recognize that each situation is worthy of study and the most intense critical analysis.

Insights

Judy L. Rowe, F.A.I.A.

A graduate of Cal Poly, Judy is a leader in the Bay Area professional community. Her network for women in architecture became so successful that it is the best source for professional placement in the Bay Area. She is presently on the Oakland Planning Board and finds that instructive, observing that architects and developers often fail to present themselves successfully.

Judy Rowe's Kaiser Permanente office has a view across Lake Merritt toward the stately county government center in Oakland. As a corporate architect she accepts the challenging position of acting as an "owner" for Northern California's dominant medical corporation.

Interview Highlights

In many ways, the corporate architect is leading the transformation of the professional practice of architecture. The direct responsibility for capital facility investments brings with it a new level of awareness.

- Architects too often think that they can write a needs statement without finding out what people really want.

- Users are becoming more educated about buildings. They want to know how much it's going to cost to heat this building, cool it, and to maintain it.

- After a hospital has been built and occupied for about three months, we do a post-occupancy evaluation, which is a real luxury. As a privately practicing architect, I never had the time or money to do this.

- We also keep a record of what we call "lessons learned." Anything that is learned on a job is sent out to everyone in our division on our computer system. Probably a couple of times a week, I'll get a "lesson learned" from somebody, and it's great.

- I think that, in the next five to ten years, it will be very hard for a practitioner who does not specialize in one building type to really be successful, because of litigation and because of computerized detailing.

- One of the things I've been struggling with is how can we help architects to be more responsive to the needs of the people using the facility, help them ask the right questions and listen to the answers.

- I think the hardest thing for an architect to understand is who the audience is, and if nothing else comes out of this book, that's the biggest lesson they need to learn.

- When we select architects we make sure their personalities mesh with the people they're going to be working with. During the interview we find out if they can actually listen and respond.

- We've developed a cost model, a model of how much a hospital ought to cost.

- We were asked to see if we could save money anywhere in the model. We looked at everything, an item that might save five cents or one that saves $1.50 per square foot. We have a ten-year capital building plan and over that period, we saved $75 million just on these sort of nickel and dime fine-tuning things.

- We're starting as an organization to look at life cycle costs, rather than just looking at the cost/benefit ratio of the first-time purchase of that item.

- I would love to see architects become involved in politics, and serving on corporate boards.

The Interview

I'm going to talk about Kaiser as a health care industry and also about Kaiser's Facility Design and Construction Division, which is my department. Kaiser serves 2.5 million members in the Northern California region, and employs about 32,000 people. (There's also a Southern California region and other regions throughout the U.S.) There are probably 200 people in the Facility Design and Construction Division, and last year alone, we did more than $400 million worth of construction in the Northern California region. So, we have a lot of customers, a lot of clients, when we go out and do a building. And, unlike many architectural firms, what we do is very repetitive.

Because it's repetitive, because we do the same kind of building over and over again, we realized several years ago that we could standardize the parts of these buildings. It's like the kids' building set, LEGO, with all the little pieces. You can fit them together differently but they all work as a whole because each part was designed to fit together and each part works. About four years ago, this department decided to find out what are the essential parts of a medical office building, and what are the essential parts of a hospital. They got together a work group of nurses, doctors, and other people—engineers, architects—and they said, "Okay, we're going to design a typical exam room in a medical office building and we're going to figure out what should go in it—all the equipment, all the furniture, what size it should be, the lighting, the flooring—everything." All these parts have been designed and my job is to make sure that these standards are current, that we do the research to make sure they're current, and to revise those standards when people run into problems. We have a long, involved process for doing this.

All of our projects, because of the scale, are managed by an architect inside the Kaiser organization, who in a sense wears two hats. He functions both as the developer and as the project manager or owner of the project. This is a role that architects are finding themselves in more and more often, for several reasons. There is usually more money associated with this role, usually less liability, and usually it's a more challenging position than just being the traditional architect. They also bring to this role their experience as architects, which most owners don't have. They've gone over that learning curve and they have all the information, which makes it easier for the architect of record, the outside consultant, to deal with them. We contract with outside architectural firms to do all the documents and hire the consultants—structural, electrical, mechanical, and so forth. We probably have 30 or 40 architects under contract at any given time.

When a project is first conceived, we give our standards to the contracted architectural firm and educate them on how to use them. Our Facilities Planning Department does all the programming. We give the outside firm a program, we give them a site, and we give them all our standards, and we say, "Okay, design a building for us." The planning department also provides a block diagram, which shows adjacencies, saying the Pediatric Department needs to be next door to the Pharmacy, or whatever. The outside firm comes back to us with a design for this building—

very preliminary block drawings. Eventually, they give us a schematic design, and before this goes through our formal review process, our department makes sure that the drawings are done in accordance with the standards that we have set. If they aren't, we do a package of drawing review comments. We say, "We'd like to know why you've done this. Can you justify this? It probably will cost more than we think it ought to cost," or whatever. After we've done that, these drawings go through what we call a "gate process" of design review, where the drawings have to get through each gate to get to the next phase of the process. We review all the drawings, the schedules, and the cost estimates, to make sure the project is buildable in the time that we think we can promise it to the medical planners.

We do the same process for design development, and for the end of construction drawings, before we start construction. Then, during construction, the change orders, requests for proposals, and substitutions come to our department and we review why people are asking to change things or substitute things. That's one of the bases for our research.

Then, after the building has been built and occupied for about three months, we do a post-occupancy evaluation, which is a real luxury. As a privately practicing architect, I never had the time or money to do this. We go out and walk through the facility, and evaluate each system in the building, whether it's the equipment or the furniture, the architectural or the interior design elements. We send a team of people, consisting of our outside consultant, our in-house project manager, and whoever manages a particular department of Kaiser. If it's an interior design team it would be the interior designer in Kaiser, the interior designer of record, and the manager of interior design at Kaiser. We write down everything that we see—successes and failures, things that we think should be learned from this project, and any corrective action that should be taken. If we find that there's a tripping hazard, for instance, we note this and tell the facility this is something they should correct right away. Then we prepare reports, which are sent out to everyone.

Finally, probably about a year and a half after the building has been completed, we go back again to make sure all the corrective actions were indeed taken, and to see if we missed anything. In other words, we may have thought that a particular material was holding up very well, and after eighteen months, we find that it didn't hold up well at all. Then we would come back and look at our standards and see what we should change. We also keep a record of what we call "lessons learned," or what we learn from this process. Anything that is learned on a job is sent out to everybody in our division on our computer system. Probably a couple of times a week, I'll get a "lesson learned" from somebody, and it's great.

All of our outside consultants have hospital experience. I think that, in the next five to ten years, it will be very hard for a practitioner who does not specialize in one building type to really be successful, because of litigation and because of computerized detailing. If you do one building type and you're always building out of wood, you're always using the same details, and you're always using the same materials, so you can have an economy of standardizing that a firm that doesn't specialize can't have. That's the other model that I see changing in the future. I've seen this happening in my 25 years of practice, and it will continue as we become more proficient with computers. In private practice I rarely did the same building type more than once. When I did have an opportunity, before I came here, to do my second YMCA, it was by far superior to the first one. But I was still "practicing" and felt that if I had gotten a chance to do a third one, it would have been great! I don't think many architects, unless they specialize in one building type, really get the luxury of doing that.

The Facility Design and Construction Division functions as internal consultants for Kaiser, although we do benchmark with other regions, such as Southern California, the Georgia region, or the Northwest. We do this to make sure that we share our learning with them and vice versa. We also benchmark with the Veteran Administration and we do visit other hospitals, such as the U.C. Medical Center and Stanford University. There is a core group of people that design and build hospitals. We have people here who have worked at Stanford and they have people who have worked at Kaiser, so a lot of information gets shared that way. We also have contacts in other organizations that we can call.

Humana used to have an organization very similar to Kaiser—their architectural facility design and construction department was internal. A few years ago they decided they didn't want to carry the burden of having that as an internal part of the corporation, so they dissolved that department. These people started their own firm on the outside and now everybody is wondering whether or not this is a more economical way to do it. Kaiser's talked about doing this and if this happened, it would give the people in our department the opportunity to sell their knowledge. We don't have that opportunity right now. Being an internal consultant denies you that market control that keeps you current with the market and keeps you in a marketing mode. Right now there's no reason for the people in Kaiser to be marketing people and there are few marketing skills here. In fact, one thing I bring is my ability to go out and make presentations to people and sell, but that's from having been in private practice for so many years.

You want to know about the complexity of the challenges that we face. In the first place, hospitals are the most complex type of building, by their very nature. Federal and state codes are very stringent and involve many inspections. In addition, Kaiser hires its own full-time inspector. The other complexity that we face is the number of users. We have the providers—the doctors and the nurses; we have the customers—the patients; and we have the engineers who maintain the building. When we do a building, all of these are our clients and we have to talk to them. So, unlike an office building or a hotel, where you might have one or two clients, every time we do a project there might be ten people in one department that we have to work with to make sure that the department functions for them, and then there will be another ten in the next department, and so forth. We're doing two hospitals right now that are replacement facilities—one's here in Oakland and one's in Santa Clara. They're probably going to be 250-bed hospitals, which is a pretty large hospital for California, and will be $300–400 million facilities. The complexity of users involved, and the process of getting the project approved by a local municipality, are monumental.

I sit on the Planning Commission in the city of Oakland, and it's probably been one of the most educational things I've done as an architect, because when architectural firms present projects to us, I see how persuasive or nonpersuasive they are, and what they think is good design. On the other hand, I'm looking at each project in terms of the city's best interests. Is it going to work from an urban planning point of view? Is it aesthetically pleasing? Is anyone going to be injured using this facility? I realize, having had this experience, that if I were to present a project now to a planning commission I'd present it very differently.

I think that's another big challenge—knowing who your audience is. I think the hardest thing for an architect to understand is who the audience is, and if nothing else comes out of your book, that's the biggest lesson that they need to learn. Architects quite often let their ego get involved in their design and talk down to the client. They say, "I know what's best for you—trust me," and the client says, "Yeah, but . . ." Then the client walks into the finished product and says, "This is what you did for me? This is how you spent my money?" I think I realized long ago that clients want to be listened to. They want to know what you can do for them as a professional—to bring insight to what they want to do, to perhaps get them to look at it a different way, to be more efficient or more visually pleasing, or to work better in the context of adjacencies, or whatever—but they want their needs to be met. They want to know that you have met their requirements and if possible exceeded them.

Another problem is that architects often think that they can write a needs statement without finding out what people really want. I talked about this post-occupancy evaluation process; we often go back and discover that needs aren't being met.

The other day, for example, we realized that we had too many outlets in an exam room. They weren't being used. The medical staff asked for an exam table with an outlet instead of wall outlets. We also realized that people were using these rooms very differently than we thought. We modified the cabinet work and put an L-shaped counter in the corner, with a sink in the middle so that they could have a clean side and a dirty side. They also didn't like having the cabinets fixed under the counter, so we found a roll-away cabinet that could slide underneath.

I find that we're fine-tuning these kinds of things based on what the users' needs are. As we walk through we can talk to the nurses and the physicians who use the facility and find out what works and what doesn't. Then we can provide this information at the front end of the next project. We don't have a set of standard activity patterns, and we expect the architect of record to meet with the users and ask about activities.

As I mentioned, we do give the architect some models of space adjacencies. For instance, in a typical hospital or medical office building, you would have a reception area, and then a nursing station, exam rooms, and the offices for the doctors. There are several ways you could put these together. We would give the architect some preferred adjacencies, but we would really leave it up to him to work with these people and decide on the best way to put the components together. This does present a problem again with the learning curve, and since I've come here, I'm learning where these holes are and I'm trying to fill them.

When we go out to talk to architectural firms, we might have twenty people at a luncheon. We have the draftsperson, the designer, and everybody in between. We say, "We went to one medical office building where the nurse's station was in the back and these people had to do a lot of walking, so when you talk to them, ask about this distance and see if it's a problem." Or, "They've lined up too many exam rooms in a row, so it makes the distance very great. This is something that you should ask about." We're trying not to dictate design, as "There's only one way to do this," and shove it down somebody's throat, but we want to point out where the pitfalls are and what has been successful, so that they know the right questions to ask. We're not trying to take design away from these people, we're trying to make design more expedient. If you don't have to worry about what's in the exam room, hopefully you can spend a lot more time talking about where they want the exam room.

We realized that for medical office buildings we probably should give them three or four options of how these rooms can be arranged to make up any department. Our hospitals are organized by departments, so we give them a template for a whole department, not the individual rooms. We give them an Emergency Department, a Surgery Suite, or an Oncology or Radiology Department, so they can't mess up the adjacencies. What I think we have a harder time with, though, is putting these larger pieces together so that the departmental pieces fit together and work well with each other.

Since we prequalify architectural firms before we interview them, we know they're all probably equally competent of doing the job. We want to make sure their personalities mesh with the people they're going to be working with, and that's probably the most important reason to have an interview. That's when we find out if they can actually listen and respond. One of the things I've been struggling with here is how can we help the architects to be more responsive to the needs of the people using the facility, help them ask the right questions and listen to the answers. It really comes down to the ability to work with people. We also have monthly partnering sessions with our in-house architect, our architect of record, our contractor, our people at the facility, the administrators at the facility, our team of interior designers, and everybody else who is involved in a project. They get together to talk about how they can best work as partners and communicate with each other.

I think communication is going to be harder and harder as time passes, because of the numbers of people and the complexities of what they're communicating. The systems we have—computers and telephones and fax machines and who knows what we'll have ten years from now—the technology is there. What isn't there is people trained to be effective communicators. And this is true of the whole profession.

We've developed a cost model, a model of how much a hospital ought to cost. We know exactly how many dollars per square foot by the structural and the mechanical elements of the building. We know exactly how much a hospital should cost. Before we start one, we tell the project manager how much money he can spend, with a contingency. And let's say construction starts today and it will be finished in four years, we can tell you what the escalation will be. So the architect has a budget for the project. Then he comes back and says, "Well, I have some site-specific problems. I'm building on a hillside so I'm going to need a different foundation," or, "The design review board in this city wants me to put granite on the outside." They may want us to add additional parking that we didn't think we needed, and these things are not in our cost model. Now, the architect may keep within the budget on other things, or he may decide to reduce the quality of something in order to increase the quality of something else. If he wants terrazzo in the lobby instead of tile, he may decide to put a less expensive material on the outside of the building to make up for the cost of the terrazzo. He has the ability to make those decisions. But here in quality assurance, every time we change the cost per square foot, we have to justify it because we're changing the cost model.

To give you an example, the other day we had a request from the hospital in San Francisco to change our typical patient room. Most of our rooms are single rooms with a bathroom and the patient sink is in the bathroom. There is also a sink in the hallway, because we want the nurses and doctors to come out and wash their hands in the hallway before they go on to the next patient's room. It's a peer pressure kind of thing. The infection control nurses from San Francisco asked us to put another sink in the bedroom. They said that when they're changing a dressing, they'll put one dressing on and then they want to wash their hands before they do another dressing, because that's how they control infection. The cost of putting in a sink at $500–$1000, when you do a couple of thousand patient rooms a year, was more money than we really wanted to spend. But we also have to consider the infection control aspect of the cost. We took this issue to the appeals board here, and their opinion was that we should take the sink out of the patient bathroom and just have a sink in the bedroom. This decision hasn't set well with anyone because now the patient doesn't have a private sink to use when he's wearing a gown that's open in the back. We're looking at another way to solve this, and it may be that having two sinks isn't really that much of a cost compared to the cost of people getting infections.

So, this department will do the research. We have a nurse who's an equipment specialist, there's a mechanical engineer who helps us with the plumbing, and we have two architects—one who does building systems and one who does hospital planning. We also have an interior designer. We'll work with all these people, and they each have a network of people that they will talk to. We may find that we're going to completely change a typical patient room, and the template that we've developed will change. But we will do that research, rather than putting that burden on the architect. I think it helps the architects because they can stay more focused. They can also set their fee and know that this is what it's going to cost and this is how much money they'll make. When I was in private practice and a question like this came up, we'd spend hours doing research—or days—and you don't get paid for that. You learn something as a practitioner, you bring this to your body of knowledge, but nobody reimburses you for it.

A couple of months ago we were asked to see if we could save money anywhere in our cost model. Everybody in our department and a couple of other departments went through the model and found 60 items. We researched every item, and we came up with 30 that we could actually quantify and get people to agree with. When I say getting people to agree, we probably talked to 100 people before we got agreement on every one of these items. Then we sent this to our review committee, they approved it, and we ran out the numbers. We figured out how much each item saved in terms of cents per square foot. An item might have saved five cents, or at the most I think it was $1.50 per square foot. But we have a ten-year capital building plan and over that period, we saved $75 million just on these sort of nickel and dime fine-tuning things.

Cost drives most decisions here, but you need to demonstrate the long-term value of some decisions. For example, hospital procedure rooms have sinks with foot pedals, so that hands don't get contaminated. The problem is that every time the environmental service people bring their scrubber around, it hits the pedal and it breaks. The pedal has to be replaced and there are fewer and fewer companies making these, because infrared controls are now widely used. Well, for a long time the cost of an infrared control was much higher than a foot pedal, so we kept replacing the foot pedals. Finally, the environmental services and maintenance people said they don't care if the infrared control costs three times what a foot pedal costs, they can maintain it and it's something that is much more cost effective, in the life cycle cost anyway.

We're starting as an organization to look at life cycle costs, rather than just looking at the cost/benefit ratio of the first-time purchase of that item. That's another change I see in the profession. In the past, architects would say, give me your money and I'll spend it for you and create this beautiful building. Clients are now saying, "I want you to build this building, but I want to know how much it's going to cost to heat this building, cool it, and to maintain it."

Users are becoming more educated about buildings. Twenty-five years ago, when I started practicing architecture, I would work with a client and have to explain what sheet vinyl was, what a product was. Today a client would come to me and say, "When you put the sheet vinyl down, be sure it looks like this." People go to places like Home Depot, and read so many magazines, that clients are much more sophisticated than they used to be, which makes it easier for the architect to help them with an aesthetic decision. But decisions also have to be based upon a cost/benefit ratio.

For example, you can say that if you want purple, you can use these three materials. This one will last longest, this one'll cost the most, and this one would look the best. In the past, I think the traditional architect would have said, "This has to be purple and there is only one material available," rather than letting the client make that choice. The architect had a limited palette of materials and design elements to present to a client. Now there is a wide range of choices, but architects often choose something for the wrong reason and don't get the client involved. The "master builder" never got the client involved in a choice like that.

I think that architecture is evolving to become more of a systemized process, rather than such an aesthetic process. You may find that people are happier in their working or living environments, but they may not have the aesthetics that were brought to them years ago, by Frank Lloyd Wright, Bernard Maybeck, or Julia Morgan, when cost was sort of a secondary issue. Now because cost is a primary issue—we have less money to spend and buildings cost more to create—I think there's an expectation for the aesthetics, but they're very much secondary to the architecture that's being produced. A lot of people feel very strongly that architecture has lost something because of that, that we're no longer practicing the aesthetic part of design.

Also, I need to mention that at Kaiser, we deviate from the traditional way in which architecture has been done most of this century, which is to get a client, design a building, do the drawings, and then hire a contractor. We are the client, we hire the architects and the contractor at the same time, and we ask them to partner with each other. But we ask the contractor to work for us and we ask the architect to work for us. We don't ask the architect to work for the contractor. We tried that and quite a few facilities suffered. We would tell the architect that we wanted to spend so many dollars per square foot and that he should work for the contractor and produce a building. We got exactly what we asked for—a facility that was so many dollars a square foot and didn't function well. Now we ask the contractor to work for us, the owner, and we ask the architect to work for us, the owner. They start at the beginning of the process together and the contractor helps the architect determine what the cost will be and the best way in which to do the building, as they're going through the design. This also changes the design of the building, this takes "god" out of the architecture or the design out of the architecture, because it is a much more pragmatic way to do a building. The contractor says, "You mean you want me to build this building on this square block? Where am I going to put my trailers and all my equipment?" And the architect says, "Oh, we could move the building over and leave you a little space." That determines the form of the building. What I'm saying is that there's another player involved now and that makes the architect less than the "master builder."

As far as developing an association of trust, I think the biggest problem we have is building a relationship of trust between the players on the team—the architects and the contractors, the interior designers and the planners, and the engineers. Often there will be a change in the design, for example, and the structural engineer will say, "My fee just went up because you changed this."

The architect says, "Trust me, I'm not going to make any more changes, so don't worry, your fee will be fine." Two months later he makes more changes and the engineer comes back and says, "My fee's going to go up again." Perhaps the contractor has had a bad experience on a previous project, and he decides that he's going to hate the architect on the next project because the last architect gave him a hard time. Developing that sense of trust between a contractor and an architect is very difficult.

I've done a lot of design/build projects where I have worked for a contractor rather than working for the owner. That whole process is based on trust—if there's no trust there, it doesn't work at all. I think as a profession we need to realize how to develop trust, how important it is, and how devastating it can be when you lose it. So I would like to see our profession take courses in ethics, and courses in building and maintaining trust, because I think it's one of the biggest weaknesses.

I have to say, as a woman architect, I've had clients who enjoyed working with me because of the bond or the trust that we developed with each other, which is different, I think, than relationships developed by my male counterparts. I was often asked to do another project because of those relationships, and most architectural firms depend on repeat clients. They develop sort of a stable of clients, or their clients recommend them to somebody else. It's that trust that perpetuates the business. If you mess up on a job, you're going to find that people won't want to come back to you, and you're going to have to work doubly hard to find new clients.

I think the architect is the right person to manage a team, but we're losing that position as we do more and more design/build or modified kinds of projects. The team manager is not always the architect. I've worked on projects where the owner has brought in a construction manager, someone who manages the entire project from beginning to end, and it's not necessarily an architect. I give seminars in project management, and my opinion is that you either know how to be a project manager or you don't. I think it's more an intuitive process than something that's learned. The best architectural designers do that one thing very well. They usually don't make good project managers. I look at people that do project management well and they usually don't make good designers. Very, very infrequently have I seen people who have been able to do both well.

Depending on the size of the firm and the size of the project, a project manager may handle everything from marketing to occupancy. But in a company the size of ours, or any comparable architecture firm, you can afford to specialize. You can have someone who does production documents, someone who manages construction, and someone who manages the marketing division. Here at Kaiser we try to have a project manager stay with a project from beginning to end. In the firm I came from—a medium-sized firm—we tried to do that also. We tried to make sure one person, at least, was on a project from beginning to end, so the client had one point of contact. Unfortunately, I think that we assume that this person is equally competent to manage all phases, and this is usually not the case. Managing the construction process takes a lot of specialized knowledge compared to managing the document production. Here, we sometimes change managers when we find someone who's better at the design part of the project as opposed to the actual production and construction of the project. Architects get into trouble when they try to be all things to all people. The client may find that he has a really good person for part of the process, and get to another phase and think, "This person doesn't know what the hell he's doing." Because what we do is so much more technical and the likelihood of litigation is so much higher than it was 20 or 30 years ago, we can't afford to be all things to all people.

I would love to see architects becoming involved in politics, and serving on corporate boards. I think the only way urban planning will ever be done effectively is to get architects into these positions. In terms of corporations, if you can get architects on boards, you can start to bring that kind of vision to corporate America. But the problem is that we don't train architects to think beyond the limited scope of what we do as architects. I look back at my graduating class and I'll bet not 50 percent of them are practicing architecture in the traditional sense.

A couple of years ago, I talked with Roger Montgomery, who's the Dean of The College of Environmental Design at U.C. Berkeley. I asked him if he would consider having a seminar for their students about nontraditional roles for architects. At first, he was very reluctant to do this because he didn't think that they should be sending the message to graduates that they should be thinking of other roles in the profession. But as the economy worsened, he realized that students need to consider this. The woman who was in this position before me went there to speak about corporate architecture as a career path. This is still pretty traditional practice, but working as the owner rather than as the architect. Some people do sculpture and other less traditional kinds of things. People have gone into computers, CAD systems. One woman offers a "temporary" service for architects. She brings in architects, sends them out to firms, and they work on a contract basis for the duration of the job. Rather than being hired by the firm with all the benefits that go along with it, and so forth, they work project by project—"piece workers." One friend from architecture school has been selling very high-end furniture for twenty or more years. I know people that have gone into research. I think there are vast opportunities for architects and they're only limited by their creativity or their innovation. It's not necessarily just where the money is, it's also where they find the most joy. I'd say most architects want to be creating something, so their innovation will take them where they find the pleasure of creating. That's what I see as the challenge—where do we decide to go professionally?

The Northern California region of Kaiser is going through a reorganization right now. We have been a centralized office here, with about fifteen major medical centers consisting of a hospital and ancillary facilities, and then a lot of small satellite facilities. We decided to decentralize our organization and develop these satellites, so there will be eight "customer service areas." As part of this reorganization we've decided to change job titles and reporting structures. Instead of reporting to a central location, people will report to medical centers. The whole purpose of this is to make the organization more customer-focused, and to give each medical center the capacity to take action. For example, if one particular center had a very large elderly population, or lots of babies being born, they could change the way in which they operated to serve these customers. People pay fees to be members of our organization, and they expect a certain level of service. If we don't provide that service, we'll lose them. So that's the overriding reason for this reorganization.

The corporation will probably ask all of us to reapply for our jobs because they will redefine all our jobs. It's very interesting to see how this affects the people who work here, the fear that it develops. I see the same thing in our profession, which is why I'm making this analogy. There's fear, there's inability to act—people get paralyzed. Eventually, I think the best people will survive and those who aren't able to make the change and learn to think and act in a different way will probably perish. Those who seize this opportunity will be part of the new organization and will make it a better place.

This type of reorganization is happening in every corporation in America—from IBM to every small architectural firm. They're saying: Let's get the fat out, let's get lean and mean, and let's make this organization work as best it can. The parallel with our profession is that as it reorganizes itself, as our profession becomes something a little different than it has been—or quite a lot different—I think you'll see a whole segment that's paralyzed, that doesn't have the capacity to act. But you're also going to see members of our profession who see the opportunity in change and grab for it, who see that golden ring out there and say, "Yeah, I gotta have this," and move forward with it. That's the most exciting thing about our profession. Yes, it will change, and a lot of us will change along with it, but we're going to lose quite a few in the process of this change.

As far as education programs are concerned, my experience has mostly been with Berkeley graduates or student interns from Berkeley. I see people who have gone through a four-year credential program and have in their hand a Bachelor of Arts degree in Architecture. They go to their first job interview and realize they can't do anything. They realize that nobody wants to hire them. Nobody told them they couldn't do anything, nobody told them they had to go to graduate school, nobody told them that no one was going to hire them, and nobody told them if they did get hired they were going to make minimum wage. That's the biggest bill of goods that I think is being sold right now by our university here, in Berkeley. If these students are lucky enough to land a job in the Bay Area, they work for very little money. They're very frustrated because they can't even pick up a pencil and draw a line with it, which they're expected to do, or operate a computer, which they haven't the foggiest idea how to do. Someone may take an occasional student under his wing, but more likely they're going to flounder around for a year or two and finally decide to go to graduate school. Well, by this time they're 23–24 years old and they go to graduate school for maybe a couple of years, work a little and go to school. They're probably 27 or 30 when they graduate. Now, they're ready to go out and make what their counterparts are making. They get a job and they say, "Hey, here I am making minimum wage again! Why did I do all this?" That's one of the biggest problems I see with the profession.

The other problem is that we as architects very much under-value what we do. We still look at ourselves as artisans, craftsmen, designers—we don't look at ourselves as business people. I'll never forget an insurance company seminar that I attended. The speaker said to us, "How many of you have made a mistake on a drawing and apologized to the owner and said that you would change it at no expense?" We all raised our hands. The speaker told us that it was a mistake to say you would correct it for free. There is no such thing as a perfect set of documents and you need to look at this as a business person and say, "Yes there is a mistake here, but you the owner are sharing in this process. Let's find the reason for this mistake and find out how best to correct it." There are also times when the architect wants a detail on a drawing, wants to see an embellishment or wants something painted a different color, and is almost always willing to work nights and weekends to do this. That's the reason why we don't make any money. You wouldn't expect a plastic surgeon to do a second operation without charging for it because you didn't quite like the results of the first operation. As architects, we don't look at what we do that way, and until we do, I don't think things will change.

***Ridgecrest Civic Center,
Ridgecrest, California.***
*(Photo courtesy of MWM
Architects.)*

Ridgecrest Civic Center.
*(Photo courtesy of MWM
Architects.)*

**John Muir Hospital,
Walnut Creek,
California.** *(Photo
courtesy of MWM
Architects.)*

John Muir Hospital.
*(Photo courtesy of MWM
Architects.)*

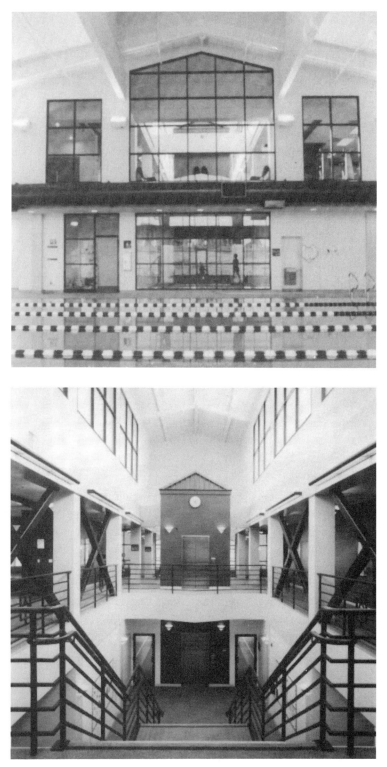

Hilltop Y.M.C.A.,
Richmond, California.
(Photo courtesy of MWM
Architects.)

Hilltop Y.M.C.A.
(Photo courtesy of
MWM Architects.)

Method No. 5
Field Studies

A well-conceived field study helps us create a disciplined exposition of the client's critical success factors. Robert Cunard, the nineteenth-century shipping industrialist, recognized that his market opportunity was in service to clients, not ship design *per se*. He designed ships to meet client requirements: he thought in terms of service when other people thought in terms of ships (Verne, 1993: 7, footnote 13). We are in the same type of business situation. The field study experience helps the executive architect think in terms of service to clients and discover new service possibilities. The discovery of opportunities and innovations originates quite often during the field study process when we critique our client's endeavors and identify exceptional ideas or faulty thinking.

Case Study Archives

Before studying field study methodology, you may wish to consider the case studies in the archives of architectural practice and business management. Universities produce cases by the hundreds to help professionals study decision-making processes in the most realistic manner possible. A succinct rationale for the use of case studies as learning tools is "Wisdom can't be told" (Gragg, 1940). A basic guideline for formulating case studies is the third edition of *Teaching and the Case Method* by Barnes, Christensen, and Hansen (1994). While devoted to the use of case method to improve instructional effectiveness, the book also contains guidelines that will markedly improve your field study work. It contains complex cases, explanatory materials, and instructive readings. When this work offers comments about good classroom practices, you can't help but think of the value of these to client relations and business development and marketing. Aren't we always educating clients about the value of our services? Aren't our persuasion strategies akin to what goes on in the classroom?

A wide range of model case studies is available through the Publishing Division, Harvard Business School, Boston. You will find the following cases most instructive: *Regency Plaza, Peterborough Court, Convenience Food Stores Site Selection at Shell Canada, Ltd., Americana, The Coolidge Block, Prospect Hill, The Architects' Collaborative, In The Shadow of the City, Habitat for Humanity International, Merv Griffin's Resorts, Sea Pines Racquet Club, The Marriott Corporation and the Warsaw Hotel, Turner Construction Company, Fan Pier, Georgetown Leather Design,* and *Lakeside Center.* These represent many of the market and project management challenges facing building industry professionals.

Basic Elements of Field Studies

The following sections present the eight basic elements of a good field study. The central strategy is to question clients along lines that are important to them and to their organization's endeavors: What did they know? What didn't they know and therefore what did they assume? What was the exact nature of decisions made? What was the justification for these decisions? Answering these questions requires full disclosure. We have to consider the issues, points of view, situational factors, dilemmas and conflicts, and market and financial analyses, while maintaining the human touch at all times.

1: The Human Touch

A major characteristic of the field study method is the value placed on the insights of those participating in project deliberations. People will always use their experience and knowledge in such deliberations, often moving beyond what the data and information on hand indicate. When it comes to making a project report, however, these anecdotes are too often omitted. When we sanitize a field study by stressing facts and numerical analysis over interpretations provided by participating individuals, we leave out what is most informative. To capture what actually occurred we must answer these questions: Who are the people involved? What are their personalities? What biases influenced deliberations? What aspects of the project were important to them? What interpretations were given to facts and situations?

To see how the human touch can be maintained in field studies, examine any recent issue of the *Harvard Business Review*. For instance, the 1995 January–February issue includes a study by Rothstein (1995) entitled *The Empowerment Effort That Came Undone*. The situation is personalized in the first paragraph when the principal character's morning is described. Rothstein notes that this was a particularly important day, because Mr. Griffin was going to proclaim a new era of empowerment at the company. If we were reporting on a childcare field study, we might set the scene by saying, "We were early for our first meeting with the new client. It was a great chance to watch children in the play area. This gave us a sense that what we achieve will affect all of these children and how they spend their day." Anyone reading this introduction would recognize the importance you give to the needs and wants of children and your commitment to their safety, security, health, and happiness. You might say directly that satisfying activities and pleasing facility features are a major consideration. However, it is more effective when people can actually visualize the situation.

2: Learning about Clients

We must develop in a field study an understanding of our client's business area, the skills required for success, the strategic directions of competitors, the expectations and requirements of customers, or if an institutional client, of the public. The standard for these undertakings is rigorous information development, in which results are confirmed or disconfirmed with facts, not opinions.

Let's return to the topic of childcare, which is an exemplary learning experience. Like so many of our projects, the childcare business demands attention to every cent, square foot, and facility feature. It is a complex individual, family, and social issue offering many opportunities for extended architectural services. Field studies are written to create a realistic portrayal of the challenge at hand. A childcare center field study would stress the extensive needs of children, not only when they feel ill or upset but in normal circumstances every day. The special needs of different ages must be considered, as well as responses to unusual situations. There is always a trade-off between concerns for the safety, security, and health of the children and the costs of operating the facility.

3: Points of View

In every field study, there are a number of possible contributors. For example, you might interview a YMCA regional director, who would be familiar with the area's total range of childcare situations, from parents who hire live-in help to grammar school children who just wander home from school on their own and hang out for the rest of the day. You may discover a corporation that has established a satellite school in conjunction with the local school district, which includes day care, at the entrance to its manufacturing facility. Since such a school district/corporate partnership would be considered a benchmark in terms of shared costs and opportunities for employees' daily involvement in the educational and care experiences of their children, you would certainly want to speak to everyone involved.

4: Situational Factors

At this point, the history of the project is reviewed. What happened after the project was first conceived? What were the preliminary market and financial analyses? Who were some of the people talked to and what did they say? Regarding significant background information such as area history, culture, geography, social factors, and political dynamics, what was found to be important? For any partnerships and alliances, how were they formed and what are the relationships between parties? Within the project, what are the lines of communication and authority? This discussion must include the constraints associated with the project; for example, the demands of liability carriers which prohibit many of the kinds of activities that children enjoy. Jurisdictional agencies also regulate childcare programs, including facility requirements and staffing ratios. You might wish to consult executives in the childcare business who operate a number of centers. This will provide an understanding of the possible economies of scale, which may alter some of the assumptions of your project.

5: Dilemmas and Conflicts

A good field study lets the reader participate in the unfolding of your understanding of project dimensions. You can be persuasive when you tell a story to which the reader can relate, stressing dilemmas and conflicts that must be resolved. For instance, a conflict may develop between those with differing views on a possible childcare center feature. The market analysis shows that many families have two working parents and that there are a number of single parent families, all leading extremely busy lives. Some take the position that the childcare center can be expanded to include a number of family support services, from grocery shopping to dry cleaning drop off, in an attempt to add value to services provided. This view is attacked by those with a traditional view of the need to focus totally on the children. A detailed characterization of when the idea of adding value through extended services developed, the support it received, and the opposition to it, is valuable.

As you undertake a field study, be particularly alert to conflicts in working relationships. These will always influence project events. Attention must be given to the extent to which these conflicts relate to organizational pressures, differences in interpretation of information, role conflicts, group allegiances, differences in management styles, lack of experience and training, and failure, on your part, to establish a sense of collaboration and shared responsibility.

6: Financial Analysis

Childcare may be a business enterprise, a social service, or a corporate/public alliance. In each instance, a complete financial picture is necessary—the value and future potential of real estate, assessed value and taxes, liability insurance, and details of occupancy costs, operating expenses, marketing expenses, cash flow, and staff salaries and benefits. These are the major reference points in almost every field study. The challenge for those in the childcare business can be appreciated when you read the following comment. "When Ms. Krause raised tuition just 50 cents a day a few years ago to $70 a week, she lost six families from her 90-child center" (Shellenbarger, 1994). Shellenbarger goes on to describe all the various cost reduction strategies employed to eke out slim margins. Such insights link financial analyses with the reality of the situation. Lisa Poelle, a highly regarded design and development consultant, shared with us a maxim that precisely illustrates the central dilemma of the industry: What is good for the child may not make good business sense for the investor.

7: Market Analysis

Every product and service has a market, and the childcare business is extremely market sensitive. If investors and nonprofit organizations spend their limited and often unreplenishable resources, only to find that parents will not use the service, this indicates that optimism took over from a good market analysis. As has been learned again and again, a market analysis cannot be based on what people say they will do but rather on what they actually will do. To this end, the field study should emphasize the anecdotal as a safeguard. It must probe beyond superficial assumptions, learning directly from the people involved. The strategy here is just like that for financial analysis: the full complexity of the problem must be addressed. Your field study should validate what was said about the competitive environment, anticipated client volume and variation, and the causes of variations in market demand. It would then produce economic models that predict performance of candidate sites.

8: Supplemental Information

These can be data tables, graphic figures, floor plans, master plans, or activity charts. Whatever is employed is selected for one primary reason: it provides a reference for or clarification of some complex feature of the case. These reference points, when they consolidate a great deal of information, simplify the task of writing. You can write to the implications of data, rather then spending words to bring together various facts. For instance, strategic responses to financial analyses can be formed while the details are presented in an accompanying exhibit.

As a forum for discussion, three examples of field studies are presented in the following sections. The first illustrates the basic purpose of every field study, the description of anticipated facility users and their expectations and requirements. The second example specifies the questioning associated with life at work in corporate, manufacturing and service organizations that depend on the attainment and support of skilled job performance. The emphasis is on the identification of key workers and their associates, their responsibilities and activities, and the organization's concern for workstation and communication and information systems requirements. The third example is a field study of a speciality food company undertaking a major market expansion. It illustrates how field studies contribute to a client's strategic thinking.

Example One: Office/Home Design Center

This field study, pertaining to Section 2.0 Facility Life Characteristics in the Knowledge Base System, must be given the closest scrutiny. This level of detail must be achieved in every field study, as it is the foundation for the development of design concepts, schemes, forms, and features.

In Chapter 1 we reviewed a case that taught us that it is possible to exceed a client's expectations and revise possibly simplistic views of architectural services—the Office/Home Design Center in Japan. Figure 6.1 presents the information developed in response to Knowledge Base System question item 2.1 Facility User Categories, which asks: Who will be active within the facility? How may these individuals be grouped by responsibilities and intentions? How many individuals does each category include? As previously noted, this is the most important question item in the Knowledge Base System. Initial characterizations of facility users too often omit people from consideration or superficially characterize them.

"Bring Life to a Building before There Is a Building"

Expectations and requirements for the Osaka project are summarized in Figures 6.2 and 6.3 as scenarios, composite answers to the five questions items in Section 2.0 Facility Life Characteristics. The scenario form is used as a means of synthesis because it is image-oriented. An image is something we can add to again and again and still maintain a cohesive overview. We have included the field study sketches by Wesley S. Ward, A.I.A., our principal partner on the Osaka project, to illustrate the value of enhancing a field study report with visual characterizations of findings.

OFFICE/HOME DESIGN CENTER: A WIDE RANGE OF USERS
FACILITY GROUP ONE: CUSTOMERS WITH AN INTEREST
IN HOUSING

- Public visitors to the center will include:
    Individuals
    Couples
    Families:
        With children
        With elderly parents
- These visitors might be interested in:
    Specific housing product applications
    Remodeling
    Buying an existing home
    Building a new home
- To these ends, the visitor might be:
    Exploring, just coming to window-shop
    Seriously seeking information
    Ready to make a major building or sales decision
- Their information needs will pertain to a wide spectrum of housing
  interests:
    Rental units
    Condominiums
    Single-family housing
    Expensive single-family homes
    Multistory business/home combinations
    Retirement units
    Resort homes

FACILITY GROUP TWO: CUSTOMERS WITH AN INTEREST
IN OFFICES

- This group will include:
    Individuals, representing themselves
    Individuals, representing a corporation
    Small groups, representing a corporation
- These visitors to the center might be interested in:
    Selective office product applications
    Remodeling
    Leasing office space
    Building a new office
- To these ends, the visitor might be:
    Exploring, just coming to window-shop
    Seriously seeking information
    Ready to make a major building or sales decision
- Their information needs will pertain to a wide spectrum of office
  situations:
    Existing home office
    Existing business office
    Existing corporation offices
    Establishing a new home office
    Establishing a new business office
    Establishing a new corporate office

Figure 6.1. Example answer for question item 2.1 Facility User Categories. (Continued on the following page.)

FACILITY GROUP THREE: HOUSING-RELATED BUSINESS
PEOPLE AND PROFESSIONALS
- This category includes potential leasees with need for:
    Long-term leased display space (major clients)
    Short-term leased display space
    Large professional office leased space (major clients)
    Small professional office leased space
  The distinction between requirements for "large" or "small" office spaces is important. When clients commit themselves to long-term or large space leases, special center privileges and services can be offered, such as prominent locations and special amenities and interior design features.
- Firms leasing space might staff these spaces with:
    Marketing and sales representatives
    Architects
    Home builders:
      Traditional
      Prefabricated
    Interior decorators and designers
    Specification developers
    Cost quotation specialists
    Purchase order clerks
    Real estate sales personnel
    Real estate financiers

FACILITY GROUP FOUR: OFFICE-RELATED BUSINESS
PEOPLE AND PROFESSIONALS
- This category includes potential leasees with need for
    Long-term leased display space (major clients)
    Short-term leased display space
    Large professional office leased space (major clients)
    Small professional office leased space
- Firms leasing space might staff these spaces with:
    Marketing and sales representatives
    Architects
    Interior decorators and designers
    Space planners
    Facility managers
    Specification developers
    Cost quotation specialists
    Commercial office sales personnel
    Commercial office financiers

FACILITY GROUP FIVE: PUBLIC, BUSINESS, CORPORATE,
AND PROFESSIONAL SUBSCRIBERS TO CENTER SERVICES
- Subscription membership in the center makes available the business, professional, educational, and training services provided to center leasees. This category of facility users includes the interested public and firms belonging to the center as professional or business subscribers who pay fees to use the center on a short-term basis. Information and office services, computer database, CAD workstation, and working drawings and specification printing can be made available through subscription, meeting the needs of small firms with limited means.

Figure 6.1 (continued).
Example answer for question item 2.1 Facility User Categories.

- Subscription members may include:
  - Public individuals
  - Small local business firms
  - Small local professional firms
  - Corporations requiring temporary business office facilities
  - Corporations requiring temporary professional office space
- Subscription membership in the center can be made available to business and professional organizations who are temporarily locating staff in the local area. "Turn-key" office facilities can be part of this service.

FACILITY GROUP SIX: EDUCATIONAL AND TRAINING GROUPS

- Within the center's exhibit and conference centers and throughout display and professional office floors, technical training and professional education events will occur. The groups involved are anticipated to be:
  - Office, home, and marketing professionals
  - The general public
  - Educators
  - Lecture and conference attendees
  - Professional seminar attendees
  - School groups
    - Individual students
    - Students—grammar school to university
    - Students—trade and technical schools
    - Students—company trainees
  - Research groups
    - Professionals
    - Public individuals
    - Community action groups
    - Government groups

FACILITY GROUP SEVEN: OFFICE/HOME DESIGN CENTER SUPPORT AND CONCESSION PERSONNEL

- These design center job categories are extensive. Employees can be categorized as:
  - Visitor services:
    - Parking attendants
    - Receptionists
    - Facility guides and attendants
    - Nurse/first aid
  - Design center marketing staff:
    - Marketing manager
    - Public relations
    - Consulting marketing staff
  - Exhibit and conference center staff:
    - Exhibits and conference center manager
    - Exhibits and conference center staff
    - Event arrangement manager
  - Professional services floor staff assigned to:
    - Computer services:
      - CAD workstation and database services
      - Internal/external information network services
      - Word processing/clerical services

Figure 6.1 (continued). Example answer for question item 2.1 Facility User Categories.
(Continued on the following page.)

FACILITY GROUP SEVEN: OFFICE/HOME DESIGN CENTER
SUPPORT AND CONCESSION PERSONNEL (continued)
Professional services floor staff assigned to:
Design center facility operations:
Operations manager
Employee relations manager
Security force
Delivery and shipment supervisor and workers
Design center facility maintenance
Facility maintenance managers:
Fire/safety inspector
Health inspector
Facility engineer
Facility maintenance workers
Office, display, and exhibit set-up crews
Cleaning crews (day and night)
Groundskeepers
Concession personnel:
Restaurant
Office supplies retail store
Computer sales and service store
Home product retail store

FACILITY GROUP EIGHT: ADDITIONAL FACILITY USER
CATEGORIES
• Every space in the Office/Home Design Center must be responsive to
the following facility user categories:
Visitors taken ill
Visitors accidentally injured
People with perception/motor disabilities:
Reduced mobility (using canes, walkers, wheelchairs)
Reduced vision or blind
Reduced hearing or deaf
People in certain psychological states:
Tired
Bored
Uncertain
Confused or disoriented
Non-Japanese speaking general visitors
Non-Japanese speaking professional visitors
Individuals requiring assistance during emergency events
and center evacuation
Design center staff with emergency and accident responsibilities for:
Vandals
Breaking and entry
Thieves
Shoplifters

*Figure 6.1 (continued). Example answer for question item 2.1 Facility
User Categories.*

There are many dimensions to a family visit to the Office/Home Design Center. People who come to the center will have different lifestyles and vary quite markedly in their familiarity with housing design and housing products. This variety of needs has been studied. What has been learned is summarized here as a narrative of a family's visit to the center. It calls attention to some of the common expectations and requirements of visitors to which the management and architectural design of the center must be responsive.

The narrative begins with the family at home thinking about their housing needs. It describes their many experiences in the center and concludes with some final thoughts they have about their experience.

1. Initial Thoughts
The Ito family has been talking about improving their housing situation. They think remodeling is their best alternative. They are anxious to find good information and get professional advice.

2. Helpful Information
The services provided by the Office/Home Design Center have been well-publicized. Since the opening of the center, a series of articles has appeared in local newspapers giving advice about improving one's housing situation. The Itos decide to visit the center. Mr. and Mrs. Ito expect that they will be well received by a trained staff, that they will find all the information they need, and that the visit will be a pleasant one for them and their children. They know the hours that the center will be open, exactly where it is located, and the available transportation.

3. Arrival
Having planned a full day's outing, the Itos drive to the center. A parking attendant guides them into the lot and, judging them to be a family on an outing, suggests they use the main entrance to the building.

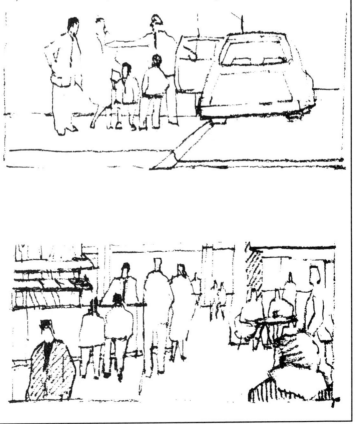

4. Entering the Center
Upon entering the building, Mr. and Mrs. Ito immediately become confused. The area is crowded and people are coming and going in every direction. There are so many signs and displays they are uncertain about what to do. Fortunately, a guide notes their confusion and asks if she can be of service. After a few questions the guide decides to escort them directly to the Housing Consultation Center.

5. Guidance

The consultant listens to the Itos' ideas about remodeling their home, and questions them carefully to determine how they can best profit from their visit to the center. A recommended itinerary is mapped and the location of each area is clearly marked, as well as the most efficient path to follow. The consultant suggests that Mr. and Mrs. Ito stop by the center when their tour is over, so that the staff can answer their final questions.

The Itos realize that the housing consultant is working for them and will be objective in helping evaluate the housing services and products displayed.

6. Exhibits

The exhibits located throughout the center turn out to be one of the most pleasant experiences of the day. Mr. and Mrs. Ito find their situation and concerns thoughtfully addressed in the exhibits. Some illustrate the housing traditions of Japan and the new types of housing being developed. The products used in a variety of housing, from apartments to resort homes, are exhibited in settings that express a feeling of quality. The housing product applications are illustrated through the use of models, full-scale depictions of remodeling under-

takings, and video presentations.

Throughout the center there are special exhibits by builders and product manufacturers. Each is designed to help people identify and understand alternatives and options.

Although the Itos are interested in remodeling , they decide to see an exhibit put on by a prefabricated housing builder. A video presentation shows how, in one day, the delivery trucks and builders arrive on the site and erect the building. The next day the family moves in. This makes them think perhaps a new home would be the most convenient and satisfactory solution for their family. The children become excited about the industrialized housing designs.

7. Displays

A Disappointing Experience. The tour of display spaces marketing services and products is disappointing. The displays are nothing more than a series of cubicles with rows of housing products and stacks of brochures noting specifications and costs. There is no way for Mr. and Mrs. Ito to make sense out of this mass of information.

An Informative and Enjoyable Experience. The tour of display spaces is very informative. The display spaces are arranged according to housing type. This scheme allows the Itos to concentrate on those home services and products that are most applicable and pertinent to their situation. They learn a great deal. Now they are ready to use the various information services provided by the center.

8. Professional Services

The Housing Consultation Center proves valuable. Now that the Itos have learned so much about various alternatives, they are ready for a detailed consultation with a housing consultant. They have achieved a new level of confidence. The housing consultant uses a variety of electronic devices and displays to consolidate information and graphically characterize the various options and alternatives that the Itos should consider.

At one point, Mr. and Mrs. Ito become concerned that they are attempting to do too much and should come back some other day. They are tired and somewhat overwhelmed. Since the Housing Consultation Center is near the restaurant, they arrange to meet the housing consultant there. Mr. and Mrs. Ito are very relieved to sit down, have some refreshments, and discuss their experiences. After a while, they feel comfortable enough to make a final decision.

The consultant escorts the Itos to the offices of the companies with which they will be doing business. Depending on what the Itos decide to do, visits will be made to companies offering housing purchase, development, or remodeling services, from design, financing, and construction to all the associated electrical, plumbing, and appliance installation services.

9. The Children

The Ito children are old enough to tour the center on their own. Many of the exhibits are of interest to them. Some include information about homes of children in other countries and describe bedrooms and various study and recreation amenities. The brochures they receive tell a story about each display. The Ito children have many ideas they want to share with their parents. The children particularly enjoyed having their own place to eat.

10. Problem Situations

Mr. and Mrs. Ito had one major problem. It was difficult to follow the suggested tour itinerary given them by the housing consultant because of the many attractions within the center. Soon they stopped following the consultant's itinerary and randomly explored the building on their own. As a result, they missed some very important exhibit and display spaces.

This has happened so many times that the housing consultation staff develop a new strategy. They create four itineraries that reduce the length of the guided visits, providing more opportunities for visitors to explore on their own. These changes in management strategy lead to the need to relocate some of the displays and exhibits and revise the information displays used to guide visitors.

11. Preparing to Go Home

Mr. and Mrs. Ito gather their children. Mr. Ito decides he might find some good ideas for his work environment by visiting the office service and products display spaces. The Ito children visit the retail computer store. Mrs. Ito decides to shop at the housing products retail store. It is always nice to find something new for the house. The housing consultant has recommended several books, so they will certainly stop by the bookstore and buy some of these books.

12. Final Thoughts

At home, thinking about their visit to the center, the Itos discuss what they have learned. Several of the decision-making checklists supplied by the housing consultation staff prove very helpful. They share all the brochures with their friends next door, who decide they are going to visit the center. The Itos want to go along with them. One thing for sure, it takes more than one visit to the center to see everything.

Figure 6.2. Scenario of a family's visit to the Office/Home Design Center.

The following is another scenario that synthesizes information derived from the application of the Knowledge Base System. Unlike an architectural program, which simply specifies facility requirements, this figure tells a complete story. The problem situations described are important because they alert the building design and land development team to areas where such problems are likely to occur.

1. Initial Thoughts

The Delta Home and Office System Corporation has developed a modular approach to cooling and heating systems for new and remodeled homes and offices. The product line is light in weight, easy to maintain, and can be retrofitted into existing structures. The ease of installation and corresponding lower labor costs for both the mechanical system modules and the electrical system elements are particularly attractive to contractors. The company's products are sold to individuals and families remodeling their homes and to housing developers and home builders, both prefabricated and traditional contractors. The office construction and remodeling market is also an area of sales activity.

Delta Home and Office System Corporation is attracted to the Design Center because both home and office market groups come to the center. People in the company have heard that the Office/Home Design Center is attracting hundreds of public and professional visitors daily. Others have said that those presently leasing exhibit and display spaces are very pleased with the marketing and sales opportunities and services provided by the design center.

2. Helpful Information

A telephone call to the Office/Home Design Center led to the mailing of an information brochure describing the spectrum of available services. Since the information brochure was so interesting, and since the center is known to play a significant role in the housing and office industry, the prospective client schedules a visit.

3. Arrival

The Marketing Office makes every effort to see that this visit is pleasant for the Delta Home and Office System Corporation representative, Mr. Kato. First, he was advised to use the parking area adjacent to the professionals' building entrance, where a space was reserved for him. The special care that went into designing the parking area's covered walkways and the entrance to the center were appreciated. Every design detail symbolizes dedication to service and attention to quality. As this entrance is used by professionals and corporation representatives, Mr. Kato is pleased to recognize and be greeted by some of his friends who are already doing business in the Office/Home Design Center. It is reassuring to know that others find it of value.

4. Entering the Office/Home Design Center
The receptionist greets Mr. Kato, and she notifies the Marketing Office of his arrival. He is greeted promptly by his host.

5. New Client Briefing

Mr. Kato is escorted to the Marketing Office, where no time is lost in providing him with all the information he will need to decide whether his company should lease space in the Office/Home Design Center.

The marketing staff conducting the briefing know it is important that prospective leasees understand that every space and space detail within the center is directed toward a specific goal, that no arbitrary design features exist, and that every space and space detail has a justification related to the expectations and requirements of center users.

It is noted that the future of the Office/Home Design Center is as much a concern as how well the center works to meet the needs of today's clients. Design, cost, and delivery systems are a major concern for the future, as well as a major market opportunity, because of the variety and variability of needs in regional, national, and global markets. The center is managed and designed to help those leasing space and doing business in the center achieve the highest possible level of adaptability to this changing market.

During the briefing, the fact that the center serves both public and professional groups is noted as an architectural and management challenge that has been successfully addressed. It is shown that great care is taken to ensure the public receives the educational experience needed to take advantage of the displays and exhibits. The marketing staff explain that the center was designed and is managed to assure that visiting professionals have efficient access to office and housing product displays and exhibits. Associated cost and space management information is explained.

Another topic of the briefing is the value of the public reaction to display and exhibit areas—this allows office and housing product producers to gain insight into how clients, customers, and the general public examine and evaluate their products. The staff describe how the center is designed to facilitate these market research efforts.

The briefing continues by indicating that the management of the center is sensitive to the needs of both public and professional visitors. Every effort is made to assure that the activities of the public visitors do not disrupt the activities of the professional user of the center. On the other hand, the public visitor is not made uncomfortable or embarrassed by lack of sophistication about office and housing products.

The briefing ends with a detailed review of leasing arrangements, leased space costs, and fees charged for the various services offered by the Office/Home Design Center. It is essential to help Mr. Kato determine whether or not his firm will profit from its investment in leased space.

During the briefing, Mr. Kato becomes impressed with the services and facilities of the Learning Center. He thinks this would be a good place for his company's training seminars. He immediately asks about space availability and cost information.

Following his briefing, Mr. Kato is invited to tour and inspect the services, spaces, and amenities provided in the Office/Home Design Center.

6. Office and Housing Consultation Center
Mr. Kato is first shown the Office and Housing Consultation Center. He can see that before the public actually enters the product display and exhibit areas, they have an opportunity to be fully informed about all that the center offers.

7. Office and Home Product Display Floors
Most of the time is spent touring the areas where display and exhibit space is leased to companies. A special exhibit is brought to Mr. Kato's attention. This area is leased on a short term basis. Since his company is introducing a new product line, the company might wish to consider arranging for such an exhibit space and schedule a major marketing event.

These display and exhibit areas cover several floors. The design center space management plan is a response to the need to make display and exhibit areas efficient for use by office and housing professionals as well as enjoyable to the public and easily understood. The floor plan circulation helps visitors find displays and exhibits that are important to them.

Mr. Kato hears how each leasee's space can be customized in terms of size and configuration of leased space, lighting system alternatives and options, outlets for power, wall fixture mounting options, fixed and freestanding partition options, telephone services, and computer system support. Mr. Kato describes some of his special requirements. Display and exhibit space features providing for such requirements are discussed.

8. Professional Services Floor

Mr. Kato is next shown the management, marketing, and information services and communication facilities that are available to serve his company and its clients. It is suggested that Mr. Kato's company may wish to lease space in this area. This would establish a base of operations for the professional and product support services offered by his company.

9. Support Services

The marketing of Office/Home Design Center leased space is promoted by the availability of a wide range of support services, all of which are inspected by Mr. Kato.

The design center staff know that potential leasees need to determine required staffing to establish, maintain, and operate displays and exhibits in leased areas. Mr. Kato notes that many of the display and exhibit areas are staffed by contracted center personnel. In addition, center information services include a computer center, word processing and database support, and sound/video, graphics, and publication production capabilities. All of these services can be contracted.

10. Operations and Maintenance

Many spaces in the center are designed to support operations and maintenance activities. Mr. Kato is told that the center is designed to facilitate the delivery, set-up, and maintenance of the furnishings, fixtures, equipment, and materials used in display and exhibits. The general and service elevators, escalators, stairs, and hallway features are explained. The aspects of the center's design and facility operations related to such concerns as safety, security, and emergency services are inspected.

11. Closing Consultaton

Mr. Kato is very concerned about the best location for his company's leased display space. Since his firm's product line requires exposure to both the office and home markets, and the two groups have different information requirements, it is suggested that two spaces be leased. Another concern is that Mr. Kato's company wants a prominent position in the center, not a remote location. It is pointed out that there is an opportunity for Mr. Kato's firm to become one of the Office/Home Design Center's founding firms. This opportunity is offered to those who lease extensive space for an extended period of time. In return, these firms are assigned prominent locations within the center.

12. Problem Situations

Mr. Kato expresses concern about the lack of quality in some of the displays. The possibility that his company's display would suffer because of the poor quality of another display is something to which the design center management staff must respond. The staff point out that the design of display spaces provides clear separation between leased spaces and that management policies set standards for display and maintenance of leased spaces. It is explained that the design center staff work hard to develop a sense of pride and cooperation among all leasees, and consideration of the goals of the entire operation. The staff hope that they have eliminated Mr. Kato's concerns in this regard.

13. Preparing to Depart

The design center staff share some of their organization's objectives with Mr. Kato.. They recognize that visitors to the center are always looking for new ideas, and that clients are interested in more than style and image. The staff assure Mr. Kato that he will find the center the best possible location for his business. The center is a place that is in touch with the

public, and there are many opportunities for market research. Observation of and informal discussions with public and professional visitors will be a valuable source of information. Discussion with center staff who come in contact with the public daily and as a result have learned a great deal about their preferences and unanswered requirements is another valuable source of product evaluation information. Mr. Kato is then encouraged to spend as much additional time as he wishes in the center.

14. Final Thoughts

Mr. Kato is most impressed by the design center staff. They are enthusiastic, well-informed, and attentive to the smallest details. Mr, Kato concludes that the Office/Home Design Center would be an exciting and profitable location for Delta Home and Office Systems Corporation.

Figure 6.3. Scenario of a corporate representative's visit to the Office/Home Design Center.

Example Two: Worker Performance and Satisfaction

Our premise is that architects, by education and experience, are highly suited to emphasize the human factor/ergonomic perspective in their work. This example is a guideline for undertaking a field study centered around this perspective, with examples of human factors/ergonomic considerations directly related to professional, technical, and service workforce performance and satisfaction. These are major themes for opportunity and innovation. Where the impasse between budget and the attainment of a high quality of life at work was once resolved by emphasizing only essential building features, now more sophisticated clients will accept additional costs that are directly justified in terms of improved work performance. Knowledgeable clients want you to fully understand the relationship between skilled job performance and profit. If you respond to these considerations and help clients develop and nuture their human resources and assets, you will find that clients are willing to commission extended professional services.

This example suggests that each item in the Knowledge Base System can be supplemented with a specific line of inquiry. Possible lines of questioning are presented. Peruse what is written, pick and choose, and apply anything that seems promising for a field study. Recognize that there is something to be learned. Test how this detailed examination of your client's situation would improve your work or lead to an extended or new service. Use it as a model of what you might create for your most challenging markets. At a minimum, speculate on the possibilities.

In this example you will find promising lines of inquiry. For instance, a number of questions pertain to identifying the types of software application programs upon which the client relies. These questions provide insights about what is important to the client. There are question that deal with the manner in which the client selects, trains, and manages personnel. Again, these provide a window into the client's world. This suggests that we must prepare our line of questioning before we invest our man-hours working to understand the client organization. It is far better, for instance, to spend 40 hours preparing a line of questioning, and then spend 80 hours with a client organization following a specific field study agenda, than it is to spend 120 of our man-hours and our client's time in a haphazard fashion, relying on serendipity to find out what is important.

Key Workers and Their Associates

Work has always been about people. Motorola, GE, Sun Micro-systems, Microsoft, Xerox, Corning, Rubbermaid, L. L. Bean, Wal-Mart, Nordstrom, Levi-Strauss, Ben and Jerry's, and hundreds of other outstanding companies and businesses, large and small, are aware that success and competitiveness is all about people. American productivity, product value, and services are again foremost in the world. Companies now recognize that whereas individuals once grew as the company grew, companies now grow only when the professional, technical, and service workforce leads the way to new opportunities. Their investment in salaries, benefits, recruitment, retention, training, and professional education is justified on this point. We see an increased awareness of these factors in public institutions such as hospitals, schools, and local and county government offices. As these institutions accelerate their transformation to competitive management systems, they too place increasingly more importance on employee satisfaction and performance and associate this with an improved quality of life at work.

Identification of key workers and their associates is the essential first step in a field study. Whether or not the design of a workplace is perfected depends upon how well the expectations and requirements of key individuals and groups of individuals are understood. In most businesses, every employee's job performance and satisfaction with life at work are important. Involve as many workers as possible in the study of needs and wants. Here, we will stress working with those identified as critical for organization success. Working with key workers and their associates provides primary sources that alert you to the full complexity of the situation.

Every investigation we undertake to understand our client's situation proceeds efficiently and effectively when the limits of the study have been clearly established. If a boundary is placed around an area of investigation, a basis is created for selectively focusing on the quality of life challenge. When we work to identify key workers and their associates, we create such a boundary. The following questions illustrate the types of queries that provide this perspective.

Who will you come in contact with daily?

Who will you see or hear from less frequently?

Which of these indviduals and groups will have special importance for you and your organization?

Are there special events that will bring in an entirely different spectrum of associates?

Are there individuals whose activities might be disruptive of your activities?

Are there individuals who will require careful consideration because of certain limitations or personal requirements?

Care must be taken when developing a listing of facility user groups. It is possible, however, to reach a point where the research effort goes beyond what is needed. The best way to proceed is to form a general listing of facility users and then develop in greater detail only those categories that appear to require refinement. The labeling of facility user categories is particularly important. Labels should help distinguish one facility user category from another. Common general labels may be used, but only with great care. For instance, use of such labels as "Technician" and "Engineer," or "Secretary" and "Office Manager," may cause misunderstanding. Such simple terms obscure many important distinctions, leading to erroneous assumptions. Categories that reflect exactly how users see themselves, or categories for people with special limitations and capabilities, require a phrase or sentence to convey the extended meaning of these special facility user categories.

Organization Dynamics

People must be given the opportunity to describe the organization as they perceive and value it. Successful field work will identify the elements of the organization structure that are particularly important. From these, we can compose descriptions of group relationships in a manner that makes the participants feel as though they have been fairly and accurately represented. First, you may ask people to describe the principal components of the organization, identifying areas of responsibility. Individuals need to talk about the history of their area of responsibility, its special aspects, and their expectations for the planned facility.

The follow-up to obtaining descriptions of responsibilities is to find out how other facility users view them. The descriptions developed are presented to selected individuals in the following form:

Here are descriptions of the activities that go on around you. How accurate are they?

What can be added or changed so that the information is more accurate and complete?

Which programs are most critical to the organization?

Which programs are unique, requiring special attention?

Or you might ask:

In which areas do you anticipate the building design and land development team will find the greatest challenge?

What individuals and groups are particularly important to your work?

What sort of working relationships do you have?

How do these compare in importance for the successful accomplishment of your responsibilities?

When you depart from organization structure how do you realign yourself?

When will this realignment most likely occur? (In emergencies? Demanding situations? When you are undermanned? In response to a scheduled event? In response to an unscheduled event?)

Worker Activities

As we work to assess people's needs and wants, we are working to identify the activity patterns to which a specific response must be formulated. Every work facility must support a wide range of daily activities. Therefore, every square meter, each fixture, furnishing and equipment item, as well as the funds expended thereon, will eventually have to be justified in terms of the activities being supported. People are willing to describe their activities. They want the architect to understand their day and weigh the importance of their activities as they do. Decisions about the extent of inquiry should be made on an individual basis. More important, complex, unique, or troublesome facility user groups require additional activity information. Therefore, recognizing the need to support the specific activities associated with identified facility user groups we must answer the following:

What are the characteristic activities of this facility user category?

What are the most important activities associated with this facility user category?

What are the skilled job performance requirements for this category?

Which activities of this category are most time-consuming?

What are the requirements for activity sequencing and timing?

What job assignments are particularly difficult to accomplish?

What are the shared responsibilities of individuals and groups of individuals within this category?

When there is an opportunity for workers to have personnel comments about their activities, then ask:

Could you tell us more about what you do? What is a typical day like for you?

Is there something you do that most people overlook?

Do you encounter unusual events that require an entirely different spectrum of activity considerations?

Which situations might disrupt your activities?

Which situations require careful consideration because of certain demanding job responsibilities?

Application of these questions can be organized by facility user category, organization structure elements, or location within the facility. An activity description that does not identify the implements, devices, and equipment used to perform a task is incomplete. To assist in the development of design guidelines, activities must be distinguished by importance, frequency, and complexity. In order to perfect physical setting features such as space plans, ambient environment, and convenience, safety, and security elements, we have to see daily activities as the facility user sees them.

Not to be overlooked are the following considerations. Recognizing that the need to respond specifically to those with permanent and temporary physical disabilities, the educationally and national language disadvantaged, and the mentally less able may require selective design responses, then:

What are the expectations and requirements of the disabled and disadvantaged for achieving a safe, secure, and convenient environment?

Work Culture

So far we have attempted to create objective descriptions of people's responsibilities and activities. We also need to know how people see themselves. This is a matter of the formulation and wording of questions. How do you get people to talk about just the right things, the things that will help develop insight? People are not too sure what is required. "Do we talk about ourselves, the people around us, or things in general?" The most serious problem is that if these inquiries are not carefully thought out, people will be superficial in their answers, avoiding what is most serious or controversial. Finally, what is found to be characteristic of people may only be accurate for a limited time, as customs, norms, lifestyles, and traditions change. What are the possible forces for change? What is the likelihood that a change will take place? Is any of this significant? These are the types of inquiry that are needed.

Because of people's reluctance to share their personal life with others, direct questions should be avoided. Individuals should be asked to review the information developed concerning organization structure and anticipated facility user activities. As they examine it for completeness and accuracy, they should be approached informally with the following questions:

What is missing here?

Is this the way we should look at things?

Is this what really concerns individuals?

How often have things changed in the past? Will things like that be likely to happen again?

What about people's feelings, concerns, and expectations for the future?

Questions about work lifestyles, customs, norms, and traditions are never set aside. The first results alert us to important considerations. As questioning that deals with quality of life at work proceeds, individuals affected by design decisions will have to be questioned again. You want to discover their real concerns for the future. The first results should itemize every possible consideration. As these topics reappear in conversations with individuals, the first descriptions of norms, customs, traditions, and lifestyles may be revised.

When dealing with the quality of life at work, it is important to study a client's management philosophy. We want to understand the way goals are pursued and what views exist concerning the human resources of the organization. Performance can be enhanced and satisfaction with conditions increased through building design only to the degree permitted by the existing management philosophy. Where the existing philosophy is beneficial to individuals, people are responsive to improved conditions. They recognize these to be a sign of regard as much as an actual improvement in the physical setting. Where the management philosophy is not mindful of individual needs, building design and land development achievements will have little effect on job performance and satisfaction. It is also a fact that when a high regard for the individual is sustained, great things can be achieved in even the worst of environments. The caution here is that these conditions must be recognized as temporary and that the future holds promise only if improved quality of life at work is forthcoming.

In a corporate setting, these inquiries will help identify subtle and important distinctions between various facility user categories:

What are the characteristic customs, norms, and traditions of anticipated facility users to which facility design and management schemes must be responsive?

To what degree do existing management styles foster the development of successful facility operations?

To what degree do existing work practices foster the development of successful facility operations?

What is the significance of work customs for facility design and management?

What impact will the project have on the existing organization in terms of changes in work customs?

Workstations

The information foundation for the design of workstations is established through application of sections 2.0, 3.0, 4.0, 5.0, and 6.0 of the Knowledge Base System. As a result of interpreting this information, we begin a more detailed questioning process:

Inventory. *What is the inventory of equipment for workstations?*

Equipment Configuration. *How will this equipment be configured at the workstations?*

Space Layout. *What space layouts best correspond to workstation activities and equipment configurations?*

When the answers to these questions are not readily available or when there is a great deal of concern about the importance of perfecting every aspect of workstation design, then we must initiate the following detailed inquiries:

Place in Process. *Where does the subject workstation fit into the total work process?*

Specific Activities. *What are the specific workstation activities?*

Output Requirements. *What are the specific work outputs required of the workstation?*

Activities Sequence and Timeline. *What task sequences and timelines characterize the activities assigned to the workstation?*

Equipment Requirements. *What are the equipment requirements of the subject workstation?*

Tool Requirements. *What are the tool requirements of the subject workstation?*

Materials Requirements. *What are the materials requirements of the subject workstation?*

Maintenance Responsibilities. *What maintenance responsibilities should be assigned to workstation personnel?*

Required Safety Features. *What safety features are required at the workstation?*

Required Security Features. *What security features are required at the workstation?*

Recognizing that the complexity of assigned tasks may exceed individual capabilities, ask:

Error Anticipation. *What task error possibilities have been identified?*

Error Mitigation. *What can be done to preclude or reduce task errors?*

Overloading Factors. What work overloading possibilities have been identified?

Overloading Mitigation. What can be done to mitigate the effects of task overloading?

Job Stress. What possibilities for job stress have been identified?

Job Stress Mitigation. What can be done to reduce or eliminate job stress?

Body Stress. What possibilities for body stress have been identified?

Body Stress Mitigation. What can be done to mitigate body stress?

Body Position. Do workstation tasks require the individual to be seated, standing, or in an awkward position for extended periods?

Body Movements. Do workstation tasks require precise finger, hand, limb, hand–arm, or eye–hand movements?

Special Requirements. When individuals with special limitatons and requirements are assigned to the subject workstation, what additional design features are required?

Considering task activities, workstation equipment features, and surrounding workstation characteristics, ask:

Input Devices. Where workstation activities center around input display devices, what steps must be taken to assure that both hardware and software features correspond to workstation tasks and activities?

Input Device Location. Where should the input devices be located?

Display Devices. Where workstation activities center around display devices, what steps must be taken to assure that both hardware and software features correspond to workstation tasks and activities?

Display Location. Considering task activities, workstation physical features, surrounding workstation characteristics, and the use of the display by other individuals, where should display devices be located?

Adjunct Work Surfaces. Is it necessary to provide a work surface specifically designed to accommodate information assessment and development activities and calculations?

Workstation Layout. How should the workstation be arranged in terms of the relationship between input device activities, information displays, and workstation activities?

Facility Integration. What is the best possible way to integrate the workstation into surrounding activities?

Recognizing that workstation design recommendations require assessment from the perspective of skilled job performance, ask:

Design Critique. Which workstation design proposals most effectively meet the organization's concern for attaining and maintaining skilled job performance?

Assigned Personnel Critique. Which design recommendations most effectively meet the expectations and requirements expressed by assigned personnel?

Recommendation Impact. Which proposals would require substantial accommodation on the part of the organization and assigned personnel?

Attaining Agreement. Which recommendations are likely to be unsuccessful unless organization and individual viewpoints are changed?

Communication and Information Systems

The following questions will help identify information development and processing tasks that are of special importance, complex or unique, and subject to information overload. Concerns identified include: ease of use, reduction of operational complexity, limiting the number of software products, providing for rapid changeover to new applications, and minimizing disruption caused by new software releases. Opportunities for application of database support, decision-making aids, and expert and knowledge system support are identified through question applications.

Workstations and associated job categories are the elemental units in the communication and information system; therefore:

Specific Communication and Information Activities. What are the specific communication and information monitoring, development, exchange, and application responsibilities assigned to this workstation?

Role in Total Communication and Information System. *In what way will the communications and information developed at this workstation be used within the total facility operations?*

Communication and Information Sources. *What elements within the total facility system provide information to and communicate with the workstation?*

Communication and Information Destinations. *What elements within the total facility system receive information and communications from the workstation?*

Important Contacts. *Which individuals and groups provide information and communications of special importance to this workstation?*

Facility System Interface. *What procedures, activities, and equipment connect the workstation to the total facility system?*

Informal Contacts. *What individuals and groups are informal sources of information and communications?*

As it is important to identify communication and information system development and processing tasks that are complex or unique, we must consider:

Task Complexity. *What is the relative complexity or uniqueness of the identified communication and information development and processing activities?*

Information Overload. *As information overload is often a concern, what sequencing, task simplification, and feedback features should be incorporated into workstation communication and information system design?*

Automated System Elements. *As it is important to automate communication and information development tasks wherever possible, what tasks are candidates for automation?*

When the workstation's place and function in the total communication and information system has been precisely prescribed, then consider:

Performance Evaluations. *What performance evaluations will help confirm that proposed designs meet task assignment and communication and information system requirements?*

System Monitoring. *When monitoring the workstation communication and information system during initial period of use, what tasks should be included in the trial?*

Perceived Function of Communication and Information System. *It is important to define the communication and information system responsibilities and activities of users. Therefore, what system description will help individuals understand the system's design, the function of various major components, and the critical detailed features of the input/output system?*

Software as an Insight

It is helpful to spend some time asking people to show you the software central to their activities. This is another source of insight as to what is important within the client organization. Therefore, you might pursue the following:

Specific Workstation Activities. *What specific workstation communication and information system activities require software support?*

Data and Information Types. *What information and data types pertain to the workstation?*

Extent of Use. *How many different workstations will employ the prospective software?*

User Interface Enhancement. *Since software design must anticipate the communication and information system operator's manner of thought and behavior, what is required of the software in terms of supporting text, graphic, and audio inputs and outputs?*

Areas of Concern. *Where will it be particularly important to assure that communication and information system technology is designed for ease of use?*

Knowledge System Support. *Since successful communication and information system activities often require knowledge support, what opportunities exist for application of database, decision support, and expert and knowledge system support within the communication and information system?*

Building the Software. *From what is known about the application situation, what are the appropriate software design criteria and specifications?*

Existing Software Products. In the context of the anticipated software applications, which existing software meet all design criteria and specifications?

Modified Software Products. In the context of the anticipated software applications, which existing software products are candidates for modification to accommodate new application situations?

New Software Product Development. If new software products are necessary, what communciation and information system activities will be supported and what are the application requirements?

Limiting the Number of Products. Since communication and information system application is best served by limiting the number and unique features of software programs, what software characteristics meet these criteria?

Rapid Changeover. Can software program changes take place in one day?

New Releases Disruption. When new software releases are introduced, what safeguards will be developed to preclude disruption of communication and information system operations?

The Organization's Concern for Skilled Job Performance

The following line of questioning helps us understand the workforce requirements of clients, as seen in recruitment and selection criteria, advancement and retention strategies, and information system, equipment operation, and maintenance training. Question items suggest the importance of anticipating the limitations and capabiltities of physically disabled, educationally disadvantaged, and less able workers. One item recognizes that as new products and technology become available, the possibilities for employing the disabled and disadvantaged increase. Health and human services alliances and family support and community development are noted as critical aspects of human resource development. While you may never apply these questions, they do identify valuable areas of inquiry.

Educational Requirements. What are the educational requirements associated with a specific workstation or complex assigned activity?

Desired Experience. *What are the experience requirements associated with workstation responsibilities or complex assigned activity?*

Required Skills. *What are the skill requirements associated with workstation responsibilities or complex assigned activity?*

Organization Resources. *Recognizing that human resource development builds on what already exists, then to what degree do the needed workforce skills and experience exist?*

Recruitment and Selection. *What recruitment strategies and selection standards are recommended?*

Existing Workforce Role in Retention. *What role should the existing workforce play in retention?*

Recommendation Justification. *What justification can be given for the recommended human resource development strategy?*

Recognizing the importance of skilled job performance, ask:

Skill Development. *What basic and advanced work skills must be developed?*

Rate of Task Learning. *How quickly can assigned tasks be learned?*

Familiarization with Operations. *What means should be employed to help personnel understand what the operation they are involved in means to the future success of the organization and the relationship between groups and individuals in that endeavor?*

Peer Associations. *What training roles can be assigned to those working with new personnel?*

Internships. *What internship programs should be established to help personnel more fully understand the operation and identify future roles in the organization?*

Scholastic and Higher Education Associations. *What training roles can be assigned to local and regional educational centers?*

Recognizing the diversity of human resource development practices and management styles, the building design and land development team must consider the following:

Management Styles. *To what degree do existing management styles foster the development of skilled job performance?*

Work Practices. *To what degree do existing work practices foster the development of job skills?*

Anticipated Work Customs. *What are the characteristic work customs, norms, and traditions to which the organization must be responsive?*

Work Culture Impact. *What impact will the project have on existing organizations in terms of changes in work customs?*

Job Performance Measures. *What job performance measures should be applied?*

Workforce Advancement. *What opportunities for advancement to more responsible and challenging work are possible?*

Skilled Workforce Retention. *What management position and strategy is needed to assure retention of skilled personnel?*

Family Life Support. *As there is a direct relationship between the workforce's commitment to company goals and the quality of life at home and in the community available to them and their families, what are the family support and community development needs that must be considered?*

Physically Disabled Workers. *What must the building design and land development team do to respond to the requirements of employees with permanent and temporary physical disabilities?*

Educationally Disadvantaged Workers. *How can the building design and land development team best respond to the special expectations and requirements of educationally disadvantaged personnel?*

Mentally Less Able Workers. *How can the building design and land development team achieve the innovative work environments required for the employment of the mentally less able?*

New Products and Technology. *What new products and technology can increase the possibilities for employing the disabled and disadvantaged and help assure a safe, secure, and convenient environment for these workers?*

Health and Human Services Alliances. *How can these public agencies be of assistance in the design of appropriate work environments for those with special expectations and requirements?*

Example Three: Understanding a Client's Situation

This example, based on a field study by Michael Palmer, A.I.A, Sohl & Palmer Architects, and Larry Wolff, A.I.A., Wolff/Lang/ Christopher Architects, illustrates how architects can play a major role in a client's strategic thinking and planning. Their work is presented here as a case study. Such studies can be used in promotional activities to demonstrate an ability to work with clients to reduce the financing required to undertake planned expansion, assure that building performance precisely supports efficient service to customers, and create a building image that is appreciated by customers and enhances the company's reputation.

Initial Field Study Findings

Gourmet Delights, Inc. (GDI) is a South Carolina specialty food company with six very popular shops and a fast-growing mail order business. This company is perhaps the most knowledgeable gourmet food purveyor in the southeast. Located in three major communities, Charleston, Columbia, and Charlotte, the shops offer quality gourmet foods, freshly roasted coffee beans, imported teas, and food preparation accessories. Premier products, an accommodating staff, and customer loyalty are the essence of Gourmet Delights. Product quality control begins with the hand selection of the finest foods from exotic locations throughout the world. Direct referral, customer satisfaction, and savvy staff dialogue are the primary methods of advertising. Gourmet Delights is a merchant of culture.

This company now faces a critical period, with plans for three new stores in the southeast and additional outlets up and down the east coast. The decisions facing GDI fall into two categories: those that affect individual stores and those related to their expansion strategy. Issues concerning individual stores may seem easier to resolve once larger, operational, and policy-driven issues are addressed, but the opposite is actually the case. While necessary innovations and recommended changes may be minor and simple, they become substantial when magnified by store volume. In combination, they form an economic model for future application.

It is a time for robust decision making and action. Gourmet Delights, Inc. is ready for growth. Recent magazine feature articles indicate that GDI is one of the country's finest gourmet companies. In order to take full advantage of growth in a manner consistent with the firm's marketing philosophy and values, a growth strategy is required. As a prerequisite, the justification for growth needs to be stated. Growth will attract investors and increase profits; it will also provide career opportunities for the people of Gourmet Delights. The quintessence of this business is its people. This is precisely what makes Gourmet Delights unique. Its staff and management are the distinctions that determine the identity of the product. The attributes of the product are important, but not as important as the identity of the people. Therefore, entrepreneurial strategies having the greatest chance of success will directly relate to GDI management and staff.

The Growth Plan

Everything from store location to the use of appropriate materials should reinforce the identity of the GDI culture, and be expressed in its language. This language can be thought of as both verbal and visual. It produces a special ambience, and a certain rhetoric. As stimulating as the gourmet products themselves, the rhetoric is creative, intellectual, and egalitarian, which are the codifiers of the language spoken. Continued customer and staff recognition of these codifiers is essential to new and existing operations. They represent the "laws," the rules of the vocabulary, that identify Gourmet Delights, and they are useful because they can be used to create a design concept for future development. These laws are both universal and particular, creating a desirable paradox for application and judgement.

George Noe, current CEO of GDI, has a flair for adventure and a carefree attitude. A veteran of the specialty food business, he opened a small shop in Charleston in the early 1980's. In the years since he founded the business, Noe has expanded on a modest scale and added five stores. With the recent explosive growth of specialty food stores in the United States, Noe feels that a more aggressive expansion plan is warranted. Armed with a profitable balance sheet, a locally renowned product, plans for a new processing plant in the works, and a new management team at headquarters, Noe feels that his company is ready to embark on a major program of growth.

Jack Hahn, the newly hired President of GDI, is in charge of organizational development, financial planning, and real estate. Hahn feels that the basics are in place for implementing a plan to open 24 new stores over the next 3 years. The immediate plan is to expand in the Raleigh, Durham, and Chapel Hill areas. The ultimate growth over a longer term would include expansion throughout the southeast, and up and down the east coast. Plans call for a total of 70 stores in the east, and possible franchises in the midwest. Of particular importance to Hahn at this time is the development of alliances with other high-quality food purveyors, which will contribute significantly to revenues and enhance GDI's image.

Wth a total of 24 shareholders, Hahn has devised a plan to finance the company's expansion through selling additional shares in the company, bringing the total shareholders to 80. One benefit of expanding the ownership structure is increased liquidity for the current owners. Previous store expansions were financed out of pocket. Revenues generated by existing stores are sufficient to handle one or two stores per year without resorting to outside financing. However, in order to arrange sufficient capital to finance the new expansion, GDI has decided that the best avenue is to combine new investor sources along with a limited number of construction loans. As the new stores become profitable, the need for outside capital will diminish.

The Organization

One area of concern, noted early in the field study, is the obvious conflict between Noe's view of the company marketing a culture and Hahn's drive to expand at a rapid rate. A certain degree of skepticism regarding "newness" is recommended, considering that a very successful enterprise is at risk, with a company culture vulnerable to insensitive merchandising and store design.

While George Noe is the inspirational and cultural leader of the organization, Hahn is the business leader. Reporting directly to Noe are Tom Kennedy, Director of Real Estate, Mary Sato, Director of Store Development, and Terry McCormick, Director of Marketing and Mail Order. Kennedy has recently been hired to spearhead the search for new store locations. His background in real estate law and experience in the southeast real estate market bring new expertise and vitality to the search for potential sites. Sato has been with the company for ten years. She started as a clerk in one of the stores, and progressed to manager, district manager, regional director and eventually to her current position. Although she has no professional training in the construction industry, she has a strong interest in construction, *esprit de corps* with architects and contractors, and the hands-on experience of working at all levels in the business. Terry McCormick, Director of Marketing and Mail Orders, is a very effective promoter, and contributes seventeen percent of the gross revenue through mail order, which is increasing at a rate of fifteen percent a year. Sales have recently jumped significantly, due to a top rating by a national consumer magazine.

Each store has only three full-time employees—a manager and two assistant managers. The salespeople work between 21 and 35 hours a week. Most are college students, musicians, artists, and so forth, and are considered the cream of the part-time labor pool. Ages range from nineteen or twenty to people in their late thirties. Compensation is considered to be quite attractive, starting at $7.50 per hour and including medical, dental, and 401(K) benefits. Hiring is very selective, in keeping with Hahn's belief that the staff is the principal articulator of the quality. Each applicant is interviewed two or three times by the manager and the assistant manager. New employees are given a total of 24 hours of training, with at least 10 hours before they serve their first customer.

Store Development Costs

Construction costs must be carefully evaluated. The total cost of developing the last few stores has soared to well over $400,000 per store, a figure that makes Hahn uneasy. In fact, a recent projection of store opening cost was $412,780. Although GDI hopes to reduce this cost through economy of scale, a thorough reevaluation of size, design, and construction procedures and practices is in order.

The architecture and interior design responsibilities have been handled by one architect since Noe's founding of the enterprise. The architect has a small firm in Greensboro, and a long-standing business and personal relationship with George Noe. Hahn has serious concerns about the capability of this architect to provide services for the accelerated growth plan. Although this firm is familiar with the intricate details of the functional requirements of the retail stores, there are nagging doubts about the wisdom of continuing the relationship. Questions have arisen about the fees being charged, and whether GDI is well served by a firm that is located so far away. Hahn believes the company should rethink its architectural services to profit from past experience and minimize future problems.

All stores use the same design vernacular, which has become a symbolic image and reflects the often bohemian character of the clientele. All facilities are situated within existing structures such as older urban buildings or more recently built shopping centers. The existing spaces were usually vacant and nondescript. Occasionally, storefronts, slabs, and plumbing had to be relocated and replaced before tenant improvements could be started. Many of the buildings required extensive renovations. Architectural construction documents were manually drawn and very little duplication was possible, due to the inconsistent nature of the shell spaces. Electrical requirements for convenience receptacles, equipment connections, and lighting were shown on the architectural plans. HVAC and plumbing designs were done on a design/build basis with the low bidder of selected licensed contractors. Once the construction documents were completed, they were turned over to Mary Sato, Director of Store Development, to submit to the various governmental agencies for plan review. Bidding was also handled by Sato, as was construction administration. The architect had only limited responsibilities during construction. Projects had been negotiated with various contractors using a contract drawn up by the contractor. Subcontracting work was somewhat competitive through selective bidding on each individual project.

Under Noe's guidance the store format has remained essentially the same, with minor changes made only to adapt to existing buildings. Although store development cost has remained relatively constant, a more aggressive growth program would require greater attention to construction cost and building performance and image in order to satisfy the new investment *pro forma* objectives. Existing GDI stores average 2,991 square feet, with approximately two-thirds allocated to sales and the other third allocated to storage, office, rest rooms, and break area. Actual sizes vary from 1,900 to 3,200 square feet. Store widths range from 16 to 31 feet. The layout of the stores has remained the same throughout the history of GDI. There is an entry at the storefront, and an L-shaped service counter with a take-out sales bar up front and a product sales counter in the back. Retail displays are located opposite the main bar area so that customers can browse the merchandise while queuing to place their order. Casework, store fixtures, and millwork have been crafted by one small cabinet shop, due to concern for consistent quality and workmanship. The design aesthetic of the stores is a very important part of the merchandising of the product. The "woodcraft" style that was popular in the 60's and 70's, represented by the extensive use of dark stained oak and other dark woods for the cabinets, shelves, and wall paneling, is still the dominant visual element. Noe has experimented with different materials and stain colors in the past and continues to prefer a limited palette of materials as an expression of the company philosophy. The quality of the finishes makes an important statement about attention given to the product. Finish materials are chosen for their appearance. Stainless steel, synthetic products, and laminates have seldom been used in any areas that are visible to the customer. The counter/bar top finish has been a major concern of Noe's for some time. It is constructed from wood veneer, requiring several coats of hand-rubbed Swedish finish. Aesthetically, this finish seems appropriate, but it is not entirely satisfactory due to high cost and susceptibility to damage. Experiments with other finishes have proved unsatisfactory.

Infrastructure

In anticipation of the planned growth, Noe has built a new facility capable of supporting the expansion plan. Merchandise is distributed daily by company owned vans. A computerized network linking the stores with the plant enables restocking on a daily basis as required. GDI's headquarters facility is centrally located and convenient to the existing stores. The facility houses corporate offices and a training facility, and is large enough to handle necessary increases in support staff for the foreseeable future.

Capital and Cash Flow Requirements

The senior management of GDI knows that the organization of cash flow and the positioning of capital is crucial to their action plan. They understand that growth must be conservative, and that the excitement of entrepreneurial actions must not disrupt daily operations. Rather than seek capital from commercial lenders, growth will be built upon equity, thus requiring very little debt. As Noe, Hahn, and the store development team contemplate the important decisions that need to be made, the overriding concern is the cost of construction for each store. Quality control and cost monitoring is crucial to maintaining sanity and meeting the budget objectives. To that end, Hahn has defined the goal of reducing store development cost to $300,000 per store. All aspects of design and construction are being evaluated to accomplish this goal. In order to develop a program for a store prototype that is appropriate to the anticipated locations, the team has been considering what steps are necessary to home-in on a model that can be fine-tuned and routinely replicated in the new markets.

GDI Field Study Conclusion

During the field study, Palmer and Wolff began to develop a strategy for maximizing the potential of GDI's expansion and construction program. With confidence that a strategy for growth can be devised that would be consistent with the company's values and philosophy, Palmer and Wolff grappled with the dilemma faced by most fresh food purveyors when they decide to expand beyond the normal rate of growth: Can quality be maintained while stretching the distribution system to greater limits? What is the optimum growth rate given the current infrastructure? Their view is that correct and appropriate responses to architectonic issues will provide answers to larger questions about the best ways to grow, aspects of competition, and new store locations. Design concept development is understood best as a series of separate but related decisions, each having an economic impact and requiring a plan of action. The following sections complete the field study report.

Confirm Customer Needs and Desires

As an existing business organization, GDI knows how to manage. There are many reasons for their success, but customer satisfaction is probably the greatest factor. Therefore, additional time out of the store is essential to rediscover the world of the customer. This is especially true for new locations that will be less metropolitan and more suburban, where different attitudes and values may exist. Moreover, existing customer values and needs may be changing to the extent that future purchases may represent entirely different needs and desires. Direct dialogue with selected customers and some random sampling is recommended to gain thoughtful insights, and reflection is needed to assess customer attitudes as they relate to company values.

To confirm their growth strategy, GDI needs to analyze all current information, and especially to identify those missing components necessary to the decision-making process. Past and present accomplishments and failures produce symptoms, which have causes; when these causes are understood, they open the door to innovation. Standard operating policies that are outworn or dated should be identified, and concepts that are no longer productive must be abandoned to eliminate unnecessary mistakes, barriers, and misdirected effort. Product and merchandise procurement, plant operations, processing techniques, and shipping routines represent certain needs vital to operations and sales. Staff and management are close to daily events, which means that potential and somewhat obvious improvements can be overlooked. Rapidly changing demographics have a major influence on the design and location of stores.

Develop Design Guidelines

The design and construction of the prototypical GDI store are dependent upon the development of design guidelines. Design guidelines produce the complete definition of all of the "model" components. For these guidelines to be correctly produced, they must be grounded on a serious delineation of all required activities, user groups, organizational relationships, space allocations, functional adjacencies, circulation systems, equipment, forms, colors, and surfaces, independent of either budget or schedule influences. Incorrect design guidelines occur when cost, time frame, or other resource dependencies are allowed to influence results, thus compromising effort and information value. Capital resources and timing are critical development factors, but they should be addressed during the design stage, not during the development of design guidelines.

It is essential that the store format continue to express the "language"—the special ambience and rhetoric—of the GDI culture. Store format, location, and even the GDI logo, establish a distinct product identity. Therefore, the notion that new stores need to "stick out" by changing the exterior architectonic vocabulary (a change in color for instance) may not be the right approach. On the contrary, it could be more rewarding, exciting, and interesting for store format to be developed somewhat as a "cult," where store identity continues a tradition of almost unrecogniz-able, common individuality. This approach is likely to continue the successful intellectual and egalitarian appeal responsible for distinguishing GDI stores.

After the design guidelines have been confirmed and ap-proved, GDI should initiate schematic design services to identify alternatives, explore options, and select a preferred approach that best meets a defined and clearly understood design concept. A focus on a true prototype store plan should be commissioned immediately. To facilitate this effort, a written program should be developed. The program should outline minimums, maximums and optimal square footage allowances and clearances, as well as staffing criteria. This exercise will reassess what has been consid-ered the minimum store space, and allow any new players on the team to learn and provide valuable information based on their past experiences and vision. We suspect that a more efficient floor plan is possible when studied in this manner. If it is discovered that 1,900–2,100 square feet is workable, construction costs will be roughly one-half the present amount. This exercise should take no more than four weeks and provide critically important information that can be used to refine the search for available lease space.

During this time, models of the prototype should be con-structed to simulate graphic plans and sketches. Scale study models are excellent for quick, three-dimensional investigations, while computer generated electronic modeling is more appropri-ate for more refined and detailed evaluations. Cost estimates, new site location analyses, and an economic feasibility study are required to confirm that facility development concepts meet profit, performance, and image objectives.

On a more specific note, most GDI stores are poorly lit, and suffer from improper "spots" of wasteful incandescent fixtures. High efficiency, color corrected T-8 fluorescent fixtures will sig-nificantly brighten overall store environments and lend them-selves to the "industrial" enamel-colored pendant fixtures customarily used in GDI stores. While energy savings may not be as important as general store appearance and product presenta-tion, these savings can pay for better quality fixtures and additional indirect or display lighting, which will decrease maintenance.

The use of natural materials should be continued. It is a distinctive element of the GDI identity that is rarely found in other speciality food stores or, for that matter, in any retail estab-lishment. This is not only a great idea, but one that becomes another of those codifiers that understate GDI identity. Substitution of other materials is not recommended. Natural materials imply ecological sensitivity and honesty. This is crucial to the perception of store interiors, packing, and merchandising. While store design should not be driven solely by environmental concerns, such concerns can be incorporated where possible in a thoughtful and meaningful way. Environmental materials include wood products that are manufactured from renewable species and recycled materials that feature ceramics, stone, glass, copper, and sisal. All of these reinforce GDI's identity and extend the philosophy of natural materials beyond current limits.

Use Modular and Factory-Finished Casework

GDI is faced with a choice between custom casework or factory-finished, modular casework. The current budget for cabinets and finish is $90,000, which can be substantially reduced to an estimated amount of $49,719. The use of factory-finished modular casework can meet GDI's aesthetic expectations, while providing the flexibility of custom design and fabrication. Cost estimates for casework are not dependent on the fabrication of the same units for each store. Although this may produce even greater cost savings than those presented, it is important that GDI maintain the ability to adapt to each new store situation. It is imperative that store location, leasing aspects, and design not be compromised by standardization of previously fabricated casework. The goal should be to standardize the cabinetry so that 90 percent of the fixtures and cabinets are modular. In order to accomplish this, there will have to be more uniformity among the stores. This can be done by selecting sites in shopping centers that are newer and more consistently organized. Changing cabinet materials will have only a minor effect on the cost. However, shopping for a production-oriented shop in the southeast, and ordering a larger volume of units to take advantage of economy of scale, will most likely result in substantial savings. End units and odd dimensions can be custom fabricated or specially detailed to account for nonstandard conditions.

Identify New Store Locations

Matching a retail line with consumers is a demanding task. On a hot afternoon in the late summer of 1994, Tom Kennedy, the director of real estate for Gourmet Delights, Inc., drove back to Charleston after his third consecutive day in the Raleigh, Durham, and Chapel Hill areas. His search for potential store sites had left him discouraged. The properties he had been shown did not match the demographic profile the company had established for its expansion program. He suspected that a different prototype might be in order for those sites located outside the Charleston area. He also suspected that the brokers were more interested in moving property than learning exactly what is best for GDI. The task of selecting sites for new stores would be best performed by in-house GDI marketing staff, possibly equipped with a computer based, geographic mapping system. Site and facility feasibility analyses of existing site, building, and infrastructure conditions is the task of the design team. More objective site presentations and lease evaluations are certain to occur if the design team represents GDI during initial negotiations, rather than depending on information provided by leasing agents.

Create Lease Specifications and Standard Specifications

Standard GDI conditions of approval and specifications for acceptance will promote faster and more efficient negotiations. Aggressive lease rates for multiple sites are obtained by applying consistent standards to competing locations. Lease specifications and standard specifications will require a collaborative effort between the design team and GDI's legal counsel.

Adapt Store Model Prototype

Once leases are executed, the development team will need to prepare and complete final construction documents to include plans, specifications, and calculations. With a definitive architectural program, a promising location, and a winning new store design, final design services can be accelerated to rapidly adapt the model prototype to each new location. Arrangements can be made with city officials to pay for an accelerated plan review, ensuring an expedited approval and building permit. Concurrently, other team members can invite bid proposals, comparing them to a historical cost database of all previously constructed stores. After signing contracts, the team can shift their attention to the actual building process.

Set Up Design and Construction Team

While the immediate challenge facing GDI is the location of new sites, the larger issue is the creation of a design and construction team arrangement that is virtually guaranteed to produce the desired results. Now is the time to get things in order. We recommend that the following steps be initiated as soon as possible. The relationship with the Greensboro architect should be changed to refocus on his expertise. As we see it, this architect is well versed in the complicated design requirements and spatial ergonomics. We envision a period of transition where, over the next year, this information and knowledge can be used to orient a new architect. The new architect will take the responsibility for construction document production and be involved in the construction phase. The Greensboro architect will be retained as a "design consultant." The quality of the present drawings for the GDI stores is inferior to documents being produced with state-of-the-art computerized drafting systems. Complete CAD drawings will create a database of floor plans, counter layouts, restroom details, and above all, cabinet/fixture details and elevations, that can be eventually used to cut production time and, consequently, save money.

A new construction team should be selected from the local area to facilitate convenience, efficiency, and mutual accessibility. A construction manager with a risk contractual relationship with GDI is preferable to other possibilities because the constructing entity joins the team early—in this case when a site location has been identified and the design team is ready to commence preparation of final documents. The construction manager with risk (CMwr) does value engineering, cost evaluation, and early procurement of long-lead items (i.e., casework), while the design team completes final documents, permitting, and approvals. CMwr overhead and profit are best negotiated with a guaranteed maximum price, while CMwr services and risk correlate to most traditional "general contractor" responsibilities. Partnering concepts will unify team members and further a team-oriented approach. In this scenario there is a potential to save $35,000 per store strictly by changing the construction contract arrangement.

Current opening costs of $412,780 can be reduced to $322,740. Consider that GDI stores (leasehold improvements, equipment, and fixtures) are costing in the range of $150 to over $180 per square foot, a phenomenal figure in today's world. It is possible to maintain leasehold improvements at $120,800 (approximately $70 per square foot), assuming that the shell of the building is adequately equipped with the necessary services such as HVAC units, storefront, perimeter shell walls, and sewer within the vicinity of the space. We feel that regional contractors should be selected in a competitive bid environment to attack these costs. In our experience, small restaurants similar in scope to this prototype have been running closer to $60 per square foot for lease holder improvements.

Equally important to the tangible construction issues is the in-house project management structure. Although Mary Sato is a talented and resourceful person fulfilling the present duties of the Director of New Store Development, we feel the structure should augmented by a person with more experience in project management. An architect with an appreciation for design would be a valued asset to the process. This on-staff architect/construction manager would primarily concentrate on the value engineering side of the problem with an eye trained on the bottom line. Administration of the building process would be improved by closer attention to the quality and thoroughness of the construction documents and by tightening up construction contracts (A.I.A. documents should be used instead of a contract drawn up by the contractor). The cost of this on-staff architect/construction manager will be between $50,000 and $60,000 per year. Amortized over an average of eight projects per year, this position will add approximately $7,000 to the cost of each new store. A side benefit of having a person with this expertise on staff is that it will allow maintenance and remodeling work to be performed in-house instead of outsourcing to an independent architect.

Sato's role would change in some ways. She would continue to be involved on the front end of the project. Her primary focus would be coordination between the Greensboro architect, the new company architect, and the landlord. Handling governmental submittals and design review liaison, maintaining conformity with the model or the prototype, and managing of the transition of the project to the construction document production mode, would make up the remainder of her responsibilities. She would continue to report directly to the CEO.

Schedule and Track Progress Growth Plan

With schedule, tracking, and reporting systems in place, construction will commence with the immediate procurement of long-lead items. Shop drawings will be submitted in required electronic format. With available data transmission technology, most submittals will be reviewed and returned the same day from the job site. Documents will be telecommunicated back and forth between the construction site and GDI headquarters, creating instantaneous record documents and allowing for fast resolution of necessary changes. The grand opening ceremony will be a smashing success, partly because early completion more than finances the celebration party. According to GDI projections, opening stores 30 days ahead of schedule can generate approximately $6,200 of profit.

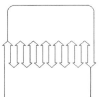

CHAPTER SEVEN

KNOWLEDGE DEVELOPMENT

Executive architects manage the crossovers between the world outside the office and the world inside the office. Working to establish opportunity for the firm, they look to the future, while carefully considering the assets of the firm and identifying where new assets must be developed. Knowledge is the foundation of this endeavor.

Knowledge Establishes a Sense of Direction

Knowledge of what must be achieved is all that most people need to begin to contribute to project success. With a sense of direction, every aspect of the project seems to improve, work speed increases, fewer errors appear, and rework efforts occur less frequently. Consider that the work of your professional associates is often delayed by stalled attempts to determine what will make a project successful. If uncertainty and unwarranted speculation are eliminated and replaced with a clear image of what should be done and how it might be done, people will start to employ their skills and insights efficiently and with confidence.

Keep a Keen Eye on the Accomplishments of Entrepreneurs

They are shaping the future. Their undertakings are creating new expectations and requirements, producing needs people never recognized in the past. This knowledge is an integral component of the strategic process. It alerts you to where people's expectations and requirements are going to change.

Develop Appropriate Knowledge Bases

The creation of knowledge is a process of discovery. This search is encoded as a knowledge base, which is a continuous stream of current and interlinked data and information formed as a model of the decision-making process. The necessary foundation for the knowledge base is the creation of information sources that are checked and rechecked for error. All information and data contain error and are subject to differences in interpretation that put people in conflict. Integral to every knowledge base is a description of availabile technology that contributes to improving the quality of life. Knowledge must always be paired with options and alternatives for action.

Realize the Potential of Technology

Within six weeks, Jeff Heller can go from project start to a dynamic, three-dimensional representation of a preliminary design that presents the building as it unfolds to facility users walking along the street, entering the building, and going from space to space. The within-space views and the views from the various windows are also dynamic. Viewers can experience the "feel" of the spaces and how they might function when the building is occupied. Recognizing that problems will come up on every project, firms have taken to linking all parties to a teleconferencing system that shows the problem in real-time by way of video cameras.

Two individuals share their knowledge development work with us in the following pages: Paul S. Chinowsky, Professor of Civil Engineering, Georgia Institute of Technology and David Gensler, M.B.A., of Gensler and Associates.

Insights

Paul S. Chinowsky, B. Arch., Ph.D.

During his professional education as an architect at Cal Poly and his graduate work at Stanford, Professor Chinowsky directed his attention to computer-based graphic and knowledge base applications that enhance the design process. These enhancements are not simple displays and database aggregates, but rather processes that blend the thoughts of the designer, project elements and constraints, and analysis into one deliberative process. Automating as much of this process as possible, to free the architect from many of the mechanical activities characteristic of design, is a feature of his research.

At Georgia Tech, Paul has found a perfect vehicle for his interests in the 1996 Olympic Games and the Renew Atlanta '96 project, which combine the academic, government, corporate, and industry sectors into an innovative partnership. He relates to us the many features of his work. The particular value of his account is that it suggests many avenues that can be undertaken by architectural firms seeking to bring enriched services to clients.

Interview Highlights

A promising lesson is that building industry professionals from every discipline are enthusiastic about contributing to an innovative undertaking. The extra enthusiasm generated by a new undertaking can often produce results that are difficult to obtain in the normal course of office practice.

- It's not technology itself as much as it is what we can do with it.

- The tools are now there to capture, manipulate, and simulate interdisciplinary realities.

- Technology can remove the barriers between the design and engineering disciplines. What does this mean for the professional practice of architecture and the concept of the executive architect?

- First, the executive architect must think as an interdisciplinarian.

- Second, he or she must be able to translate technology into a professional service or the enhancement of traditional services.
- Third, while people think the research perspective can encumber a business enterprise, the executive architect must be committed to the rigors associated with research.

The Interview

First, let me tell you about the opportunity we have before us, a once in a lifetime chance for students, educators, and building industry professionals to study the expansion and rehabilitation of an international urban center. During sixteen days in the summer of 1996, the spotlight will focus on Atlanta as two-thirds of the world's population witnesses the Olympic Games. This audience will see the result of a one billion dollar design and construction effort completed within the Atlanta metropolitan area. Our goal is an in-depth documentation of the whole process, including infrastructure, transportation, permanent and temporary construction, urban landscapes, and urban rehabilitation projects.

Renew Atlanta '96 is a massive documentation effort that will be translated into the National Archives for Urban Rehabilitation, Planning, and Design. We will create what people in our profession have always needed: access to case histories at an unprecedented scope and level of detail. Educators and professionals from around the world will have electronic and Internet access to information from which to fundamentally impact professional, planning, development, and educational activities at many levels of complexity and for many disciplines. Government officials will have the same opportunity to find support as they prepare for the demands of the twenty-first century. These archives will be used to educate and inspire future generations of architects, planners, engineers, urban designers, and construction managers.

I'm sure you are most interested in the technology for all of this. Of course, it's not the technology itself as much as it is what we can do with it. I guess, most of all, I'd like you to envision the foundation we are creating—captured real-world situations for the classroom environment. The tools are now there to capture, manipulate, and simulate the complexities and interdisciplinary realities. In particular, advancements in video technology are providing the capability to create libraries of design, manufacturing, and construction case histories. Specifically, we are using state-of-the-art computer technologies to integrate multimedia case study information into courseware supporting design and construction education. For the Renew Atlanta '96 project we will be documenting on video the construction process for the principal Olympic facilities: the aquatic, basketball, tennis, velodrome, and archery centers, the hockey stadia and the shooting, rowing, and canoeing complexes. There will be additional elements such as Centennial Park, an urban plaza comprising 2.5 million engraved bricks; the Olympic Village, which will be turned into dormitories for Georgia Tech and Georgia State University; and the International Broadcast Center, which has the special feature that it can be completely disassembled within ten days of the completion of the Games. Paralleling this effort, we will document Atlanta's rehabilitation of infrastructure and housing throughout the metropolitan area. This includes transporation, urban landscapes, public works, and low-income housing—everything that Atlanta is doing for the Olympics and the twenty-first century. As a final component of the project, the researchers are exploring the possibilities of placing the case studies on the Internet as a basis for introducing a common framework to which design and construction researchers from around the world can continue to add interdisciplinary case studies. While this component of the project is still in its early stages, advances in distance learning and on-line services are setting a clear path to follow.

Technology can remove the educational barriers between the design and engineering disciplines. Combining design perspectives, interviews with sponsors, designers, engineers, and contractors, site development events, and the guiding statements originating with public officials, governmental staff, and the full spectrum of concerns and advice from all faculty disciplines enhances the probability of introducing the true nature of the professional experience into the educational arena.

Let me tell you about our project documentation effort. Interdisciplinary teams of students travel to construction sites throughout Atlanta twice a week to document and study design and construction processes. This is undertaken through the use of state-of-the-art videotape and editing equipment. Students are introduced to each of the projects through the use of plans and interviews with project designers, managers, and consultants. Based on these introductions, primary design and construction processes of interest are selected by each of the disciplines. These individual selections become the framework for scripting the comprehensive documentation. For instance, the Olympic Tennis Center is being constructed in an environmentally sensitive area requiring minimal disruption to the surrounding environment. Given these conflicting requirements, the study team will be able to characterize the continuous evolution of the designs and construction processes in response to the negotiations between project participants. Documenting the evolution of these negotiations from abstract concepts to physical solutions, we gain understanding of the intrinsic complexities of large-scale projects and the role of interdisciplinary cooperation in bringing a project to completion.

Of course, a major difficulty is maintaining continuity from project inception to project completion. The strategy for this means recognition of the project issues and a mutual agreement as to what these are. Sometimes to achieve this we need to do more in-depth study. For example, the Olympic Field Hockey Center site in downtown Atlanta spans a rapid transit subway tunnel in the center of the site. The tunnel creates a design and construction difficulty because spectator stands and the field of play have been designed to span the tunnel. To resolve the problem, a team of structural designers, construction engineers, and transportation engineers are developing a structural scheme and construction process that will eliminate the need to place any direct loads on the tunnel and the need to place heavy equipment on the tunnel during construction. This situation is an excellent example of a problem that could not be solved by a single discipline. The complete understanding of issues here enables the documentation effort to be precisely directed.

What does all of this mean for the professional practice of architecture and your concept of the executive architect? First, the executive architect must think as an interdisciplinarian. Second, he must be able to translate technology into a professional service or the enhancement of traditional services. Third, while people think the research perspective can encumber a business enterprise, the executive architect must be committed to the the rigors associated with research.

In our work we did recognize a number of lessons learned. Foremost is that new endeavors must be undertaken with caution. The extra enthusiasm generated by a new undertaking can often produce results that are difficult to obtain in the normal course of office practice. Further, someone must act as the stage creator who inspires interest and engages people with the challenge of a complex problem. When we give people the opportunity to step out of the normal course of events and explore the intricacies of a new opportunity or promising innovation, their response far exceeds original expectations. Another lesson we learned is that, to obtain maximum benefits from an innovative process, significant preparation is required. In our profession it may mean obtaining critiques from builders and clients. Additionally, as the number of projects being studied increases, the logistics component of an undertaking increases substantially. Thus, the participation of a number of people in preliminary work is a safeguard for future success. A promising lesson is that professionals from every discipline are enthusiastic about contributing to an innovative undertaking. People are always more than willing to accommodate your requests.

Georgia State Dormitories, Atlanta, Georgia—host site of the Olympic Village. Capturing a large project on videotape from beginning to end requires close interaction between the designers, constructors, and research team members. Here we see two of the Renew Atlanta '96 student researchers filming the site from a distance to obtain an overall perspective of the project.

Clark Atlanta Athletic Stadium, Atlanta, Georgia—host site for field hockey. To obtain a complete understanding of a project and enhance the educational experience, students must be placed in the center of a design and construction project. Here, documentation of the stadium grandstand is obtained from the future location of the stadium field.

Morris Brown Athletic Stadium, Atlanta, Georgia—host site for field hockey. The cooperation of design and construction professionals provides opportunities to solve complex issues such as constructability and cost. Here, we document the installation of precast stadium components, which require less time and cost to complete the project.

Georgia Tech Aquatics Center, Atlanta, Georgia—host site for swimming, diving, and water polo. Large-span structural systems require a combination of design, engineering, and construction expertise. In this picture we see the multiple structural systems required to create an open space large enough for world-class competition facilities.

Georgia Tech Dormitories, Atlanta, Georgia— host site for the Olympic athletes. Long-term usage of a facility requires extensive planning and architectural programming. The Georgia Tech dorms represent state-of-the-art facilities including telecommunications, electronics, and distance learning centers.

The creation of the Renew Atlanta '96 documentation effort archive requires the efforts of many people and the advanced capabilities of today's computer and video equipment. Increased cooperation between the design industry and academia will permit both the executive architect and the next generation of designers to benefit from respective areas of knowledge.

Insights

David Gensler, M.B.A.

David Gensler is a valued resource. With his degree in economics from Dartmouth, an M.B.A. from Stanford, and management experience with national firms, he brings to Gensler and Associates an understanding of the challenges facing major corporations and companies. David is totally engaged in developing his area of service and expertise within the firm. We had one hour to speak with him before he was off to another meeting.

Interview Highlights

There is a strategy that says by adding skill sets outside the traditional architectural profession, we will achieve a greater impact on our clients. We can integrate the various disciplines and collaborate to provide a product or service that is greater than the sum of the parts.

- In the mid-60's the process was schematic design, design development and construction documents.
- In the mid-70's the process was programming, schematic design, design development and construction documents.
- In the late 70's and throughout the 80's, the profession developed a discipline called "strategic facilities planning," in which people with different skills performed a process that precedes programming.
- This produces an output that isn't ready for schematic design, but it defines the organization in a way that allows the program to be set to meet the organization's business requirements, or to support the organization's business objectives and strategy.
- Now architectural practitioners are working on the idea of servicing clients throughout their entire organization life cycle.
- The competitive model for the future moves toward an account relationship, as opposed to a project-by-project relationship. This means client relationships all the way up and down the organization, knitting ourselves into the fabric of the client's organization.

- To achieve all of this, you have to know how to frame questions, how to pursue information, how to analyze information, and how to help organizations think about their strategic options.

The Interview

In terms of knowledge development that helps us to set the benchmarks, helps us understand the market and the client, and supports the organization's strategy, there are multiple tracks for achieving that vision. It starts when you're identified as a "future of the firm" professional, and typically a vice president or managing principal takes responsibility for trying to expand your horizon in terms of what is appropriate for you to be doing to develop your professional skills. It may be a suggestion that you read *The Wall Street Journal* or books about management, business, international economics, technology, or whatever. Then there's continuing education, which deals with the professional skill set of architecture. And then there is a strategy that says by adding skill sets outside the traditional architectural profession we will achieve a greater impact on our clients. We can integrate the various disciplines and collaborate to provide a product or service that is greater than the sum of the parts. We work together regularly, we educate each other, and we can develop a vocabulary that we can use to identify and address problems as we see them.

For instance, my background doesn't lend itself to the design process, but rather to defining problems and objectives, which occurs well before the traditional design process starts. Primarily I am involved in pre-design and post-design services. Pre-design is what we call strategic facilities planning, where we identify an organization's business objectives and create a facilities plan that supports those objectives. In post-design services, we develop tools that our clients can use to realize a greater value after we have traditionally left the project. These are primarily facilities management, technology management, and human resource management tools.

We use this "little d" and "big D" terminology, which is like "micro" and "macro." We try to discover the big concept that we want to achieve, the bigger picture within which we need to be working, rather than just jumping right down to fabric and finishes. It involves understanding what the "big D" design is on this project, or what the "big D" design problem is, as opposed to, "I've got to fit 100 people in 10,000 square feet, how am I going to do it?" It's understanding the work process, work flow, technology impact, regulations impact, and organizational design's impact on facilities strategies. So, my role is two-fold: one is internal and one is with the clients. I'm supposed to spend about 50 percent of my time in providing services to clients and 50 percent in helping to develop our firm to be more effective, whether it's financial policy, or recruiting, or strategic vision of building new business.

Maybe I can summarize the development of Gensler and Associates from a strategic standpoint. In the mid-60's, when we started, our process included schematic design, design development and construction documents. That was how we delivered our services. We competed effectively and differentiated ourselves in the market because some of our founding principals understood our clients' vocabulary and their business. We developed design solutions in a way that responded to their businesses. In the late 60's and early 70's, Gensler and Associates, along with a lot of other organizations, developed professional programming as an institution.

So, in the mid-70's the process was programming, schematic design, design development, and construction documents. We also did some construction administration, which became even more prevalent. In the late 70's and throughout the 80's, we developed a discipline called "strategic facilities planning," where people with different skills perform a process that precedes programming. The output isn't ready for schematic design, but it defines the organization in a way that allows the program to be set to meet the organization's business requirements, or to support the organization's business objectives and strategy.

Now we're working on the idea of servicing our clients throughout their entire life cycle. We talk about it all: planning, programming, schematic design, design development, construction documentation, and construction administration. We want no part of the situation where everyone gets in line, and we all compete, and it becomes price competition because it's such an amorphous service that no one firm can really be differentiated, other than based on relationships.

While we've always been a relationship-oriented company and built our success on forming relationships with individuals, we're now trying to move toward an account relationship, as opposed to a project-by-project relationship. This means that we have relationships all the way up and down the organization, horizontally and vertically, so that we knit ourselves into the fabric of an organization. And we follow the organization all the way through its life cycle, providing value at every single point. Now we need to start delivering service that adds value from the time the project's finished until the client starts planning to remodel or move on to another facility. We have occupancy management services, we've done outsource planning, which helps organizations free up space when they become constrained, and we have facilities management services, which is my specific area. We're now trying to take these services to the next generation and transform them into resource management, as opposed to facilities management.

We've developed a practice that we call "Gensler Information Solutions," and we're taking the emerging integration of relational database technology and graphics, CAD technology, in order to deliver significantly more user-friendly systems that give people the information they need to do their jobs. It helps our clients make better decisions because they make decisions based on information that is accurate, timely and appropriate, as opposed to whatever they feel is the intuitive right answer.

The typical entry point is a map of an organization's facilities. It might be a world map if it's a global company or it might be a map of Los Angeles if it's a local company. You enter in through this map, as a metaphor for navigating through the organization's resources, and you basically point and click at facilities, and drop down to a lower level of information. So, if I started out with a map of the U.S., I might click down to a map of California, and then drop down to a map of my facilities in California. I might drop down to a campus, down to a building, down to a floor, and then do a query based on that floor. The query might be, "How many IBM PC286's with four megabytes of RAM do I have?" It might be, "How many paper clips do I have on this floor?" You can track anything, but one of the most critical aspects of the system is that it helps an organization determine cost-justifiable tracking. Tracking paper clips is not cost-justifiable; tracking PC's and their exact configurations may or may not be. Many organizations right now want to, at a minimum, start charging back square footage to departments, so that people become more sensitive to the cost of their facilities and start using it as a limited resource as opposed to a free resource. If people get space without having to pay for it, they'll use more than if they have to pay for the space. If you force charge-backs, you force your organization to utilize space more rationally.

Historically, many organizations have avoided charge-backs because the cost of getting accurate, appropriate, timely data has been overwhelming. The money spent gathering the data chewed up any value they might have created by utilizing space more effectively. Now we're at the point where we can deliver that process in a cost-effective way. We can determine what space goes to what department, how much it costs, and allocate it back to the department. This helps organizations to better understand their resources and allocate those resources more cost-effectively than they've ever been able to do. The system is primarily driven by two things: it is integrated relational database and CAD technology in one application, and two, it's very user-friendly. A departmental manager, or an operations/maintenance manager, or a CEO, could actually get the needed information from a PC, as opposed to having to go to the high priest of technology and say, "Please can I have some information because I need to make a decision?" If you want to use it today, and then again in two weeks, and then again a month later, you can actually get the information that you need to make an information-driven decision.

I should say that while our information solutions tools certainly would be capable of aiding an organization to make capital investment decisions, this may not be appropriate for supporting the decision-making process. This tool is more of a snapshot in time, and less of a rigorous, statistical, analytical tool for determining growth trends. One of the things that we're helping our clients to address is the fact that extrapolated growth projections are no longer as valid as they were fifteen or twenty years ago, when the world was changing at a much slower rate. At that time one could feel more comfortable saying, "Well, if I've been growing at five percent a year for the last three years, then I'm probably going to grow at five percent a year for the next three years." Change has become so discontinuous that you can't base the future on the past as readily as you could years ago. I'm not sure when it happened, but it's certainly less relevant today.

The organization that has just discovered that programming is an appropriate discipline might ask, "Well how many inches of file cabinets do you have, and how many people are you going to add?" Basically, they're extrapolating the future based on the current situation, and that's where we think we're leapfrogging into the next generation of problem-solving solutions. In our strategic facilities planning practice, we are helping organizations to develop visions of their future. We go through a process of developing alternatives and gaming with our clients on different probabilities for different scenarios, and developing a scenario that they feel most appropriately addresses what they're trying to achieve. Then we develop a facility strategy that helps them to achieve that vision, as opposed to one that becomes a constraint on their ability to achieve that vision, or one that ends up driving business decisions, as opposed to business decisions driving facilities decisions. It requires a high focus on facilities flexibility—expansion, contraction, and exit strategies. How do you build a facility for this purpose, knowing that five years from now you may not even be delivering this service? It becomes much more of a strategic visioning process than a rigorous statistical extrapolation.

Gensler Information Solutions is also related to the idea that our historical output has been analog output—construction documents on paper. In the future we will provide digital output, electronic files instead of paper, even to contractors and subcontractors. A client will certainly want a system that will continue to provide value as the space is occupied. The system needs to be updatable and queriable. It must be a tool that the clients can use to understand and manage their facility over time. It's like the changes in cars: we've gone from stopping short and listening to how much gas sloshes around in the tank to the point where we have a gas gauge, odometers, speedometers, and all these gauges, which help us to understand what's going on with our "auto resource." Now we're delivering systems, which is what information solutions is about—providing the information people need to understand the facility and teaching them how to use it effectively.

On the issue of knowledge development, our strategy is similar to designing a race car that's going 200 mph. We are taking off the wheels and putting on new wheels, redesigning the windshield and putting on the new windshield, while the car is racing. I've got pressures on me to be billable, and I've got to get the projects out the door. I don't have the luxury of having a venture-funded side business that's going to go off and tinker, and has a mission of moving into the next century. We're trying to pull our clients' entire organizations into the next century while they continue to do their work every day.

The culture here is such that everyone is under the same level of accountability and stress to perform and deliver and be billable and be profitable. We're constantly looking for leadership—that's our biggest constraint in terms of achieving our vision of success. I've never worked harder for as little money, and frankly I've never had more fun. That has a lot to do with the fact that I believe this organization is meeting the challenges of an entire industry and leading the industry into the future, and it happens to have my name on it, which is tremendously exciting.

This industry is basically built on the concept of the virtual corporation. On every project we bring together contractors and subcontractors, designers and real estate brokers. Every project is an entity unto itself: professionals come together at the beginning of a project, disband when the project is over. It is recreated with new members for every project. We are struggling with that concept.

I think Charles Handy's book (1994) and a number of other books have challenged us to think "Do we have the appropriate types of people here? Are we deploying them in the appropriate way, as permanent employees or contractors or associates or partners or staff people? How do we do that more effectively?" I don't think we have the right answers. We were probably closer to it before we even started the discussion than we thought we were. We probably are more fluid as an industry than we think we are, because we think of ourselves as units, as organizations unto ourselves, when the organization really is the entire project. In a professional services firm like this, the relationship you build with other professionals over time is so critical to being able to deliver value. The learning curve of bringing new contract labor in on a project, and then letting them go and bringing new ones in for the next project, has too much overhead.

We're challenging the ways we've organized ourselves in this company. We have to bring in different kinds of people, and we've talked a lot about the kinds of professional skills that we need. Over the last four or five years, we've hired people with real estate backgrounds. That was a slam-dunk. Everyone knew that if we broadened our practice just one tick out of architectural design, we would need an understanding of real estate. We also have technology professionals, and we realize every day how much we need that expertise. What we call architectural/technology integration is becoming critical to the success of projects. Value is achieved by delivering not only a physical environment that supports the work, but by delivering both a virtual environment and a physical environment that are integrated, that together support the work. Of course, we must accommodate the physical cabling plan and get from the point of access at the building to the desktop, but we are asking additional questions. Do we need to accommodate video teleconferencing? Do we need to accommodate certain kinds of transmission rates because we're going to have virtual reality? Do we need to accommodate high data requirements for graphic transfers between different functional groups or within functional groups? We need to consider theses technology-related issues so that we can deliver a more holistic environment that supports the person trying to do his or her job.

I bring a different skill set to our firm, and because I have a high quality pedigree in terms of Dartmouth and Stanford I have some credibility. People are willing to listen, and as they listen they realize how much they've been missing because they don't have that type of educational background. These are very intelligent people, so it's not a question of intelligence, it's a question of training and education. They don't have the framework to even recognize certain types of issues. I was at an interview last week with a managing principal of one of our offices, and we each asked different questions because we come from such different perspectives. He was amazed at the direction the interviews took because I was there, as opposed to where they would have gone without me. I asked sets of questions that were totally outside his scope of knowledge. Whether it was technology or business strategy, or organizational strategy, or just basic strategy-type questions, it was outside his framework of understanding. It was like the lights went on. He said, "Now I understood the concept of strategic facilities planning and how it differs from programming." That's not a very easy thing for many architects to understand.

I took a 50 percent cut in compensation when I came to this organization. I did it for a very personal reasons, but I also did it for professional reasons. I can make a perfectly adequate living here and I can have more impact on society than I can in other industries. I can also have a lot more fun, because I'm in an industry with a very creative group of people. These professionals are as creative, if not more so, than any other group with whom I've worked, and I've worked with some of the great software companies and leading banks and investment firms in this country. Those people are tremendously interesting, challenging, and intelligent professionals, but none of them, day in and day out, think more creatively than the people at Gensler and Associates. After I made my decision to join the firm, I went to a staff meeting and right away I could tell that this organization was different, and that was exciting to me.

I was in the securities industry, working for the Pacific Stock Exchange and Morgan Stanley, before I went to Business School. Then I worked for Microsoft between my first and second year of school. After I got my M.B.A., I worked for a management consulting firm doing strategic and marketing consulting, primarily to software companies. Then I became CFO of a health care information services start-up, and then I was recruited here. I've only been here for two years, and initially I had three or four small roles on strategic facilities planning studies. Then I had the lead role on the strategic facilities planning study for an international fast food company.

I worked on the study with Ed Friedrichs, who is an intuitive strategic facilities planner. He knows in his gut what the right answer is—by listening, by hearing. He thinks as a business professional. I don't have his 25 years of experience in this industry to relate to, but I know basic, generic strategy. I know how to frame questions, how to pursue information, how to analyze information, and how to help organizations think about their strategic options. My role is really that of a facilitator. I could do the very best job on a project, and if the outcome were horrible, it wouldn't be a reflection on my performance. On the other hand, I could do a terrible job and the outcome could be wonderful, and it still wouldn't be a reflection of my performance.

One job is not a valid sampling for understanding whether or not I know what I am doing. But considering what we did for the international fast food company, I think it was leading edge work for an architectural firm. I approached it like a management consultant. Our design professionals tend to be caught in an architectural paradigm. I believe the way to add value is to change the way an organization acts, or improve how it acts, as opposed to delivering some report. We produce presentations with statistical analyses, with status information, there are questions, there are recommendations, but there is no report. People say, "Where's the report? I want to be able to pull out a report and say here's the study for that client." But that's not what it's about; it's about facilitating a process of understanding their options, developing a recommendation about where they ought to go, and why.

I've said a lot about facilities, but I also need to talk about the human resource. This is the most expensive resource in an organization, with facilities in second place. Historically facilities have been managed as a line-item expense. The lower you can get it the better, with the optimal solution probably zero. When you start thinking like that—optimizing the parts rather than optimizing the whole—you miss a tremendous opportunity to optimize the ways in which facilities impact the human resource. Does the facility support work flow? Does it support the self-image of workers? Does it allow people to feel good about where they go every day and make them want to go there every day? The facility impacts recruitment and retention. It impacts a customer's perception of who you are and what you're doing. It has all those non-quantifiable impacts of your performance as a whole.

I have yet to see any study that does an even adequate job of trying to tie facilities to any effect on performance, positive or negative. There are minor kinds of indicators that there is a least a Hawthorne effect, that you can change things and things get better. However as far as the bottom line is concerned—how will this affect profit—I don't think it lends itself to analysis.

We have a client who publishes a newspaper, and he says that one of their guiding principles is that they make a custom product every day. And that's really what we do—we make a custom product for every client. Even prototype rollouts for retail are customized. It's not cookie cutter work. So again, it's like a statistical sample of one. How can you measure the impact on an organization? And the value of design is an ephemeral thing. If you could put it on a scale of one to ten, today I may do a six, tomorrow a four, the next day a nine. If I start asking about the impact of Gensler's design, there is no consistent design output to correlate to something. It becomes a very confusing analysis and ultimately, even if you produce something, nobody's going to believe it!

After 25 years and doing work here and there, the only justification I can give for spending money on facilities is to ask the person, "What have you done at your own home lately? How much have you spent on furniture? How much wallpaper have you put up? Why are your improving that environment out of your pocket?" Or, "Do you like to go home at night? If not, do you think if you had a nicer house you'd like to go home? Do you spend time in your house? Does it affect your mood? Does it make you feel good if your room is messy, if you have paint peeling on the walls?"

It has an impact. We all believe that; you can prove that. The question is, so what? The reality is that many people in management will choose according to the impact on the bottom line—

which is the least cost, the least space possible. Now we're trying to help organizations understand how they can achieve a high-quality environment, a high-performance environment, for the least possible cost. That's the trade-off that we make, but we don't want to forget one and just focus on the other, because then the optimal solution is not to have a facility. Some organizations today are trying to do that: they work at home, they use technology to communicate. Maybe in the future, far in the future and in some other world, we'll all work through virtual reality. We'll all feel like we're together when we want to be and we'll all feel like we're apart when we want to be. But that's not today's world.

Someone said something interesting to me recently, to the effect that it is the discretionary effort that you get out of your employees that differentiates you from your competitors. If you don't treat your people well—and that includes how you house them—you won't be able to get that discretionary output, that discretionary effort on their part. People perform at very different levels, based on whether they feel like they want to work harder or not. What we try to do here—and we fail and succeed at any given moment—is to recognize that we're all human beings, we're all professionals, and we all have something to add. There's a kind of commonalty, and it's about getting, as the Japanese try to do, extraordinary output out of ordinary people, because it's impossible to always get extraordinary people.

Sitag International, Irvine, California. *(Photo: N. Merrick.)*

Sony Theater, New York, New York.   (Photo: M. Lorenzetti.)

Oracle Corporation, Redwood City, California. (Photo: S. Takata.)

Champs Sports, Bloomington, Minnesota.
(Photo: D. Wheelock.)

Westlake/MacArthur Park MetroRail Station, Los Angeles, California. (Photo: M. Arden.)

John Wayne Airport, Orange County, California. (Photo: S. McDonald.)

Method No. 6
Research Techniques

We are constantly challenged to understand the world of our clients and client organizations. In Chapter 4, the discussion of client assessment strategy considered the importance of learning about and learning from clients. In Chapter 5, the Knowledge Base System was presented as a set of questions that help define the full complexity of our attempt to identify the expectations and requirements of clients and facility users and the translation of this information into design concepts, schemes, forms, and features. In Chapter 6, the field study discussion indicated that detailed information about people's activities is essential. None of this work is possible without the ability to ask the right questions and, just as important, to obtain reliable answers. We need research techniques to develop patterns of behavior based on identified customs, traditions, and lifestyles, to determine preferences, and to gain an understanding of the factors that produce and maintain preferences. We need techniques that provide individuals with an opportunity to speak for themselves, to answer questions as they would like to see them answered and, even more important, to tell us what the important questions are. We need the means to gather a great deal of information about the personal views and experience of individuals, such as concerns, perceptions, and values. The research techniques in the following sections help us to see and hear from clients and facility users directly, to identify with clients and facility users, to understand their situation, share their insights, and encourage them to state their needs. If people are uncertain about the future, we want to share this uncertainty. If goals and objectives come into conflict, we want to collaborate to achieve the best possible compromise. We can expect to benefit from the feelings of cooperation and openness created by the techniques presented.

Group identification, study sessions, interviews, systematic observation, activity analysis, questionnnaires, and preference assessment techniques have been selected because these research techniques build upon the skills of architects. Architects acquire skills in listening to people. They are sensitive to the cultural heritage of individuals and communities. Above all else, they are diligent and thorough in the handling of details. These are skills upon which we can build. There is a second aspect of importance that influenced the selection of research techniques. Our fee structure is limited, we are always pressed for time, and man-hours must be conserved. This means we need techniques that work within these constraints of funds, time, and available personnel.

A Typical Two Weeks of Research

The research techniques selected as companions to Knowledge Base System and field study applications are economical in terms of man-hours involved. Building design and land development professionals studying research techniques expect to find something useful, not something esoteric and strange. Research techniques must have readily recognized boundaries. The team must know when to end their inquiries into facility user expectations and requirements. While it is important for the behavioral scientist to continue questioning, the limited time available to building design and land development teams requires an economical undertaking. Only what is critical to the project at hand and effectively employable should be studied.

Applying the research techniques presented in the following sections with thought and care, two members of the building design and land development team can accomplish a great deal in two weeks. The two-week schedule of activities in Figure 7.1 suggests the recommended sequence of application for strategic research. Guided by the Knowledge Base System and the detailed lines of questioning associated with field studies, this work will be efficient and of immediate value. The recommendation to form a liaison committee and to meet informally with people on a daily basis should be noted.

Group Identification Techniques

The goal here is to identify the groups that will occupy and influence activities within the planned building or land development. Almost all building value, performance, and image objec-

	Day 1	Day 2	Day 3	Day 4	Day 5	Day 6	Day 7
8 to 12	Meet with liaison committee	Study sessions	Interviews	Systematic observation	Review study session	Review study session	Charette
12 to 1	Lunch with liaison committee	Lunch with facility users	Lunch with liaison committee	Lunch with facility users	Lunch with client	Lunch with liaison committee	Charette
1 to 5	Study sessions	Systematic observation	Interviews	Interviews	Activity analysis	Charette	Charette

	Day 8	Day 9	Day 10	Day 11	Day 12	Day 13	Day 14
8 to 12	Meet with liaison committee	Study sessions	Interviews	Activity analysis	Activity analysis	Work on design guidelines	Work on design guidelines
12 to 1	Lunch with liaison committee	Lunch with facility users	Lunch with liaison committee	Lunch with facility users	Lunch with client	Interview	Interview
1 to 5	Study sessions	Systematic observation	Interviews	Interviews	Work on design guidelines	Work on design guidelines	Work on design guidelines

Figure 7.1. A two-week schedule of activities.

tives are related to how people work and live in association with one another. It is often easier to think in terms of groups rather than individuals; this simplifies the image of what will occur in a building. Additionally, group characteristics tend to endure and are aspects for which the building design and land development team can plan effectively and confidently. Groups endure because both organizations and individuals use groups as a means for structuring activities to achieve objectives. Organizations and individuals depend upon a wide variety of groups to achieve their purposes. Neighborhood studies may involve family, peer, interest, activity, street, and transitory groups. Community studies might pertain to territorial and non-territorial groups that exist within public and private, historic and cultural, religious and political, and local and regional organizations. Facility studies by themselves are often based on groupings of individuals who conduct their daily affairs within the facility.

The purpose of the following procedures—progressive survey and group identification technique—whether applied at a facility, neighborhood, or community level, is to identify important groups and to determine how individuals perceive their roles. These procedures directly answer question items 2.1 Facility User Categories, 3.1 Family Life Groups, and 4.1 Community Life Groups in the Knowledge Base System

Progressive Survey

The progressive survey procedure may be used when it is necessary to identify a large number of individuals and groups spread over a wide area. An illustrative application of the progressive survey approach is presented in Figure 7.2. The procedure was used in a study of the recreational preferences and concerns of users and potential users of a U.S. National Forest. The resulting information helps those responsible for forest management and environmental planning maintain an awareness of the full spectrum of forest users.

The term "progressive" is suggestive of the application procedure. As described in Figure 7.2, the initial survey was distributed to selected Forest Service personnel, who were asked to write down as many different forest users as they could. This information was edited into an initial listing of forest users. This listing was then given to another group of Forest Service personnel, who were asked to review the work of the first group. These people were encouraged to add or delete users and revise the first listing as they saw fit, in order to obtain a complete spectrum of forest users. The first group was given the same opportunity to revise the listing. In the final step of the progressive survey, the public was asked to review the results and contribute suggestions. The systematically accumulated results provided a thorough and complete answer to question item 4.1 Community Life Groups in the Knowledge Base System.

APPLICATION RESULTS OF THE PROGRESSIVE SURVEY

Figure 7.3 contains the information resulting from the progressive survey in the National Forest project. It will help you realize the potential of this method for your work and further your understanding of the extent to which you must be aware of facility users, their identity and activities. Note the detailed attention paid to helping the building design and land development team understand the forest experience. A review of Figure 7.3 should convince you that it is possible to identify and characterize all users of a facility or planned development.

NATIONAL FOREST RECREATION AND ENVIRONMENTAL PLANNING STUDY

What Type of Project Is This?
In this part of the planning study, we are attempting to identify all the Forest users, acquaint ourselves with their activities, and determine the significance of this information for recreation and resource development programs. What we are doing is based on our concern for the Forest visitor, seen as the individual and family users, community organizations, interest groups, local recreation-related business firms, state and local governmental agencies, United States Forest Service personnel, and those not now directly benefiting from our various educational and recreational opportunities.

What Are We Doing?
We are distributing to 30 selected Forest Service personnel a workbook in which they will be asked to write down all the various types of users of the Forest they can think of. This is the first step in a "progressive survey." After the workbooks are collected, we will edit the findings and prepare an initial list of Forest users. In the next step, this listing will be sent to another group of Forest Service personnel. They will be asked to review the work of the first group and revise the first listing as they see appropriate. The original group will certainly be given the same opportunity. Findings will again be edited, seeking to establish the most complete listing of Forest user categories. In the final step of the survey, the public will be given a statement of the project's purpose and a response form. In this form, they will be asked to review the results of our work and add to the list those who have been overlooked. After a full and verified listing is completed, the activities and preferences of these users will be studied, working to identify specific expectations and requirements to which the recreation and resource development plan must be responsive.

Why Are We Doing This?
As you know, our forest has the highest recreation visitor use of any National Forest and is spread over 630,000 net acres. How would you go about establishing the most extensive listing of users possible? How would you assure the completeness of your listing? We are taking an approach that centers around those most knowledgeable, the Forest user. This approach is also the one that is the least demanding of Forest Service personnel time and one that will clearly demonstrate to the public the breadth of our concern.

What Would We Like You to Do?
Each of the sheets making up this workbook refers to a general Forest user group. Would you please write down all the specific users you can think of that fall into the preliminary user group categories. Thank you. We will keep you informed of our progress and findings.

> **User Category No. 1:** *Individual and family users in your area*
> This is your first task. Think for a second of all the various people you have seen in your area of the Forest (such as family backpackers, solitary backpackers, a person injured on the trail or on the road, someone whose car won't start, the tow truck driver who comes along, vandals, snowmobile riders, fly fishermen, leisure drivers, "crusiers," picnickers, rock hunters). Please write down as many individuals, types of users, by situation, interest, or activity, as you can think of. When you are finished with your listing, pass it on to a friend. You'll probably get another 50 users added to your list. Before you start writing, look at the rest of the workbook. It will help you understand what we are doing.
>
> 1. _____
> 2. _____
> 3. _____

User Category No. 2: *Community organizations in your area*

This is your second task. We can identify such community organizations as the Sierra Club, Girl Scouts of America, Retired Senior Volunteer Program, and Lions Club. What we need to know are the names of specific chapters, patrols, and clubs in your area. We would like to contact as many such organizations as possible, and have them help us in our work. You can see what we are after here. We don't want to miss contacting any local organization that might help us in our recreation planning study.

1._____
2._____
3._____

User Category No. 3: *Interest groups in your area*

Please list here the names of such interest groups as your local recreational vehicle club, rock climbers' association, fly fishermen's club, ...

1._____
2._____
3._____

User Categoy No. 4: *Local recreation-related business firms in your area*

Please list here the names of local businesses and services that play an extremely important part in the activities of the Forest users (shops, tackle and bait stores, lodging, . . .).

1._____
2._____
3._____

User Category No. 5: *Federal, state, and local governmental agencies in your area that play an important role in your work or the activities of the Forest visitor*

Please list here the names of the agencies that play an important part in your work and in the activities of the Forest visitor (San Bernardino County Crippled Children Services, State of California Parks and Recreation: local office, U.S. Fish and Wildlife Service: local office, . . .).

1._____
2._____
3._____

User Category No. 6: *United States Forest Service personnel in your area*

Please list here all the various people who support your activities (trail maintenance crews, summer recreation program leaders, . . .).

1._____
2._____
3._____

User Category No. 7: *Those not now directly benefiting from our various educational and recreational programs*

Please list the various circumstances that define those who do not visit the Forest and benefit from what is offered (those without transportation, those never hearing about our programs, those fearful of being in a forest because of lack of experience, . . .).

1._____
2._____
3._____

Figure 7.2. Progressive survey procedure.

LISTING OF NATIONAL FOREST USERS

Fifteen categories were required to cover the complete spectrum of forest users. The titles given to each user category are conversational labels that will help the forest user see him- or herself in the work and deliberations of the Forest Service. An attempt was made to organize users according to type of activity and type of forest experience, and the environmental characteristics of these activities. Each category is broken down into management and planning elements. This information should be available to the forest manager and planner at all times and used as a reference when decisions are formulated to ensure that all users, potential users, and nonusers have been considered. This information may be used in public meetings and cooperative efforts to demonstrate the level of awareness being maintained by the Forest Service.

1. Let's Go Fishing, Hunting, Collecting, . . .

This category identifies those forest visitors who, to an acceptable or unacceptable degree, come to catch, hunt, collect, and gather things that are natural to the forest, such as:

   a. Lake fishermen, stream fishermen, ice fishermen, fly fishermen, social fishermen (retirees often fish daily), bow fishermen.
   b. Hunters (deer, quail, dove, pigeon, squirrel, rabbit, bear, duck, snake), bow hunters, frog giggers, trappers.
   c. Collectors and gatherers of flowers, pine cones, mistletoe, piñon nuts, bracken fern, mushrooms, bark, rosehips, acorns, berries, dried "anything."
   d. Collectors of spring water.
   e. Family woodcutters and dead Yucca plant, oak burl, manzanita burl, and pine slab cutters.
   f. Rock hunters, gold panners, and prospectors.
   g. Scavengers.
   h. Fossil collectors.
   i. Artifact collectors.
   j. Insect collectors.
   k. Wildlife, flower, and nature photographers.

2. Let's Go Boating, Riding, Skiing, . . .

This category identifies those seeking a special recreational experience in the forest that requires directed services and planning support, such as:

   a. Motorboaters, canoeists, sailboaters, water skiers, water scooter users, ice boaters, skin divers, rubber raft users, rafters, model boat hobbyists, ice skaters.
   b. Horseback riders (roadside and trail), packers, burro racers.
   c. Downhill skiers, cross-country skiers, snowmobile users, tobogganers, sledders, dog sledders, snowshoers.
   d. Bicyclists, skateboaders.
   e. Kite flyers, model plane flyers, rocket launchers.
   f. Hang gliders.
   g. Rock climbers.
   h. Target shooters, plinkers, participants in turkey shoots and muzzle-loading events.
   i. Those who work on private cars.

Figure 7.3. Listing of National Forest Users.

3. Let's Go into the Back Country
The spectrum of back country and wilderness users includes:

  a. Educational and scientific field trip participants.
  b. Hikers (solitary, families, groups, organizations).
  c. Trail riders and packers.
  d. Cross-country skiers and snowshoers.
  e. Sportsmen.
  f. Historical buffs, writers, movie makers, artists, photographers.
  g. Military personnel on survival training.
  h. Forest enthusiasts.

4. Off-Road Vehicles Help Us Enjoy Lots of Things
Off-road vehicles are the basis of the forest recreational experience for:

  a. Dirt bikers.
  b. Trail bikers.
  c. Four-wheel drive vehicle enthusiasts.
  d. All-terrain vehicle enthusiasts.
  e. ORV campers (individuals, families, groups).
  f. Racers.
  g. Rally participants.

5. Let's Drive Up for the Day
Many different people fall into this basic recreational category:

  a. Picnickers.
  b. Photographers.
  c. Sightseers.
  d. Shoppers.
  e. Stream toe-dippers and waders.
  f. Bicycle riders.
  g. Leisure drivers.
  h. Snow enthusiasts.
  i. Solitude seekers.
  j. Hitchhikers.
  k. Swimmers.
  l. Nudists.
  m. Lovers.
  n. Dog walkers.
  o. Wildlife observers.
  p. Day hikers.
  q. Strollers.
  r. Joggers.
  s. Partiers, beer drinkers, wine-tasting partiers.

continued on page 288

6. My Family Likes to Camp in the Forest

The campground is the center for many forest visitors (individuals, families, informal groups, organized groups) who may be:

a. Experienced campers.
b. Inexperienced campers.
c. Well-prepared campers.
d. Ill-prepared campers.
e. Those using a campground as a base for other activities.
f. Weekenders.
g. Those on an annual vacation.
h. Socializers who enjoy being with others.
i. Those who seek solitude and peace and quiet.

7. My Friends and I Get Together to Enjoy the Forest

This category stresses the importance of the forest to the informal activities of youths and young adults. Just about every activity seen in the forest or in the city can be associated with this group, which includes:

a. Local residents.
b. Visitors from nearby.
c. Neighbors and friends organized for their own purposes.
d. Visitors from throughout Southern California.

8. Our Organization's Activities Depend on the Forest

Many people who enjoy forest recreational experiences belong to a club, interest group, or organization, and find that association with others is a necessary part of an enjoyable visit to the forest. Such groups include:

a. Conservation clubs.
b. Riding clubs.
c. Fish and game clubs.
d. Motorcycle clubs.
e. ORV clubs.
f. Boating and sailing clubs.
g. Gun clubs.
h. Winter sports clubs.
i. Folk and square dancing clubs.
j. Hang glider clubs.
k. Rescue clubs.
l. Mountain men clubs.
m. Sports car clubs.
n. Historical societies.
o. Bird watcher clubs.
p. Garden clubs.
q. Service clubs.
r. Fraternal organizations.
s. Church groups.
t. University outing clubs.
u. Heritage, cultural, and ethnic clubs and organizations.
v. Scientific and professional associations.
w. Organizations for children, youths, and young adults.
x. Cross-country bicycle clubs.

9. Our Camp Helps People Enjoy the Forest

There are many private and public camps that provide forest recreational experiences. Such camps are:

    a. Boy Scout, Girl Scout, PAL Club, YMCA, YWCA, YMHA camps.
    b. Private camps.
    c. Music camps.
    d. Church camps.
    e. Religious conference centers.
    f. Private conference camps.
    g. RV camps.
    h. Privately run campgrounds.
    i. Trailer parks.

10. Our Agency Helps People Enjoy the Forest

Recreation often takes place in the context of programs, services, and facilities provided by:

    a. Fire departments.
    b. Departments of the State of California.
    c. Departments of county governments.
    d. Departments of local governments.
    e. Water districts.
    f. Hospitals.
    g. Humane societies.
    h. Museums.
    i. Departments of the U.S. Government.
    j. Public and private schools.
    k. Universities and colleges.
    l. Private organizations offering social and human services.

11. Local People, Services, and Businesses Contribute a Great Deal

The forest communities and residents (permanent or seasonal) provide one context for the recreational experience, such as:

    a. Markets, hardware stores, sporting goods stores, liquor stores, retail stores.
    b. Motels and resorts.
    c. Newspapers.
    d. Garages, towing and repair services.
    e. Home appliance and equipment repair services.
    f. Restaurants, bars, and taverns.
    g. Winter sports facilities and concessions.
    h. Marinas.
    i. Stables.
    j. Golf courses.
    k. Rifle ranges.
    l. Transportation companies.
    m. Telephone companies.
    n. Automobile clubs.
    o. Medical services.
    p. Ranchers.
    q. Miners.
    r. Loggers.
    s. Recreation resident permittees.
    t. Homeowners.

continued on page 290

12. The Forest Service Helps People Enjoy the Forest
The forest recreational experience is directly or indirectly dependent on:

    a. Maintenance crews.

    b. Fire crews, fire control and prevention staff.

    c. Youth and young adult corp leaders and crews.

    d. Scientific, engineering, and technical staff.

    e. Resource development and planning staff.

    f. Recreational planning staff.

    g. Summer recreation crews.

    h. Office staff.

    i. Information and education services staff and volunteers.

    j. Administrators, managers, and supervisors.

13. Some People Can Ruin It All for Others
Situations which are undesirable or difficult to handle can be caused by:

    a. Drunks.

    b. "Outlaw" motorcycle and car gangs.

    c. Violators of forest rules and regulations.

    d. Drug users and sellers.

    e. People dumping trash.

    f. Litter bugs.

    g. Vandals.

    h. Arsonists.

    i. Transients.

    j. Thieves.

    k. Disorderly, bothersome, and inconsiderate people.

    l. Intolerant and discriminatory people.

    m. People avoiding fees.

    n. Runaways.

    o. Wood poachers and others who destroy or remove natural forest features.

    p. Fugitives.

    q. Occult groups.

    r. Nondocumented illegals.

    s. Escaped mental patients.

    t. Animal poachers.

    u. Muggers, rapists.

    v. Incompetent and careless drivers.

    w. All those who threaten the safety of others.

    x. All those who contribute to the deterioration and pollution of the forest.

14. Sometimes Emergencies Come Up
Emergency situations require special attention. Those most likely to require assistance would include:

    a. Lost or stranded hikers, hunters, campers, and pets.

    b. Those who can't deal with vehicle-related problems (vehicle needs tire chains, vehicle is stuck or breaks down, driver needs directions or information).

    c. Medical emergencies (illness or accident).

    d. Suicides.

    e. Those involved in fire and disaster situations.

15. Let's Open the Forest to Newcomers

The Forest Service is highly concerned with those who do not benefit from what the forest has to offer. The spectrum of potential users and nonusers is broad, and includes the following:

Potential users:
a. Those who need more information.
b. Those who need to be reached through promotions.
c. Those who will come for only one recreational experience and no other.
d. Those who are bothered by rules and regulations.
e. Those who are disappointed by lack of facilities.
f. Those who are bothered by crowding and traffic congestion.
g. Those who are disturbed by forest deterioration.
h. Those who are disappointed by lack of fish, game, wood, and so on.
i. Those who don't like the design of the recreational facilities.
j. Those who need new facilities designed for special interests and needs.

Nonusers:
a. Those who do not own proper equipment and clothing.
b. Those who find the forest experience more trouble than it is worth.
c. Those who have language problems.
d. Those who do not feel comfortable without familiar faces or friends.
e. Those who find no match between personal recreational interests and the forest environment.
f. Those who have special physical or sensory limitations requiring special attention.
g. Those who cannot afford this type of recreational experience.
h. Those who need more promotional literature (such as personal communication, encouragement, invitation, or services).
i. Those who depend on others or public services for transporatation.
j. Those who think the forest is for those with a great deal of experience.
k. Those who are fearful of strange settings.
l. Those who would feel isolated and fearful of others.
m. Those who feel likely to experience discrimination.
n. Those who want to see specific areas devoted to their preferred way of enjoying themselves.

While the study site has the highest average daily use of any U.S. National Forest, the survey required only 80 working hours to administer and verify. As noted before, we have selected only those research techniques that satisfy our typical time and funding constraints.

Imagine beginning a project presentation with the exhibit shown in Figure 7.3. In a few brief minutes the entire complexity and challenge of the project is revealed. People will see that what you are proposing as design concepts, schemes, forms, and features is more than speculation. Your proposal is justified, and because people can see that you have worked to take their needs and wants into account, it is readily acceptable.

Directed Group Identification Techniques

What can be achieved with the progressive survey may also be sought on a smaller scale by utilizing a directed group identification technique. In the most favorable situation, people will be quite willing, during a study session or interview, to describe and discuss their feelings about group activities and their personal role. In other cases, it may be necessary to ask one group of individuals to help define another group, because the prime group will not talk about themselves or is not available. When developing such a technique, Harper and Harris (1975) used law enforcement personnel to determine the structure of criminal organizations. They cite a number of state agencies that have followed this procedure to improve their understanding of organized crime. Figure 7.4 illustrates how the group identification technique may be used to identify neighborhood and community groups.

Step One
Prepare a description of your study objectives: "The Neighborhood Renewal Committee wants to be sure that every individual and family, community organization, interest group, business firm, shop, public service organization, and those not heretofore identified as members of the neighborhood, are considered during this renewal project. We want every planning step and design decision to respond to the entire neighborhood. We need people who can help us identify community leaders and neighborhood groups, and who can help us understand how they relate to one another."

Step Two
Ask some members of the neighborhood to review your statement of objectives. Ask them to tell you how it sounds and what should be changed or added, so that those asked to participate in the study sessions will feel the project is worthwhile.

Step Three
Set up and schedule as many study session groups as are necessary to assure that your results are representative of neighborhood and community concerns.

Step Four
In each study session, ask the participants to list as many members of the neighborhood as they can think of, with particular emphasis on neighborhood leaders, active groups, problem groups, and those least likely to be well represented during the renewal project.

Step Five
Divide the listing into logical groupings and indicate the relationship between groupings.

Step Six
Ask all study session groups to review one another's results.

Step Seven
Edit the collected information into the clearest possible description that takes into account and gives identity to all neighborhood groups and sources of influence.

Figure 7.4. Neighborhood/community group identification study.

Study Sessions

Study sessions may be defined as crucibles for interaction between participants, resulting in new information or reevaluation of existing information. Study sessions are the most efficient and effective way for building design and land development teams to obtain the necessary background for understanding the client's and facility users' project perceptions. As individuals talk to one another and work to complete the tasks assigned them in the study session, the team will become acquainted with the client's situation in a way that would not be possible if they just jumped into the project and started to ask general questions. Study sessions will be used to acquaint the participants with the scope of concerns identified in the Knowledge Base System, to examine the way spaces are presently used, to resolve conflicts, and to formulate appropriate design features. In another type of situation, the study group might be asked to review the results of research efforts and to help prepare conclusions.

The basic procedure, illustrated in Figure 7.5, is to assemble a group of seven or eight individuals, with additional groups as necessary to achieve a balance of experience, views, interests, and intensity of feeling about the design project. The participants are assigned both individual and shared tasks, centered around the Knowledge Base System. A record of progress is maintained, and there is a summary and critique of results.

There are some problems associated with the selection of individuals for participation in study sessions. Individuals may be recommended for inclusion in deliberations only as a courtesy and may have nothing of value to contribute. Individuals may be suggested who have already closed their minds and are not willing to extend discussions into the realm of alternative thinking. Important individuals may be overlooked: those who know more about the project than anyone recognizes, those who have a history of being argumentative and yet do tend to make significant contributions, and those who are not viewed as being sufficiently important in the client's organization and yet have valuable insights. The best strategy is to keep participation open. Deliberations can begin with those made available; as more is learned about the organization and its situation, new individuals can be identified, contacted, and asked to contribute. It is best to schedule study sessions before conducting any interviews or group meetings, because study session results provide a basis for iden-

The objective of these study sessions is to meet with those who will occupy the leased facility, in order to identify preferences for location within the building, to help resolve conflicts when more than one group wishes to be located in the same area of the building, and to determine the most desirable arrangements of interior spaces.

Step One

Give copies of the building floor plan and the Knowledge Base System question items to a study team that is representative of the new occupants. Review both documents carefully so that participants understand what information is needed and what decisions are required.

Step Two

Provide each participant with two-dimensional cut-outs of equipment and furnishings corresponding to their current inventory. Ask the participants to respond to the following:

If you were being moved into the building tomorrow, what location would you choose, and how would you arrange your equipment and furnishings? There are no restrictions on location or arrangement. Paste the cut-outs you have been given on the floor plan to show your plan for the space you have selected. At our next meeting we will share the results of your work. In this way, we can understand one another's preferences and work out a scheme that is satisfactory to everyone. You have also been given a set of questions, a Knowledge Base System. This information is very important to the development of the facility, and I would like you to answer as many of these questions as possible before our next meeting.

Step Three

In the second session, the pasted-up floor plans will be displayed. Participants will be able to review all suggestions and discuss necessary compromises.

Step Four

Review the answers to the question items in the Knowledge Base System. Summarize this information and share it with participants. Prepare conclusions and proposals based on this information, and provide all participants with an opportunity to critique these conclusions and proposals from the standpoint of their own background and experience.

Figure 7.5. Sample outline for study sessions with corporate personnel: facility lease project.

tifying important questions and facility user concerns. When the building design and land development team representatives participate in study sessions, they gain an initial understanding of how people view the project, what problems are in people's minds, and the way people like to talk about the project. This experience then helps the team form a more effective agenda of research questions. Without this background it is difficult to conduct interviews and group meetings effectively. The agenda presented must make sense and be well-directed or participants will tend to skirt topics of importance.

PUBLIC MEETINGS, A TYPE OF STUDY SESSION

People want a voice in the design and use of their buildings, streets, parks, and cities. They want to be more than spectators and consumers in a world designed and managed by remote professionals (Sommer, 1972: viii). This statement introduces a particular form of community participation in the work of building design and land development teams: public meetings.

The strategy of collaboration and shared responsibility that is common to all the research techniques must be maintained in these public meetings. It is best to avoid confrontations that produce a win or lose spirit. The results of Knowledge Base System applications can be extremely helpful by clarifying the situation for everyone involved. Descriptions of people and their activities will demonstrate to those present that their needs and interests concern the developer. The important characteristics of the project can be identified and illustrated by means of graphic presentations and photographs. The building design and land development team should also discuss information that supports the direction the project has taken. With this type of briefing, the developer can provide a clear context for discussions and help participants develop and maintain objectivity. Informally stated, the team needs to present information that takes the heat off the proposal and maintains instead a focus on the resolution of the problem situation.

CITIZEN PARTICIPATION

Design and planning review board meetings are a familiar example of one form of citizen participation. Developers appear before review boards for every type of project that influences neighborhood and community life to present goals, means, and proposals, to answer questions, and to provide and obtain information that clarifies the review process. What is often a threatening situation for both the developer and the interested public can be a worthwhile opportunity for information exchange if the building design and land development team is well-prepared.

There is probably no other type of project that generates greater challenges and pressure than one that has become a community issue. If the developer is to survive public hearings on such a project, it is essential that he or she identify and understand the issues related to the allocation of community resources. Whatever the exact nature of the project, the developer will be held responsible for an accurate and comprehensive understanding of community needs. Public officials, administrators, and citizens demand that developers recognize that an inappropriate master plan can limit and inhibit programs, fail to support community needs, and be incompatible with the existing sociocultural dynamics of individuals, families, and community organizations.

Although many attempts have been made to use citizen participation programs to identify needs and develop acceptable design objectives, experience with citizen participation has revealed a number of puzzling situations. One puzzle pertains to attitudes. In situation after situation one finds little correspondence between attitudes that people express publicly and what they actually do. Sometimes it seems that citizen participation programs actually create, through the stimulus of pressure groups, feelings and attitudes that exist for only a short time. Citizen participation programs will be worthwhile only if enduring behaviors become the focus of attention. Another puzzling aspect of these programs relates to the role of the design professional. On one hand, the purpose of such programs is to enlist the support and participation of individuals, families, neighborhoods, and community groups for whom the development is significant. The developer is asked to participate, to provide advice, and to complete a thorough analysis of the project. On the other hand, the professional participants will often focus on physical development, thereby losing sight of the close linkage between neighborhood and community life and land developments.

These two crosscurrents usually conflict throughout the citizen participation program. The public participants worry about neighborhood disruption and long-term community problems, while the professional participants are concerned with the success of the project from a physical standpoint. As a result, citizen participation programs tend to be quite unsuccessful. Advocates of action create false expectations, few individuals are satisfied, and only the barest needs of neighborhoods and families are met. This conflict between citizen participation and professional management of a project is so intense that the developer often assumes the role of community organizer and information processor. Traditional roles are disrupted, participants are immobilized by confusion, and few structures, if any, are built to anyone's satisfaction.

Fortunately, while shifting attitudes and roles may result in confusion and conflict, they can also be the basis for an effective citizen participation program. The building design and land development team wants participants to try new roles, to see things from a different viewpoint, and to recognize the complexity of the situation. It is important, however, to guide these meetings by first providing all participants with a description of the full complexity of the situation, a precis of the Knowledge Base System. This helps produce involvement that remains in context and avoids becoming destructive. Without this common starting point, participants will work to have their own opinions appreciated rather than attempting to understand others and striving to reach a compromise.

Interviews

Individuals can be very analytical when they discuss their experiences and suggest ways to enhance the settings for their daily affairs. People will want to talk about their situation, requirements, and expectations. When an interview is completed, the building design and land development team should know what an individual wants, what he or she thinks others need, what is most important and least important to the individual with regard to the alternatives for the planned facility, and, most helpful of all, the thoughts and feelings behind all the various statements made. A good interview makes it possible for team members to see beyond facility users' suggestions, use their experience to interpret what is being suggested, and lead the individual into a discussion of design possibilities never before considered. Seen in this fashion, the interview is the beginning of design.

While this method is simple in application and presents an opportunity to obtain valuable results, the information obtained will be significant for building design and land development only if the undertaking is directed toward obtaining information that does not require interpretation prior to application. If participants do not know exactly what is required and are not guided to that end, the information obtained may require so much interpretation that misunderstanding results. This consideration, of course, applies to all research applications.

Before any interviews are conducted, an agenda of questions is selected from the Knowledge Base System. There are many questions that can be asked, but it is essential to decide which are the most important questions. The purpose of the interview is to ask questions that will motivate people to talk in a manner that is both informative and insightful. Since this will occur only if they recognize the importance of what is being asked, the questions selected for the interivew must be important to the project as well as to the individuals involved. It might be necessary to ask a question in different ways, depending upon who is being interviewed.

With the assistance of the member of the building design and land development team who represents the client's interests, individuals will be selected for interviews. The selection of the right people with which to work is the greatest challenge in Knowledge Base System research. Candidates for interviews include individuals knowledgeable about the client's stituation and intentions, selected users who have firsthand knowledge of daily affairs and particularly important activities, and those who, though not prime users of the planned facility, have a particular interest in project success.

The most suitable form for interviews is the informal interview, which is essentially conversation—conversation initiated by an explanation of the building design and land development team's position and structured by only a few key questions or comments. While the informal interview may be less than systematic, it helps develop an understanding of the private world of meaning of the user. A well-conducted informal interview is likely to foster a high degree of motivation and interest because the person being interviewed feels that his or her observations and opinions are really important. Individuals are able to use their own idiom, to organize thoughts in their own way, and to bring up any aspect of the situation that concerns them personally. The goal is to create the type of interview in which, at the end, you might find the individual saying, "I never realized I felt that way" (Terkel, 1972: xx–xxi). The importance of the free-flowing, unstructured interview is demonstrated when conversational data drawn from naturally occurring encounters is compared with the results of formal interviews. The bulk of the significant data usually comes from less structured situations (Van Maanen, 1973: 409).

Although informal, conversations with individuals should be guided by specific informational objectives. Required information can be written in the form of questions; these can either be given to the individual and used as a means for maintaining selective focus, or kept at hand and used as a checklist to assure that the conversation has covered all the topics. The interview can be structured, calling attention to a particular problem, yet avoiding overdirection. This can be done by showing the individual a photograph of the area of interest and asking if he or she is acquainted with this place or has had experience in similar situations, asking the individual to recall his or her past experience and comment on recollections. Contrasting situations or different physical settings may also be depicted visually, along with a question asking the individual to express his or her interpretation of the significance of what is shown.

Preference Assessment

The purpose of preference assessment is to determine how environments create incentives for cooperation, satisfy the needs of individuals, produce constructive attitudes, and develop more positive alternatives for personal activities. Responses to such challenges can never be entirely adequate unless they are based on a through understanding of users' customs and preferences.

In the U.S. National Forest study, for example, after user groups were identified, interviews and study sessions were used to determine preferences for various land development alternatives and options. This work was guided by the preference survey portrayed in Figure 7.6. It should be noted that the survey does not simply ask for random opinions and preferences. In order to produce results that can be logically assessed, questions are organized in sequence, from the initial thoughts of the forest user, through a possible range of activities, and concluding with final impressions. Preference research must always have some kind of logical structure that guides those surveyed toward the established information objectives.

The following three Figures, 7.7, 7.8, and 7.9, provide examples of how preference information can help us understand the activity patterns that will serve as a means to maintain a total focus on the needs and wants of a specific forest user category. Remember that research is not conducted for informational purposes; it is undertaken to provide verified images of what must be taken into account. While these three figures could have been written as specific recommendations, this would lessen their value as focal points for discussion and deliberation. This is the way to realize the full potential of a building design and land development team. Further, while the level of detail in the exhibits presented here and in the preceding chapter may seem excessive, it is exactly what is required to attain an improved quality of life at work, at home, and in the community.

WE WANT TO UNDERSTAND WHAT A TRIP TO THE FOREST MEANS TO YOU

The questions presented here are designed to help the Forest Service understand what the forest means to you. This is a common sense approach. We want to know what you like to do in the forest and what your problems are. We want to plan and manage the forest with you in mind. Please answer these questions as they apply to you, your family, and any neighborhood group, club, or organization with which you are associated.

1. **INITIAL THOUGHTS**
   A trip to the forest can mean a great deal.
   a. What do you most look forward to when you begin to plan a trip to the forest?
   b. Has anything, at any time, kept you from visiting the forest, even when you wanted to go?

2. **INFORMATION**
   The more we know about the forest, the more we will enjoy it.
   a. What sources of information about the forest do you depend on?
   b. Is there any type of information that you would like the Forest Service to provide?
   c. What do your friends say about our forest?

3. **PREPARATION**
   A trip to the forest requires a lot of preparation.
   a. What do you, your family, friends, neighborhood group, club, or organization do to get ready for a trip to the forest?
   b. What problems do you have in organizing a trip?

4. **TRAVEL TO THE FOREST**
   Travel can be a problem to all of us.
   a. What means of transportation do you use?
   b. Have you had problems with travel to and within the forest?

5. **PICKING YOUR DESTINATION**
   It is important to be able to identify easily a suitable area for your purposes.
   a. What information do you depend on for picking a place to go in the forest?
   b. How difficult is it to find a place that fits your needs?
   c. What should be done ahead of time or after you get to the forest to help you locate the best place for your enjoyment?

6. **RULES AND REGULATIONS**
   The Forest Service uses rules and regulations to ensure an enjoyable experience for everyone and to protect the forest environment.
   a. What rules and regulations have detracted from your forest visit?
   b. What rules should be more strongly enforced?
   c. What rules and regulations need to be introduced to help you enjoy yourself and protect the places you go?

7. **IN ROADSIDE AREAS**
   Many of us use roadside areas for the day.
   a. What roadside areas do you prefer?
   b. When do you use this area?
   c. What do you usually like to do in the roadside areas?

8. **IN DEVELOPED AREAS**
   There are a lot of campgrounds and recreational facilities in the forest.
   a. What campgrounds and facilities do you find the most enjoyable?
   b. When do you usually go to these areas?
   c. What do you like to do in these areas?
   d. What should be done to improve these areas as a place for recreation?
   e. What do you like to do when you go outside of these areas for a short trip?

9. **IN DISPERSED AREAS**
   There are many opportunities for backroad travel in the forest.
   a. What backroad areas do you visit most frequently?
   b. When do you go to these areas?
   c. Why are you attracted to the backroad areas and what do you do there?
   d. What should be done to improve these areas as a place for recreation?

10. **IN BACKCOUNTRY TRAILS**
    The forest provides a great number of backcountry trails.
    a. What backcountry areas do you prefer for hiking and trail rides?
    b. When do you like to take a backcountry trip?
    c. What do you do along the trail and once you get into the backcountry?
    d. What should be done to increase your enjoyment of the backcountry?

11. **IN TOWN, CONCESSIONS, AND PRIVATELY DEVELOPED AREAS**
    Many recreational opportunities are provided by private operators and businesses.
    a. Which of these facilities do you use?
    b. When do you usually go to such a facility?
    c. What do you like about these developments?
    d. What should be done to improve the facilities and services provided?

12. **PROBLEM SITUATIONS**
    If we think we are going to have problems in the forest that we can't handle, we will either go somewhere else or worry about them while we are in the forest.
    a. What problems concern you the most?
    b. Do you see people around you with problems and wish that someone would help them?
    c. What minor problems detract from your enjoyment of the forest?

13. **PREPARING TO GO HOME**
    The last hours in the forest are spent preparing to go home.
    a. What do you do to help maintain the camp and forest areas before you leave?
    b. What do you wish other people would do to make the forest ready for the next visitor?
    c. What difficulties do you encounter as you prepare to go home?

14. **TRAVEL HOME**
    The trip home can either be a pleasure or an irritating chore.
    a. What are your biggest problems on the trip home?

15. **FINAL THOUGHTS**
    The Forest Service wants you to come back again.
    a. What do you usually recall as the most pleasant part of your visit to the forest?
    b. What do you usually recall as the worst moments of your visit?

Figure 7.6. Preference assessment format.

Figure 7.7 illustrates the extent to which we must go to characterize individuals and groups of individuals with limited capabilities. In the activity pattern detailed in Figure 7.8, we can see that the same level of attention must be given to what we consider common situations.

This statement serves to remind the forest manager and planner that there will always be groups who will not enjoy the forest without special consideration. Unless we study these special situations and find out exactly what is needed to support such recreational activities, a great number of potential forest users will be overlooked. Some people need detailed consideration and study because they come to the forest looking for a very special recreation experience. Boating, riding, skiing, and similar activities require detailed consideration. In the case of the trail rider, for example, you do not simply park a truck and horse trailer and go off into the forest. Space for unloading is needed. Safety and containment for the animals are principal requirements. Other forest users have to be alerted to the presence of trail riders and pack animals. Each recreational activity of this type requires special facility and space allocations, as well as necessary rules and regulations to enhance the recreational experience, protect the forest environment, and provide safe and convenient conditions. The activity pattern shown here characterizes another group requiring special consideration, those with physical, mental, and emotional limitations. While it describes the needs of those on a nursing home outing, it reminds us to maintain a high level of awareness of all those who cannot enjoy the forest unless special accommodations are provided.

1. INITIAL THOUGHTS
The elderly who live at our nursing home are always interested in new challenges, opportunities, and companions. Even if what we do in the forest in the way of recreation is similar to what we do at home, a change in routine and travel is important to us.

2. INFORMATION
One of the most enjoyable parts of an outing is finding out all we can about the history, environment, wildlife, and conservation aspects of the setting.

3. PREPARATION
Maintaining a controlled diet is critical for many of us. All our meals are planned ahead. The planning that goes into providing for the individual needs of each participant is what makes an outing a major project for the staff.

4. TRAVEL TO THE FOREST
We always look for a camp located within an hour's drive of the nursing home. We certainly expect the roads leading to the camp to be in good condition, free of holes and dust and anything that could cause our vans to get stuck.

5. LOCATING YOUR DESTINATION
The Forest Service has always provided us with maps, good directions, and estimates of road conditions.

6. RULES AND REGULATIONS
As requested by the Forest Service, we make our reservations well in advance. The regulation that creates difficulties for us is the one that keeps organized campgrounds away from other campgrounds. We like to watch other people's activities and see new faces.

7. IN DEVELOPED AREAS
Our trips usually last two nights and three days. We usually look for three cabins housing five people each. Our group is interested in fishing and excursion boating, education sessions, sunrise and sunset services, shuffleboard, stargazing, and table games. We certainly need an approved water supply, barrier-free cabin and bathroom facilities with heat, comfortable seating around the campfire, sheltered cooking, dining, and activity areas, and level outdoor paths and activity areas.

8. PROBLEM SITUATIONS

Our average age is 68 and almost all of us suffer from multiple health problems, including diabetes, obesity, glaucoma, hypertension, and heart disease. All conditions are controlled by medication, requiring refrigeration. A telephone is essential. Stand-by emergency service should be no more than fifteen minutes from the campsite.

9. PREPARING TO GO HOME

Our group has always taken the greatest care to clean up the camp. One thing we always do is have everyone put on a fresh change of clothes, so as to be as comfortable as possible for the trip home.

10. TRAVEL HOME

We always stop off at a gift shop and a mail station on the way home. It is very important to us to be able to send postcards and letters off to our friends and relatives as soon as possible.

11. FINAL THOUGHTS

The only regret we have is that to date it has been impossible to travel to the Forest in winter. What we need is some inexpensive accommodation for one night. Since we find it difficult to walk in the snow and ice, we need an enclosed and heated area with a view of winter sport areas.

Figure 7.7. Needing and using special facilities.

The campground is the center of the forest experience for many visitors, for a weekend or longer. Particular sources of enjoyment and a wide range of activities are noted here.

1. INITIAL THOUGHTS

Our initial thoughts are always the same. When is the best time to avoid crowds both on the road and in the campground? How can we make reservations? Should we depend on Ticketron to assign a nice site or take a chance and hunt for a good site once we get to the forest?

2. INFORMATION

If a camping trip with my family is to be successful, I must plan for the entire family, help the children enjoy themselves and still cook meals, keep things clean, and also find a few quiet moments. I want to be able to plan in advance for the entire outing. With this in mind, I really wish the Forest Service would send me a complete outing packet that describes everything available to the family camper in the way of forest facilities, possible activities, special campfire programs, where to swim and fish, what problems to expect, and what to do in case of trouble.

3. PREPARATION

Part of the fun of a family outing is delegating things to the members of the family. This way the trip belongs to everyone. No one is just along for the ride. It would be nice to have a checklist of things to do to get ready, particularly if there are things I could assign to the children.

4. TRAVEL TO THE FOREST

We wish people would slow down coming down the hill. It is hard to point out things to the children and still dodge those who drift around curves.

continued on page 304

5. LOCATING YOUR DESTINATION

Though we can always go back to the same campground we stayed at before, it would be nice to be able to find new places, better places. If there was an entry station where we could get advice, rather than having to find things on our own, it would be a great help. Once the family gets to the forest, they want to set up camp and start having a good time. No one wants to spend any more time in the car than they have to.

6. RULES AND REGULATIONS

As far as the things we do, there aren't any rules that interfere with having a good time. In fact, we find the campgrounds where the rules are enforced are the most enjoyable.

7. IN DEVELOPED AREAS

We like campsites that are not packed together. We like campgrounds that provide nice clean restrooms, picnic tables, water, firewood, and trash pickup. It would be even nicer if there were showers and electrical hookups. Camping near a stream or lake is always best. At the same time we like to get as far away from the road and busy areas as possible. I guess we are looking for a forest utopia. Once we get set up, we do all kinds of things: take hikes, stroll the trails and go exploring, visit with people, set up horseshoes, enjoy the scenery, relax, and sightsee. We camp during spring and fall and sometimes during the summer. We would like to camp in the winter, but it seems that it is almost impossible with the present facilities. On one-day trips during the winter we have seen some people camping and going snowshoeing and cross-country skiing. We would be happy if we could just bring the kids and let them play in the snow and at the end of the day get them dried off, and warm and cozy.

8. PROBLEM SITUATIONS

We always worry about the children getting lost, having an accident, or being bothered by people. It is hard to do anything other than act as a playground monitor or stand guard over our car and belongings. I would certainly like to know if there are campgrounds where rangers are around to help us watch things, ready to help if we need it. We wouldn't worry so much if we knew that someone experienced in handling emergencies was always available, particularly if they knew how to get a stalled car running. Car worries have prevented us from coming to the forest more often than anything else. You might not think it is a problem situation, but when our children were small we never came to the forest. It would have been nice, but it is impossible to cook, keep small children clean, get them to the toilet, and not worry about them being knocked down by people not used to seeing small children in campgrounds. If some campgrounds were specially designed for families with small children, it would mean a great deal to more families than you realize. Did I forget to mention noise and those damned ORV's and motorbikes?

9. PREPARING TO GO HOME

More than anything else we would like bigger restrooms, with more countertops and sinks, and enough space to let us clean up the children and get them ready for the trip back.

10. TRAVEL HOME

Going out of the forest on a hot Sunday afternoon is the worst possible experience. Some genius should help solve that problem.

11. FINAL THOUGHTS

The best feeling of all was the fact that we got away from the house, and though things were crowded, we did have a few quiet moments, sat by the campfire at night, hope we have helped the children appreciate the forest as a forest, not just another place to mess around in. The forest should always remain a special place.

Figure 7.8. My family likes to camp in the forest.

An essential need of every building design and land development team is the ability to provide benefits for facility user groups that have never before been taken into consideration. Figure 7.9 addresses this issue.

The Forest Service is highly concerned with those individuals who have never benefited from what the forest has to offer. With all that is known about recreational experiences and what can be readily provided, any evidence or concern for underutilization is best considered as the need to reach, inform, and serve at a highly personal level.

The need to guard against bias is probably foremost in everyone's mind when they think about opening the forest to the "nonuser." Those seeking to open the forest must realize that they will always be influenced by their own experience and culture and as a result may misinterpret the behaviors and preferences of others. It is always essential to work in collaboration with those who bring a different point of view to forest management and planning.

Another bias factor is related to the fact that demographic information frequently obscures important cultural differences. Individuals may assign quite different attributes, values, and meanings to the forest, which are not apparent in statistical summaries. One bias that is particularly detrimental for future planning stems from the labels we use. Such labels as "black," "Chicano," "foreign," and "disabled" can be so powerful that many of the behaviors of individuals and groups can be overlooked entirely or profoundly misinterpreted. These safeguard considerations point to the need to go beyond the general appearance of people and their behavior and give recognition to individual needs.

1. INITIAL THOUGHTS
These are often mixed. Negative impressions are common: It's not for me. I have better things to do. The word is out; the place is boring, dirty, and has little to offer. You are on your own. A lot of my friends feel ill at ease with so many strangers around. But these can be balanced by positive impressions: My dad used to take me; maybe I should take the kids. Lots of people suggest it for a weekend. I feel more at home there than I do anywhere else. People are really nice and want everyone to have a good time.

2. INFORMATION
Information must reach both individuals and groups and must be very real, not abstract. It should depend on pictures, simplified maps, drawings, and simple directions and suggestions. It should stress the personal recreational experience. This means people should be informed about what they can do, about things they can do with friends, and about someone nearby who can help arrange and plan a trip. Word of mouth, the grapevine, and the persuasive friend or neighbor must be relied on as much as more general means of information dissemination. The key is to approach the nonuser on two levels: on the personal, individual-to-individual level, and in terms of his or her connection with a particular community, interest, or cultural group.

3. PREPARATION
Those who are encouraged to visit the forest must be told what aspects of the trip require preparation. The Forest Service should consider providing a service to help individuals, families, and groups to get ready for a trip to the forest. Problems in organizing a trip can be noted and first-time users can be told about problems they might face in the forest and what to do about them.

4. TRAVEL TO THE FOREST
Travel is a problem for many individuals and may make a trip to the forest impossible. Assistance in the arrangement of transporation would be a role for the Forest Service. For those able to make their own arrangements, a travel packet containing route and emergency services information would be helpful.

continued on page 306

5. LOCATING YOUR DESTINATION

The first-time user of the forest needs all the help that we can give him or her. For the newcomer, the forest is a strange setting and what is now available in the way of information is of minimal use to the inexperienced. What is behind all those signs along the road? What goes on there? What is a good destination for me? How does the reservation system work? Who will help me once I am in the forest? These are questions to which information can be directed.

6. RULES AND REGULATIONS

The Forest Service uses rules and regulations to ensure an enjoyable experience for everyone and to protect the forest environment. As presently explained, only those with a background in the forest can read between the lines and interpret what is said. Certainly, the inability to read English is a problem for many potential users of the forest. When these rules and regulations are critical, a friendly smile from a forest ranger and an encouragement to use the forest thoughtfully is needed.

7. IN ROADSIDE AREAS

This is a place to begin to provide for the needs of those not now benefiting from what the forest has to offer. The first places seen along the road should be as attractive and inviting as possible. Particularly on weekends, these areas should be staffed and used as places to distribute information packets.

8. IN DEVELOPED AREAS

While the forest has value as a recreational resource, the first-time user will miss many things without guidance. The first trip must work out well or all the promotional efforts will be wasted. For example, campgrounds can be perceptually confusing when crowded or empty. What lies beyond the campground can remain a mystery. An escort service in the developed areas will overcome many of these problems.

9. PROBLEM SITUATIONS

Discrimination is a concern for many possible users of the forest. People will segregate themselves, of course, as they follow their own interests and preferences; if discrimination operates to do do this, however, few will return to the forest. Right now this is a silent issue and hard to see. For instance, many people have felt excluded from the forest experience because what they bring with them doesn't seem as adequate as what other people have, and the things other people have seem out of reach. Campground designs that offer more amenities and require less equipment can help eliminate such subtle aspects of discrimination.

10. PREPARING TO GO HOME

The Forest Service should devote a period of time to informally contact new visitors as they prepare to go home, offer assistance, and find out what has worked for the visitor and help plan another trip.

11. TRAVEL HOME

Travel tips can help prevent problems on the road and provide for that last chance to encourage a return visit.

12. FINAL THOUGHTS

Programs and services directed to the nonuser must emphasize promotion, communication, and more personal direct services. The area is so complex that it would be best to begin a series of outreach efforts in a target community and find out what works well. San Bernadino would be an ideal target community because it is within a short distance of the forest and contains a large number of nonuser groups. In the case of the nonuser, planning for the future means research, experimentation with new ideas, and, above all, collaboration and shared responsibility between the Forest Service and the local community.

Figure 7.9. Let's open the forest to newcomers.

Activity Analysis

If the building design and land development team studies a children's playground, they will readily understand what is being suggested for activity analysis. Children will be seen running, throwing, swinging, jumping, climbing, falling, rolling, tumbling, balancing, creeping, hiding, digging, skating, skateboarding, and cycling. To place these activities in order, they may be classified according to user group, game, or event. As the team considers these activities, they will form associations between activities and environmental features. Jumping, rolling, tumbling, crawling, and digging will bring to mind landscaping and ground cover possibilities. Balancing, climbing, swinging, and falling evoke thoughts of bars, ropes, poles, and safety features. Cycling, skating, and skateboarding are associated with hard surfaces, flat and contoured. Pushing and hitting suggest wide fields of view for monitors, so that these activities can be spotted and controlled before they develop into fights. Each game and recreational event brings to mind additional environmental features needed to support anticipated activities. Activity analysis follows this commonsense approach to identifying important building design and land development considerations.

The First Step in Activity Analysis Is to Determine Which Facility Users Must Be Given Special Attention

These users include people under constant and prolonged stress: assembly line workers, emergency room staff, police officers, single heads of households, detention facility staff and inmates, and those in understaffed environments. The activities of people prone to fatigue or boredom—clerk typists, bedridden invalids, students, military personnel, prisoners, fast-food service employees, draftsmen, and copy and reproduction workers—may be considered in detail. The team may wish to consider people likely to become disoriented or confused: travelers, first-time facility users, those caught in emergency or crisis situations, and those who are unable to read or understand the local language. Another category might include those who are emotionally unable to deal with anything other than a perfectly designed environment, such as the senile, children, and adults with learning disabilities, individuals who are easily frustrated because of a biochemical dependency, and those with emotional problems. Some individuals may require special consideration because of physical disabilities that affect vision, speech, or motor movement and coordination. Some individuals will be selected because of a stressful work situation due to job pressures, detailed and demanding work, or the critical nature of their tasks. Individuals who are particularly important to an organization may be singled out for special attention to emphasize that their concerns and needs are paramount. Listings of individuals to whom activity analysis should be applied may be quite lengthy when the situation being studied is part of a complex culture employing advanced technology and expanded services.

The Second Step in Activity Analysis Is to Determine Which User Activities Are Important

Even simple movements of disabled individuals (walking, grasping, reaching, sitting) should be given the closest scrutiny. For these people, common daily events such as bathing, cooking, or mailing a letter can assume major importance. Similarly, the activities that make up the daily routine of ward nurses, clerk typists, and laboratory scientists and technicians may also need to be carefully studied. Certain activities may also require attention because of the characteristics of the facility being considered, such as long corridors, stairs, common spaces, limited space, distracting operations, and hazardous areas. Detailed attention must be given to activities that are likely to cause stress, fatigue, boredom, or confusion, as well as detailed, demanding, or critical functions. Lack of support for such activities will adversely affect convenience, safety, and security.

After identifying the individual and group activities toward which activity analysis will be directed, the building design and land development team selects the best approach for determining the important relationships between people, their activities, and the immediate environment. Interviews, study sessions, and systematic observations are all possible methods for activity analysis. It should not be difficult to determine which will work best in a given situation. The method selected and its application will depend on the kind of results required.

The Final Step in Activity Analysis Is to Depict How Activities Vary by User, Event, and Space

The more specific and quantified the results of activity analysis, the more value they will have. Activity sequences are frequently used as a guide for space planning. The sequences of activities occurring in a physical setting should be described as completely as possible. As this may involve a large quantity of information, the challenge is data reduction. The activities occurring in a particularly important space are arranged as a sequence of actions and communications, accompanied by a column which shows time of occurrence. Sometimes a sequence of activities can be graphically illustrated, such as the semi-pictorial representation contained in Figure 7.10.

Activity analysis requires that occupancy, movement, and communication patterns be characterized, developing activity data in the context of spaces and the circulation between them. Mapping and flow diagrams are excellent formats for depicting occupancy and movement patterns. These diagrams rely upon the association between a visual figure and an indicated number of users rather than a listing of spaces and corresponding numbers of users, as in a table. While this information can usually be

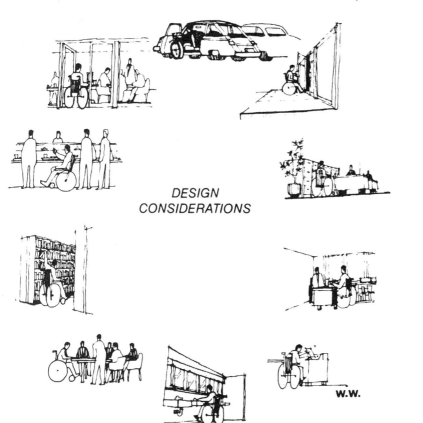

DESIGN
CONSIDERATIONS

Figure 7.10. Activity sequence.

shown in a table in less space and with less effort, the figures in mapping and flow diagrams convey significant additional meaning to the reader.

Communication Matrix

Quite often the goal of activity analysis is to develop a communication matrix, showing how individuals, groups, and spaces are linked in order to accomplish a particular task. This information is important for medical facilities, educational centers, museums, libraries, and government and business offices where information must be routinely developed, stored, retrieved, presented, and exchanged. Even in the area of housing, particularly large housing projects, information may be the key to convenience, safety, security, and the prevention of facility misuse. The first step in developing a communication matrix is to identify each means of communication. The next step is to develop a suitable communication log. Measurements of frequency of exchanges and the numbers of individuals involved are achieved by asking participants to maintain a log for a specified period of time.

When both the formal and informal aspects of communication between individuals is important, then a special study may be required. A survey may be used to identify the relationships between group members as perceived by the members themselves (Figure 7.11).

Systematic Observation

The results of systematic observation are primary data sources that are particularly valuable for characterizing the client's situation and maintaining a direct concern for anticipated facility users. Observation results are also a valuable means for motivating people to participate in research. No design or plan, no matter how worthwhile, can withstand public scrutiny by itself. People want to see themselves in the work of the building design and land development team. Observation results, shown in interviews, study sessions, and public meetings, are evidence that care has been taken to understand the existing situation. Observation results can also serve to double-check the results of other research technique applications.

The purpose of these questions is to identify the people you work with every day, those who are essential to the performance of your job, and those who contribute to the success of your day. With this information, we will have a better basis for arranging your work environment to meet your needs.

Please write your name and department in the lines below. On the following lines please write in the names of three co-workers with whom you have direct contact on a daily basis. It may be helpful if you read through the questions before listing these names.

Name_____

Department_____

Co-workers:

1._____

2._____

3._____

Please write the number corresponding to one co-worker only in the space provided. This means that for each question you wll select the one individual who is most closely related to the question asked.

____1. Which of these individuals is your most important source of job information?

____2. Who supervises or guides your work routine?

____3. When you need an opinion or wish to discuss a work-related matter before making a decision, to which of these individuals do you usually go?

____4. To whom do you most often give information?

____5. Which of these individuals, if any, frequently comes to you for advice or assistance?

____6. Whose work do you supervise directly?

____7. With whom do you spend most of your time during the day?

____8. Which of these individuals is likely to affect your work the most if he or she is absent or otherwise unavailable?

____9. If appropriate, with which of these individuals are you most likely to share a computer network and database?

If you feel you would rather not answer the following questions, please omit them. However, we would put this information to good use when determining the best way to increase your enjoyment of your day at work.

____10. With which of these individuals do you most often have lunch?

____11. Which of these individuals, if any, do you frequently see outside of working hours?

Thank you for your help.

Figure 7.11. Communication network survey.

In observation programs, the building design and land development team studies individual and group activities and the surrounding environment, using notes, sketches, photographs, and videotapes to record findings. It is important to remember that many design decisions made will be influenced by observation results, which makes it essential to devise a thorough and systematic observation program. The observer cannot simply follow his or her eye, for any observer may be overwhelmed by the complexity of the situation to such a degree that the approach becomes random and loses its representativeness. First impressions will readily indicate what is interesting, but they will seldom help determine what is significant.

A program of systematic observation is undertaken because it is possible to establish justified design objectives for a new facility by observing existing facilities and the activies of users. The time spent on systematic observation is particularly justified when one is confronted with a situation that is new, or one that is complex or highly variable. Even when the building design and land development team is experienced, it is not unusual to find that systematic observation results have saved them from making a serious error in judgment.

Observation can yield many important insights concerning the general characteristics of the study site. For example, a one-day excursion through a downtown shopping area can provide a range of interesting and insightful impressions. In public spaces with broad fields of view, you become aware of the varied and rich aspects of the study site. You recognize that the range of sociocultural character is both broad and select. You note which displays are of interest and which goods draw the attention of passing shoppers. If you are alert, you will recognize which of the actions, movements, and facial expressions are in response to particular events or to spaces with special features. You become aware of which sounds, lights, and spaces appear to attract the attention of shoppers. Your observations might center around a plaza that offers space for the stroller, the active child, the socializing youth, and the pensive individual watching the flow of water in a fountain. You may observe the flow of traffic and the ease or difficulty in obtaining preferred parking in the shopping area. The results of these observations may evolve into a statement of the human and physical characteristics that produce a shopping environment. At the very least, you have guarded against relying too heavily on your own past experience.

The building design and land development team need not restrict attention to situations that are similar to the study topic. Observations can come from all types of facilities if they contain significant design features. Even an unsuccessful design may contain details that are significant for deliberations. The whole study may take the form of a post-occupancy evaluation, demonstrating that various design features make the environment responsive to user expectations and requirements or fail to support individuals and their tasks.

The extent of observation can be controlled in several ways. While on site, as the observations of actions, movements, spaces, and objects begin to accumulate, the building design and land development team can step in at some arbitrary point and decide whether or not a sufficient basis for representativeness and inference exists. If not, the team can compare the cost of continuing with the expected increase in information. This is more than a trial-and-error approach. Individuals have intuitive statistical capabilities, which can be used to approximate how much more information is needed. In fact, people actually tend to use this skill too conservatively (Peterson and Beach, 1967: 43). When relying on observer judgement to direct the study, you must carefully assess your approach (Figure 7.12).

The observer may also control the extent of observation by establishing a sampling plan prior to entering the study site. It may be more beneficial to observe the study site only during important time periods, rather than all day. The building design

---

While preparing for a program of systematic observation, the critical questions to be asked are:

- Have we chosen a study site that will help achieve our informational objectives?
- Will the site be available to us?
- Under what restrictions will we be operating?
- Will we have to be on the site continually, or can we set up a sampling scheme?
- If so, should we observe activities every day, hourly, or at another time interval?
- Will the selected time periods be representative of the activities that occur at other times?
- To what degree will our presence affect the situation?
- Will there be uncertainty about what to observe?
- Will the observers be consistent in what they pay attention to and what they document?
- If it is anticipated that there will be a problem with consistency of observations, how much training should we give observers?
- Do our observational goals match up with the situation, or should more effort go into their development?

Figure 7.12. Assessment steps for systematic observation.

and land development team might select from a number of possible events those of particular significance. People can be classified according to individual characteristics or activities and their behavior sampled in proportion to their numbers in the study situation. The sampling unit may be a portion of a downtown area, a city block, or a section of a housing project. A natural way for the team to control a study is to arrange observations according to the building units and spaces which are identified with the facility type under consideration. Whatever is selected for observation, the team does so because it is willing to take the results of sampling and infer from them the characteristics of the total situation.

Questionnaires

If the building design or land development problem indicates the need for input from a large number of participants, the team may elect to use the Knowledge Base System as a questionnaire survey. The first step in questionnaire development is to review the Knowledge Base System question items to identify areas where information is inadequate and can be conveniently or economically obtained through a questionnaire. Once the information objectives for the questionnaire have been established, the form and extent of the necessary information are determined. No question items should be selected until these two tasks are accomplished. Without this specific target, it is impossible to form a thoughtful series of questions. Even more important, this preparation will keep a questionnaire from becoming a catch-all method; it is this tendency that quickly discredits questionnaires in the eyes of the individuals asked to participate.

Although the questionnaire survey is widely used, it is also frequently misused, overextended, and distrusted. In addition, many people dislike or are not motivated to respond to a questionnaire because it places them in a highly structured and passive situation. Despite these disadvantages, a skillfully designed Knowledge Base System questionnaire can obtain information from a large number of people with considerably less effort than that needed for some of the other research techniques, and may in some cases cause less embarrassment or inconvenience.

Development Considerations

The questionnaire depends almost entirely on words. It involves asking questions, in one form or another, to gather information about individuals' experiences, activities, habits, opinions, customs, goals, and preferences. In order for this information to be of value, great care must be taken both in writing the questions and in sequencing the order in which they are presented. It is also necessary to find people interested enough in the project to complete the questionnaire and who adequately represent those affected by final designs and plans.

Questionnaires should not be used just to obtain general information, as people resent being such a source. They prefer to be questioned in a way that lets them work to the best of their ability. Questionnaire items must be specifically directed to the resolution of important issues, indicating the reliance being placed on the questionnaire results and each individual's contribution.

Questions can take two forms: closed or open. Closed questions provide a number of answers for the individual to consider, with the option to chose one or more. Although closed questions require little time or effort to answer, they may generate very little interest or motivation and are difficult to write. In order to prepare alternatives that will elicit significant information, a great deal must be known about the background of the individuals who will be answering the question. Closed questions are suited to the preliminary stages of a study, as well as to later stages to confirm information and conclusions drawn from other methods, to check on the acceptability of design decisions, or to determine preferences for specific design features. Respondents will be more willing to provide information when they see that much work has already gone into the project. Closed questions that convey a sense of urgency to resolve key problems reflect serious intentions. Any person participating in a closed-question survey has the right to expect that the questions presented contain answer choices that express his or her viewpoint. If this is not possible, frustration must be eliminated by providing space in which to provide opinions or criticisms about the contents of the questionnaire (Rosier, 1974: 113).

Open questions allow the individual to answer in his or her own words and to discuss any aspect of the situation that he or she considers important. Open questions require time, thought, and effort from the respondent, however, and as a result of individual differences in the way questions are answered, this type of question is more difficult to summarize than closed questions. On the other hand, an open question creates more interest and helps determine how strong the respondent's feelings are (Cannell and Kahn, 1968: 565). It is possible to combine questions of both types in any Knowledge Base System questionnaire, and it is not necessary to limit the questionnaire to words only. It is often also useful to include photographs or drawings that illustrate objectives or depict various alternatives.

Bouchard (1976: 381–382) reviewed the literature on questionnaire formulation and suggested that by keeping the following questions in mind, the building design and land development team can avoid mistakes and ensure an effective final result: Is each question clearly written, easy to read, and necessary? Are the questions specific or do they contain more than one idea, making them difficult for individuals to answer? Are questions embarrassing, repetitious, or likely to bias following questions? Is the arrangement of questions reasonable and likely to maintain motivation? Where necessary, were statements provided that put the questions in a proper context? Finally, were an introductory statement and a concluding statement included that indicated the purpose of the questionnaire and expressed appreciation to the respondents? The questionnaire, then, must be clearly written and well organized. It is essential to avoid questions that cause embarrassment or hostility, confuse or mislead the respondent, or encourage an automatic, thoughtless response.

Unlike the social scientist surveying a group or organization, it is not difficult for the building design and land development team to get people to complete and return questionnaires. The client's representatives take on this responsibility. It is preferable that the questionnaire be personally administered on an individual basis. When it is only possible to administer questionnaires on a group-by-group basis, it may still be necessary to schedule individual sessions for those who are unwilling or unable to furnish information through a questionnaire—those who have not learned to read, people with visual or physical handicaps, those with scruples about filling out forms, and those who demand individual attention (Rosier, 1974).

CHAPTER EIGHT

VALUE, PERFORMANCE, AND IMAGE

The ability to provide services within the three-fold criteria of value, performance, and image is the most marketable aspect of professional architectural services. To prevail over the competition in the building industry, we must promote in the minds of prospective clients the extraordinary value of this professional service. To provide value, the executive architect should develop, market, and deliver a complete service to clients, which may include everything from financing consultations to building maintenance. We must be known for husbanding our client's investment, increasing his or her returns, and guarding every cent in a budget. Scheduling is a major component of value; investments begin to perform only when we are far enough along on a project for clients to start selling property, leasing space, or for the client to occupy the new facility. In the realm of performance, our clients must be assured that when they contract for our professional services, the spaces, buildings, facilities, and land developments will perform in the context of project objectives and every client expectation and requirement. This means we must promote with those judging our services the recognition that achievement of quality of life at work, at home, and in the community is the demand we place on ourselves. In regards to image, design achievements that reflect the images appropriate to our client's situation and expectations will always be the heart of our service. There is a slight caveat here: if we make design style our principal offering, or permit clients to maintain this stereotype, we markedly undervalue architectural services.

Insights

Douglas H. Austin, F.A.I.A.

Doug Austin, a graduate of Cal Poly, is special. No architect we have met is more successful in achieving building value, perform- ance, and image on every project. The Austin Design Group has offices in San Diego's golden triangle, a center for research closely associated with the adjacent University of California, San Diego. The building's grounds offer the unique amenity of a large Japanese garden. The office is spacious and comfortable; each associate has plenty of room to pile up drawings and documents. The compan- ionable atmosphere mirrors the way these people work together.

Interview Highlights

Doug addresses the topics of value, performance, and image from the perspective of client relationships. Read this interview with care. Every insight and method developed in the preceding pages is verified.

- You have to build a relationship of trust and confidence with the client, whether it's in the RFQ or not. We begin by selling ourselves to the client as a team that listens.

- The more you communicate with a client, the better the rela- tionship is. We need to teach ourselves to do it more often and at critical times.

- Sometimes we do extra things, that clients don't expect from architects. When a client has a fund raiser we can provide graphics or other assistance.

- Sometimes we can introduce a client to a bonding company, or an investment or capital firm. It's amazing how much clout you have when you bring money to the table.

- One of the things we are looking at right now is the possibility of partnering with a local company that provides information about comparative real estate prices to appraisers and brokers.

- One thing we do sell is true value engineering. We say that a lot of contractors say they do value engineering, but they don't. They do cost cutting. They'll tell you how to save money but they won't tell you how to add more value for the same money.

- We've done a lot of overseas work and we've learned that if you really want the business you have to be prepared to stay there, and be there, because they're not interested in here today, gone tomorrow.

- We do a wide range of projects, which means we're less likely to get taken out by one shift in the marketplace.

- We try to find out as much as possible about the client and his situation before we ever get to the interview. We do more "homework" than anyone else.

- You hate to communicate bad news, but the earlier you do it, the better off you are. I tell my staff I want to hear good news right away, but I want to hear bad news even faster.

- One of the ways we handle the challenge of a wide range of projects is through a highly interactive design process, where programming and design overlap.

- We use charettes with great success for us and the client. One thing to watch out for is that you don't jump to a quick or obvious solution as a result of the "group think."

The Interview

I guess the challenge of working with clients and client organizations is probably the same challenge that we have with human relationships in general. It may sound trite, but communicating with the client is one of our constant challenges, from the time we're first trying to get their attention and communicate to them who we are, what we do, what makes us different, what makes us special, and why we're a good choice for them, to the point where they've moved into the building and they have questions. I know we don't do enough communicating with our clients after they've moved into the building. In fact, in our profession, it's rare.

Throughout the process, it is a challenge to communicate effectively, to keep things on track. In general, the more you communicate, the better the relationship is. We need to teach ourselves to do it more often and at critical times. This is especially important when there is bad news to share—when this is going to cost more than the client wants to spend, or there is a problem with the building department, or we've made a mistake. We hate to communicate bad news, but the earlier we do it, the better off we are. I always tell my staff that I want to hear good news right away, but I want to hear bad news even faster.

We do a wide range of projects. We do large master plans, hospitals, churches, and we still still do custom houses—and that challenge of communication is there with every one of them. One of the ways we handle this challenge is through a highly interactive design process, where programming and design are somewhat overlapped. We'll start by doing some basic research to familiarize ourselves with the client's situation. We get to know as much as we can about the site, the building department that we'll be working with, and various other issues. The more sophisticated the project or the client, the more thorough we have to be. If it's a house, we give the clients a thick questionnaire and then get together with them to get their imaginations going. With an organization like a hospital or a municipal agency, or perhaps a school, we have to do more preliminary research.

As soon as possible, we try to get all the people involved in the project together and go through a process that has been referred to as "designing out loud," or what we call a "charette." Some designers are intimidated by this, but we find it invigorating. The communication during this process is very good. For example, we designed an operations building for the City of Oceanside. The new building was going to house departments from several locations, and some of these people didn't get along very well. During the charette process, they had to communicate with each other as well as with us, which was very helpful for the project. Afterward they commented about how healthy it was for their organization.

There are a couple of things we need to watch out for during a charette. One is that we don't jump to a quick or obvious solution as a result of the "group think" or group mentality, and fail to see a potentially better solution. This happens when one person has a good idea and everybody else says "aha!" and we don't look for other possibilities. If people can draw back a little bit, or go off by themselves and come up with individual solutions first, we have a greater variety to consider when they come back to the table. People will buy into their solution, defend it a little more, and more possibilities will be explored. So we have to have the skill to manage the power and chaos of these meetings and make sure we look at enough potential solutions, working from quantity to quality. We also need to use "people skills" if we get into a situation where one person is dominating a meeting. We try to draw the others forward and balance the group dynamics.

It can be equally challenging to communicate effectively with clients during the design of a single-family home. For example, we are doing a house in Aspen, Colorado, for a family that currently lives in Oregon. This project is a communications nightmare for a number of reasons. The first is that the house is in Aspen, the client lives in Oregon, and our office is in San Diego. Under the circumstances, it would be difficult enough if we were building the house from scratch, because Aspen is one of the most restrictive communities I can think of in terms of building any-thing. But we're actually doing a significant remodel of an existing structure. The program for the new home includes an in-home office, which makes it even tougher. In addition, the client—the man—admits that he cannot visualize anything in three dimen-sions, yet he is absolutely passionate about this project and wants to understand everything. This man is in the business of hiring product design professionals so he talks the design language, he knows a lot of designers and he understands people very well, but he can't visualize three dimensions to save his life. We're also working with a very tight budget, and the family's demands are higher than their budget. They fired another architect because he came in somewhere between 70 and 90 percent over budget.

The most interesting thing to me is that the husband feels it's terribly important to communicate about this project. He is like a convert to the interactive design process. I flew up to Aspen and lived with the family for a week, and we would design until we either got to a block or we wanted to go skiing so badly we'd just head out the door. There were times when we'd be up until two in the morning.

With a family, the process is a little different than when we go through an organized process like the one for the municipal building. It's more intuitional, I suppose. I never know when I'm going to wake up in the middle of the night and just start working again. One night—and this happened at least twice while we were up there—they got to the point where they understood what we were doing and thought, "This really makes sense, let's go with it." Then the next morning they came in and brought up a new issue, one that they really hadn't referred to before. In this case it was, "We think this house is going to function well, but this has to be a family house; this has to feel like a family house." Since that can mean different things to different people, I asked, "Okay, what does that mean to you?" Their concern was that the house needed to feel safe, particularly in terms of the stairs, and also that it needed to have zones. Other issues came up as we went through this process, which would significantly change the design each time.

As I've already indicated, we try to find out as much as possible about the client and his situation before we ever get to the interview. We have to build a relationship of trust and confidence, and the one thing I tell my people here is that trust is going to be an important issue, whether it's in the RFQ or not. There are many very, very competent firms competing for business right now, so the selection process depends as much on personal factors as it does on competence. Do people trust you? Do they feel good about you? It's very difficult to create that kind of relationship in a one-hour interview. But if you go out there and you really look interested, word gets around within their organization. Even if they say they're not going to talk to any architects, you bug whoever you can and you find out as much as you can.

As an example, we picked up a job at Francis Parker School at one time. There was some excellent competition when we went after that job, but we did more "homework" than anyone else. The headmaster had a lot of visionary ideas. One of the things that he saw, which I felt was significant, was that the school needed to provide more than an education, that they should encourage kids to hang out there after school. Since many families have two working parents, there are a lot of latchkey kids, and he felt it was important to create a sort of community center where the kids would be in a supervised environment and yet feel free, not institutionalized. By the time we went in for the interview, they'd seen our faces on campus a lot, so they knew we were highly interested. We had chatted with as many people as we could to find out what was really important to them. This is a private school that has been around for a long time, and when we went in there we were able to give them a history lesson on their own school, which was good. We talked about why that was important to what they were going to do, from a master plan standpoint. After the interview I heard that they had been predisposed to give the job to somebody else, who'd done work for that school for a long time, but our interview changed their minds. It wasn't the interview—of course, we had to be "on" at the interview, but they knew something about us, they had spoken to us ahead of time, and when we got to that interview we sure knew a heck of a lot more than anyone else did about what was important to them!

So we've found that building a relationship of some trust before we have a job is important in getting the job. However, when you're dealing with a large institution, it's hard to do what we did with that private school.

When we went after the student union building at U.C.S.D., for example, we were up against a number of top firms, including I. M. Pei and Arthur Erickson. The competition was awesome. Another firm, KMD, had asked us to team with them and we assumed that since they were so anxious to go after it, they must have done a lot of student union buildings. I remember being so surprised when I found out they'd never done one, although they'd done some retail and commercial projects that were maybe somewhat related. We'd never done one either! I remember thinking, "How are we even going to have a ghost of a chance?"

So when we went into that meeting, we said, we're going to have to sell this team as a team that listens. We're going to have to talk about pieces of things and how we're going to invent something with them. We're not going to give them something we've already done, we're going to create something unique and appropriate for this situation. Fortunately, Herb McGlaughlin from KMD is a master at interviews, at breaking down the "us" and the "them." I knew what I wanted to say, but I was pretty stiff. He just came in and sat down in the middle of all these people, took off his coat, loosened his tie and rolled up his sleeves, while I started to talk. I said, "One of the things about Herb that you'll find different from any other architect you're going to see today is that he's more interested in you than any of them are and he can prove it. He's done more post-occupancy evaluations—his firm is one of the few that has spent the money to document those experiences." Well, his presentation was very relaxed and informal, but he came across as genuinely interested in their unique desires and that carried the day. We did get the project, and we've had the chance to do other jobs up at U.C.S.D. since we developed a relationship during that process.

Throughout the entire process, there are ways to develop an association of trust. Listening with an empathetic ear is a big plus. I'm going to harp on this, probably because we still don't do it nearly well enough. Try to put yourself in the other person's shoes, understand the pressures he's under, and find out how you can impact his life in a positive way. It'll differ from one client to another. If you're dealing with a developer who is working with banks and is constantly leveraged to the hilt, he's going to have a whole set of pressures that are different from an institutional client like U.C.S.D., even though they both want to keep a project on time and on budget. It's important that we relate to them.

The reality on any job is that things are going to go wrong, if the project has any sophistication at all—and I think any architectural project is sophisticated by definition because there is so much going on in three dimensions. We can make a mistake—we do make mistakes—or something can happen to the team and the project. Somebody comes up with a moratorium, or the cost of a material suddenly becomes very high. A hundred different things can go wrong, but if we're in there talking to people and they understand that we're really trying, and if we get them involved in solving problems instead of doling out "Who's to blame this time," it really helps. Of course, with some clients, it's a waste of time—we never change their attitude—but most clients will get to "What can we do about it?" One of the things we try to do is to have some potential solutions in mind when we're presenting the problem.

Sometimes there are things we can do that are extra, that clients don't expect from an architect. This economy revolves around money, and if your client is, for example, Tri-City Hospital, they'll have fund raisers from time to time. You can help with those by providing graphics, a dance band, the wine, or what have you, or by just providing some "creative juices."

Another thing we're trying to do is become more aware of financial aspects of projects—what are the sources of capital, and what's happening with those sources. Sometimes we can introduce a client to a bonding company, or an investment or capital firm. I took a number of trips to New York, a lot of trips to Saudi Arabia and Kuwait, and identified people who were interested in investing, so from time to time we put people together. It's amazing how much clout we have when we can bring money to the table! The point here is that you need to find out what you can do to help a client solve his problems, and it goes beyond just design issues.

So again, communication is so critical. We can always do a better job. I think it helps just to be aware of it. It is important to have communication at various levels within any organization, both ours and theirs. We'll generally assign a project manager for each project, and it's that person's job to communicate on a day-to-day basis. Our firm is just too large to have everything flow through me, but I have to be careful not to allow a client to feel abandoned. This is an interesting management challenge. On one hand, we want to empower our people here, to give them the responsibility and authority to get a job done. On the other hand, the client wants to have some interaction with the key principals in the firm. Even though the project manager may be a stock-holder, the client realizes that he's not where the buck ultimately stops.

During one project, the employee who was assigned to be in charge came to me and said, "Do you realize that at every impor-tant meeting with the client, you're there. How am I ever going to get to the point where they believe in me? They feel like unless you bless it, it's never going to happen, and it's not going to be right." So I started backing away and let him truly take charge of the project, but I made a critical error. I didn't keep enough contact to make the client feel comfortable. This employee then decided to leave our firm and he took this client with him. I went to talk to the client and told him that we'd like to continue to work with him on this project and that we'd be happy to have the departing employee work with us as a consultant. The client said, "Why should I do that? As far as I'm concerned, this person *is* Austin Design Group. Where have you been?" We ended up losing that client.

So it's a balancing act, and I'm still learning. I need to have enough contact with the client to let him know where I am, keep track, make sure I understand his goals, even if it's just a phone call every once in a while to say, "What kind of job are we doing?" Of course, the level of involvement varies with different clients— for example, I find that foreign clients, especially, are very intent on working with "the boss." Institutional U.S. clients are more tolerant.

We've done a great deal of overseas work and we've learned that if you really want the business you have to be prepared to stay there, and be there for them. They're not interested in here today, gone tomorrow. If we stay there, we can get the work, but we have to be prepared to pay the price. It's expensive, because it's easy to make cultural, legal, and political mistakes. It's tough to get paid, so we have to be careful about that. We did one project that was a fantastic project, master planning the 280,000 acre island of Batam across from Singapore, but it took us probably a year to collect the last $100,000. We practically had to resort to extortion to get the money. These people are much better negotiators than Americans are. It's also even more relationship-oriented. In America you might hear, "Well, he's one of the good old boys, so he's getting the work." But it's nothing like it is overseas. Everybody out there is an influence peddler and is a cousin to somebody, but you have to be sure you connect with the right people.

The foreign clients we've met do like our expertise. One of the things we found is that they admire American architecture and American architects. I think they feel that American architects are the most creative designers in the world, which is an advantage from a business development standpoint. In some countries, such as Japan, we were also at an advantage because we were cheap. In Indonesia, on the other hand, we were very expensive. We were maybe five times as expensive as an Indonesian firm, so we really had to bring something of value. Most of the time we have to partner with an existing entity. One of the designers from our office, Tom Elliott, is in Indonesia full-time now. He's no longer working for us—he's on his own. The Indonesians are willing to pay a design principal, but they don't want our complete production staff because Indonesian architects can produce it so much cheaper than we can. While Tom's been over there, he's landed more work than he can handle. I hear he's not getting rich, but he's getting a lot of opportunities to create, which would be difficult in San Diego these days.

As far as client relations are concerned, I've already mentioned that foreign clients want to deal with the top principal. So, if you don't want to be there all the time yourself, you have to set somebody up who appears to be a principal. When we were working in Kuwait, I had somebody over there whom we had designated as the "President" of the firm. I was "Chairman." Well, our "President" got deathly ill and had to come home. I had to go over there for the charette, and then I had to keep going back. They couldn't believe the "Chairman" of the firm actually rolled up his sleeves and drew pictures. They liked that very much. It was interesting for me personally and it was an adventure, but we're much, much more selective now in what we'll do overseas. One of the main reasons is that it takes deep financial resources.

Another challenge of working with any client has to do with money, with trying to remain profitable. Everybody assumes, I think, that architects make more money than they actually do and have larger margins that they do. In reality, the margins are extremely thin. Even in the good times, the margins are thin because it's very competitive and we have to do so many projects at a fixed fee. Every architect I know complains that they don't make enough money, and they're right.

The other problem is that, unlike even an engineer, an architect doesn't know when he's done. It's art! We're never done! It almost seems that, as an architect, the better you are the less likely you are to stop when you hit your budget. You keep going because you want to make it better and better, and what's driving you isn't the money: it's doing something you're proud of, doing a good job. Then when things get tough, most architects find it difficult to be as ruthless as they should be. We're eternal optimists, we don't want to let go of staff as quickly as we should, and any reserves that we have go quickly. I'd say that if we could make 10 percent on every project, we would be very happy. In reality, we probably make 20–30 percent on some projects and lose 20–30 percent on others, and come out with an average of about 5.8 percent, if we're having a decent year. That doesn't leave much room for surprises.

As I said, our firm does a wide range of projects. We consciously set out, right from the beginning, to avoid becoming "niche" architects. In some ways, that has been a good business decision and in other ways a bad decision. It's bad because we are always learning on the job, every time we take on a new project. That's expensive and reduces our profits. Also, in today's market, many people become specialists and it's difficult for us to compete with firms who say, "This is our specialty—this is all we do." From a business standpoint, if one's in the right niche, that's great, but it can be risky. So we have been diverse, which means that we're less likely to get taken out by one shift in the marketplace, but it's always going to be with thinner margins and we have to hustle a little bit more.

Another reason we got hurt during the recession is that a number of our private clients, as well as our institutional ones, went bankrupt and left us holding the bag. When we're piling through a project at $40,000 to $50,000 a month, and all of a sudden the client is 60 days behind on his bills, we can lose a pretty good chunk of money very quickly. Then if the client goes bankrupt, it's a loss. We had a very wealthy client—he was a billionaire—and yet he left us high and dry for $280,000. These days we're trying to be more careful, and not just assume that the client can pay his bills. Even though our direct cost may not be the $280,000 that we're owed, if we knew then what we know now, we'd have tightened our belt earlier, and we would be in a much better position today.

In terms of trying to differentiate our firm in the eyes of potential clients, I'd say that the charette process is one way that we do that. This process is still unique enough that clients are impressed by the fact that we want them involved in the design and decision-making process all along the way. Another way to make our team distinct is by getting together with other experts, such as architects and consultants. We're also "teaming" with contractors, clients, and so on, up front, to try to avoid getting into destructive adversarial situations, where everybody's pointing the finger at everybody else and trying to cover their own fannies.

We work with a lot of contractors early on in projects because we feel that they bring something to the table—a focus on cost— that the architect really has a hard time providing. Contractors are constantly faced with what's happening with materials and manpower—the cost of wood versus the cost of metals, what is easy to get and what takes a long lead time, as well as the cost of various processes (this is where the big cost decisions are made). It's awfully embarrassing, not to mention expensive, to have to go back, after the working drawings are half or fully done, and say, "Gee, we really blew it. We should have looked at a totally different structural system."

We've heard that facility management services are a growing method to attract new clients or keep clients coming back. We haven't gotten involved in this like some firms have. However, we do offer a complete spectrum of design services, which includes tenant improvements, interior design, structural and civil engineering, landscape architecture, and so forth, so it shouldn't be hard to do it. For example, we have all the information on the complex in which our office is housed on CAD, and if someone wants to do something here they are likely to come to us. We're finishing a relatively significant space planning job for a tenant who's moving into 150,000 square feet here. So, I guess this might be considered, in essence, facilities management.

One of the things we're looking at right now is the possibility of partnering with a local company that provides information about comparative real estate prices to appraisers and brokers. They found an architectural firm in New York City that has detailed information about most of the buildings there on CAD, and they sell the information to brokers looking at buildings on behalf of clients. The president of the local company is interested in expanding its services, and has approached us. Because they're already set up to sell information, we probably would just provide CAD services and share in the profits.

Right now we're constantly looking for new opportunities to provide space planning and interior design services when companies expand in existing facilities or move from one building to another. If we now become known as a repository of existing information, the brokers in town are going to think of us every time they have a client moving from one space to another. At present, we see a potential in San Diego for increased business in tenant improvements. Eventually, as space gets gobbled up, which is finally beginning to happen again, we can do new buildings and build-to-suits. Because clients may look at their alternatives with us and ultimately decide that a build-to-suit is the way to go.

One thing we believe is that good design doesn't always cost more to build. We have examples of projects that have life in them, that have elements that go beyond just putting up four walls, that have a sense of spirit, and yet they were done within a given budget, within a set of economic parameters. I love to tell the story about a client who came to me and said, "Don't even think about trying to win an award on this project—I'm not sure you're even going to want this project. This building is going to rent for one reason and one reason only—because it's cheap." I said, "Really—so it doesn't matter what it looks like?" He said, "Right." I said, "Very interesting—so, in other words, I can do anything I want, as long as I hit your budget and your basic parameters?" He kind of rolled his eyes, and I said I'd be very interested in taking on this project. For me it became a real challenge: a budget of $12.50 per square foot to enclose about 120,000 square feet in three or four buildings. This was to be what is called an "incubator" industrial building. Somebody who's building skateboards or widgets, or whatever, moves into 1,500 square feet of space because it's cheap and he or she just wants to get the business started.

When this project was finished, it got published, it was on the La Jolla Museum of Contemporary Art tour, and it did get recognition in a design award program. We told the jury the developer story in cartoons when we presented it, because at the time—this was the early 80's—we felt like we were getting handed all these tough design problems with low budgets. I think the jurors understood what we were up against. It also helped change what happened to similar buildings in the future. Up to that time, every tilt-up down here was basically a big box with a racing stripe around it. We started taking the pieces and pulling them apart, using pattern more dramatically and changing some of the forms. We found that there were a number of things that we could do to make that project more exciting, more fun, have a sense of spirit and add a little dignity to the lives of people who were going to work there. We heard other architects say, "How did they get away with that?" But the buildings leased up very quickly. Now, it may have been that they only leased because they were cheap, but we think that they leased even faster because of the design.

I have to admit that I wish I had a stronger database to prove that point. We can say, "Well, we feel confident that a contented cow gives more milk," and there are examples such as the Levi Strauss building. I heard that they did a study showing that sick days and absenteeism went down and that they had a more productive work force, but if somebody asked me the percentages, I couldn't quote them. With companies who are contemplating a build-to-suit, we have to be a little more sophisticated about how we convince them to spend more money on the physical environment so that their people will be more productive. The principle is a little easier when your client is doing leased space—if your buildings are leasing faster, you can show that good design sells. You can demonstrate that if you provide a better mousetrap, or something, you do true value engineering.

One thing we do sell is true value engineering. We say that a lot of contractors say they do value engineering, but they don't. They do cost cutting. They'll tell you how to save money but they won't tell you how to add more value for the same money. They won't give you those innovative ideas that show you how to push the limits. I tell a story about the first house I did when we went out on our own. There were two identical one-acre lots, next door to one another. Our house was 2,850 square feet and I think the house next door was a little over 3,000. They spent about $110,000 to build that house and we spent $100,000. Those houses ended up selling 45 days apart—the house next door sold for $265,000 and the house we did sold for $415,000. Our house got published; it won an award; and it made the client more money. That man is still our client today, and this was eighteen years ago. I tell that story a lot—about the synergy of putting three-dimensional pieces together and how you make a difference.

As far as value engineering is concerned, we did several things that made a difference. We kept the house very simple, but there were times when we told the client to spend more money. In those days, wood houses were a hot item. It was right after Sea Ranch and everybody wanted a wood house, but most people were using tight-knot cedar. Now that's the finish material that everybody's going to see, when you put it on the ceiling or the outside of the house. We suggested that the client use clear, all-heart redwood, even though it cost twice as much as cedar. For the amount of board feet involved—about 5,000—he was going to spend $5,000 more to make the house look and feel totally different. We also used fewer walls to divide space, which made the house feel bigger than the one next door, even though it was actually smaller. We used levels, we had a spine running down the middle of the house where light came in, and we had a tree right in the middle of the house. People assigned a value to this house that was far higher than what we spent, because we put the money in the right places.

Every once in a while we get a corporate client who's sensitive to the value of good design. One company, Elgar, had chosen to have a building built for them by a developer, to house the corporate headquarters, their research department, and some manufacturing. The developer came to us and said, "Look, I'm taking you to the meeting with me because you're not going to believe what these people want, and I don't want you to think I'm just jamming this down your throat." So I went with him and discovered that they wanted to be moved in and operating by July 5, and this was December 1. This was an 87,000 square foot project with a budget of $15 a square foot for the raw shell. Now, that didn't include the site or interiors, but that's still a very, very tight budget. After the meeting, the developer asked if I wanted to do it, and I said, "Do you know what this means? This means we'd have to get this building in to the Building Department by January 15 to have any hope at all. We'd have to grease all the skids at the department to get this thing out and you'd have to start construction before you have a permit. You're going to have to take some risks and work it out with the title company, and you're going to have to find a contractor who's willing to work night and day to get this thing built that quickly. But do you know how many decisions will need to be made? We're going to have to live with this client."

Well, we signed a contract with the client on December 7 and the CEO came to meet with us. He brought a picture of the

U.C.S.D. Library that Perreira did—have you ever seen that building? Probably $200 a square foot and would take two years to build, or at least fifteen to eighteen months. He said, "This is what I'd like," and he was dead serious. We did exactly what you're doing—we burst out laughing. He looked at us like, "What did I say that was so funny?" We said, "Do you know what the budget for this building was? Do you know what the time frame was? Look, we admire the fact that you want a good building—this is a dynamic building. Why do you want this building?" He said, "Because I want a building that doesn't look like every other tilt-up out there. Our most important asset is our employees and we want a building that is going to make them feel special. We want a place where they can live while they're earning money. I want a building so good, not only are people proud of it, we want it to be published, we want it to win awards."

We told him that we could probably do that on his budget, but that it wouldn't be the U.C.S.D. Library. We warned him that he'd have to be very open-minded and consider possibilities he might not have thought about, which might push the barriers a little bit. He said, "Great" and added one more comment. "My wife is really interested in interior design. Would you have a problem if she worked with you on this team?" We looked at each other and thought, "Boy, who set this up? Is somebody filming this?" and said, "Sure. Why not?"

It turned out that this client was very open-minded and his wife turned out to be a real asset. She was in there as part of the design team and she understood what we were going through. She helped sell some of the innovative features such as bold use of color, shifting the building elements around, and creating a great sense of entry. In addition, several of their key people were in our office practically all the time, making decisions. It was a great effort, and we did get it built on time. It was published in three magazines, it won an A.I.A. Honor award and building industry honor award. Elgar was happy—they have offices all over the globe and they still talk about this one. It would be hard to measure how it's produced in terms of productivity, but they're still happy with the building and the developer made a profit— happy story.

I find that most clients respond better when they sense that we're passionate about what we're doing, which also helps to sell a good design. Right now we're designing an outlet center, which is going into a California desert town. Once again, this project has a tight budget. Our project manager was talking about doing this or that because he thought the client would like it. I said, "You know what? I think the client will like it if *we* really like it, and so I think we've got to go in there and have some guts. We've pushed our budget as hard as we can on this thing. If we go any further, they're not going to be able to lease the place and they know that. They have to understand that they can't have the little Mexican village they'd like to have because it would cost 25–30 percent more to do that right, which means we'd be forced to do it wrong. But they can have bold, strong, simple design that is well suited to the desert and still within their budget." We were able to sell the idea and they got excited about it because we had passion for it. So we've got to remember that we can sell good design. Sometimes we get too timid and the client will sense that we don't really believe in it. He'll say, "This guy's not sold on it—why should I be sold on it?"

What do I do to stay up on management ideas? From time to time I'll read books, but more often I read periodicals. I've also belonged to a couple of organizations that have been very valuable. One was called TEC, The Executive Committee, which was made up of top executives from businesses doing at least $2 million of work a year. It had a wide range of members—not just architects but all types of executives—and it met for one day a month. The first four hours we'd have an educational resource—some person would come in and talk to us on topics ranging from "Managing Chaos," which involved getting the most out of diverse groups, to "Modelnetics," which was like a communications software idea for management. We actually hired the guy from Modelnetics to come and talk to our company about the things that face us as managers, techniques to use in certain situations, and things to watch out for. The second four hours of the TEC meetings, we'd just talk to each other about our individual business problems or opportunities.

The other organization that has been great for our business and for me personally is Young Presidents Organization, or YPO. It's a potent group because all members must be president of a company with at least 50 employees, billing a minimum of $5 million a year, and have reached the position of president prior to turning 40 years old. YPO's motto is "Better Presidents Through Idea Exchange," and it presents forums and places for you to exchange ideas with other managers, presidents, and entrepreneurs. It's an international organization and resources are brought in from all over the world. My stint as chairman and education chairman for the San Diego Chapter gave me an opportunity to travel to meetings as far away as Santiago, Chile, which was fascinating.

YPO concentrates not just on business, but on the total person. Any president of a sizable organization is going to be isolated. They can't really be friends with their employees—it just doesn't happen. They can be friendly but they're not going to share their deep, dark secrets. We spend so much time at work it is hard to develop other close relationships. YPO forces us into situations where we become close to people who share a lot of the same problems. There are people from different kinds of businesses—I'm the only architect, which has been a real advantage from a business development standpoint. I'd say that probably even in a bad year, we get in excess of a million dollars in fees because of that association. YPO also suggests books and present resources. Ken Blanchard, who wrote *The One-Minute Manager*, has been an honorary member of the Las Californias Chapter, and he acts as a resource for us all the time. The YPO network has been fantastic. It provides access that we just wouldn't have if we were out there duking it out on our own.

We've also spent a lot of money over the years on business consultants. I would say, in retrospect, that I wish we had chosen people who were closer to our profession. Our profession is so unique that if I were going to hire an outside consultant now, I'd want it to be somebody who really focuses on architects. At first I though it was good just to get a sort of "broad brush" of what management is about—get the principles and try to apply them. But now I'd like to have specific formulas. Hey, if something works, I want to know about it.

My involvement in the A.I.A. has also been helpful in a lot of ways. I must admit, even at the national level, many meetings were intensely boring, but every once in awhile gems would come out that would make it all worthwhile. I found the research for "Vision 2000" to be fascinating. Another time an A.I.A. resident fellow came in and talked to us about the research he did for his book, *In Search of Design Excellence;* that was also great! It was also very interesting to follow the design team that redesigned the graphics for the A.I.A. The Gold Medal presentations were perhaps my favorite. They gave me an education on some of the best in our profession, people with really distinguished careers. Often I learned more from the people who didn't win than from those who did. The A.I.A. also was an opportunity to network within our profession. It was nice to be in a situation where we could forget about competing and really get to know each other. A guy from Iowa is not as worried about revealing trade secrets, so I could find out what kind of problems he's had and how he handled them.

One thing I wanted to talk about here is that, as a company, we've had lots of "retreats" where we talk about where we're headed, what markets we want to go after, and so on. We constantly have this debate about, "Do we want to specialize?" But one of the things that always comes up is that we need to train our people better. They're just sort of learning on the job. We've tried to have outside resources come in, and we have developed some manuals, but they're not systematic enough. So one of our big concerns is ongoing education—we talk about it and we want to do it, but we never find out how to really do it, how to integrate it, and how to find the time and the money. This is definitely a role that the universities could play.

Scripps Clinic—Carmel Mountain Ranch, San Diego County, California.

Scripps Clinic—interior.

Sporting Club—
Lakeshore Towers,
Irvine, California.

Sporting Club—interior.

"Julian Retreat"—private residence, Julian, California.

Upper Deck Company, Carlsbad, California.

Arjons Plaza—Research and Development Park, San Diego, California.

Elgar Corporation, San Diego, California.

Method No. 7
Decision Support Systems

The themes of this book—leadership, strategy, client relations, working with clients, quality of life, knowledge development, and value, performance, and image—in combination with the associated methods of critical thinking, thorough analysis, client assessment strategy, the Knowledge Base System, field studies, research techniques, and decision support systems, focus on what makes a firm competitive and esteemed by clients. The most salient characteristic of the insights and methods developed are their flexibility and responsiveness to new endeavors and enterprises. Because the application of the material contained in this book will vary as much as the spectrum of possible client situations and services, we need some anchor points for decision making and work in progress. To this end, we present first a scenario referred to as the "open entry, open exit" project and then outline how we might work in this context. Next, we use the project to illustrate Decisions Support Softwares' decision-making aid, Expert Choice. Expert Choice is a device for establishing weighted criteria and assessing the relevant importance of objective and subjective factors in the deliberative process. Finally, we discuss the utility of relational database programs, an exacting and efficient means for project history retention and retrieval.

"Open Entry, Open Exit" Project Scenario

For purposes of this discussion, let's suppose that an electronic manufacturing corporation in Hsinchu Science Industrial Park, Taiwan, is investing in advanced memory chip applications associated with an attempt to markedly increase the features, quality, and reliability of their product line. The success of this enterprise depends on the availability of technicians with many advanced skills. For a time, the corporation trained its own people; however, the complexity of new manufacturing processes is now placing demands on the corporation's in-house training program that cannot be met without a significant improvement in their education and technical training programs. The demand is great. It takes a total of 1,700 hours to move a new employee through the three training stages: Technician Levels I, II, and III. Corporate officials decide to discuss their situation with a local Junior College of Technology. They find that the present curriculum is too basic for their needs and designed for students able to attend regularly scheduled classes. The inflexibility of class schedules does not meet the needs of a corporation that uses shift changes and overtime to achieve manufacturing objectives. Another aspect of this problem is that when the corporation's technicians attend scheduled classes that take them out of the work setting, their place in the manufacturing process must be filled by someone else. This means a possible decrease in productivity, and involves paying the replacement as well as the student, which doubles training expenditures. The corporation needs a flexible educational opportunity that accommodates the variable schedules of their manufacturing personnel. This need is so great that they offer to build a new facility for the junior college in return for the development of a more advanced and accommodating program.

The college administration and faculty suggest an "open entry, open exit" program as a solution. They say it is possible to develop and maintain an educational setting that is open 24 hours a day year round, with the exception of national holidays and the last day of each month (for maintenance). Relying on a combination of programmed learning, which permits self-instruction, and faculty supervision, a flexible and yet economical program can be established. According to their concept, all the required educational materials will be crafted for a computer-student interactive setting. Students can come in at any time, work on educational assignments, and leave any time they wish. Students can be on the job when required and pursue their studies in the computer-student interactive setting during nonworking hours. It is also noted that, with the appropriate technology, distance learning could provide for study at the corporation's facilities. The college suggests both undertakings.

Within this project concept, the task of the building industry professional is to develop the new facility and the distance learning capability. As you might anticipate, the building design team will include college administrators and faculty, corporation managers and engineers, and the technical workforce. Each of these stakeholders will have his own preconceptions, some personal and some related to the corporation's objectives. Each group will have ideas about the design of the building, the interior architectural spaces, workstation and telecommunication features, and required amenities. As one stakeholder group expresses its expectations and requirements and design suggestions, the other groups will learn more about the total situation and reform their own ideas as a result. Building design professionals will work with the stakeholders to discover the unique requirements of this project. Equipment and furnishing designers and manufacturers will contribute their expertise. Government representatives from the Ministry of Education will support the project. Success in this venture may lead to new national education strategies. High school administrators and faculty may wish to participate, as they see this as a means for accelerating and enriching the educational opportunities for selected students. Certainly, other corporations facing similar needs will want to become sponsors of this project. In a short time a national showcase will have been created.

Two Faulty Scenarios

Now let's examine this project from the standpoint of two scenarios that characterize situations that are not uncommon. The "open entry, open exit" project begins with an empty room and a blank blackboard. The first person to enter is an architect. What can he or she do? Given the project concept statement, the architectural professional can go to the blackboard and conceptualize the whole building. What would be the significance of this accomplishment? Very little. It expresses only a single point of view, where many are required. A second designer enters the room and helps sketch the interior architectural spaces. What has been achieved? Again, very little. These two professionals are relying on their professional training and experience without the knowledge and experience of those most familiar with what is needed. Let's have the client enter the room. He sees the schematic design presented on the blackboard, derived by a process invisible to him. Since he cannot understand what has been achieved, he rejects the proposal or, even worse, pretends enthusiasm without the intent of approving the concept. The two professional designers, not recognizing that the client's intention is to help them save face, begin to ask a series of questions about the client's requirements. As information is placed on the blackboard, the initial work of the design professionals is revised to reflect what they have learned from the client.

As a reflection of only three points of view, the design solution is still very remote from the full complexity of what is needed. The final product will be only the most meager type of building. Facility users occupying the building will find that nothing has been customized for them. Nothing has been perfected in terms of what is needed to support their activities. Certainly, there is no indication that any of their preferences have been considered in the design process. They conclude that it would have been better to buy an existing building, even if it met very few requirements, and create their own space features. This would mean discarding all of the expertise and experience of building design professionals who can assure that what is developed realizes the full potential of the capital facility investment.

A different scenario might be that the entire building design team enters the room together to work on the "open entry, open exit" project. Each takes a portion of the blackboard and begins to work toward a final problem solution. In this situation, there will be a lot of shoving and fighting for room to work. There will be no central focus. Professionals and stakeholders will go off in many directions. The result will be a blackboard full of ideas, without any synthesis or justification. In this case, there is no reliable outcome. Some of the people will then be asked to leave the room until candidate project concepts and design schemes, forms, and features have been developed. When they return, they study what is proposed. Since the process of deliberation is not visible to them, they question everything. They begin to revise, alter, amend, and redirect what was developed. The result is chaos, with no product. Finally, the team gives up and two or three people are given the responsibility for completing the project.

A More Promising Scenario

Whether acted out in a few days or over several weeks, the appalling aspect of the two faulty scenarios is that they exaggerate only slightly what are common experiences. The best that can be said is that when the work is finished an adequate and reasonably attractive building has been produced. In fact, this is a common description of new buildings—adequate and reasonably attractive. Our decision-making strategy needs to achieve so much more on behalf of the client. First, we do want a room full of ideas, but without the chaos. Second, we want to develop a building design and land development team that works efficiently and with a sense of cooperation, collaboration, and shared responsibility for project success. Third, we want a visible process, where all team members can see the whole deliberation sequence unfold. The following is the strategy we recommend for the "open entry, open exit" project.

SELECT THE BUILDING DESIGN AND LAND DEVELOPMENT TEAM

You received the "open entry, open exit" project contract, in the first place, because your Taiwanese clients saw that you were prepared to work with them with a sense of collaboration and cooperation in the context of what this means in Taiwan. Now you expand the team to assure that all perspectives are represented in deliberations. Appropriate team members are selected. Once assembled, the team is asked to suggest additional members who may have been overlooked. This is the way the executive architect works: take considered action and then ask for critique.

REVIEW THE KNOWLEDGE BASE SYSTEM

The team is now ready to investigate the elements of the Knowledge Base System. There is no doubt that it is best to let team members select the Knowledge Base System question items in which they have an interest. Some members will wish to deal with the full scope of sections 2.0 Facility Life Characteristics and 5.0 Critical Circulation Patterns, and some will give in-depth attention to 6.0 Interior Architectural Spaces. Others will move directly on to sections 9.0 Facility Space Arrangements and 10.0 Facility Design Image, while some will begin to consider 11.0 Facility Site Plan. When more than one member selects a question item, a collaborative effort is assured.

TEAM MEETING AGENDA

As results are reviewed, there should be two types of team gatherings: formal and informal. While formal agenda are set for project milestones, informal meetings should be the rule. Team members must share their data, information, and situation interpretations on the most frequent basis possible. Dialogue, critique, and experimentation with concepts and ideas will keep the process productive. From preliminary discussions to facility occupancy and beyond, the team will remain intact.

What is undertaken has all the dynamics of a game of chess. Like chess pieces, the team members will have different roles and capabilities. The scope of work has opening, middle, and end steps. Many strategies and methods are applied, yet the end game is always in mind. As in any process in which events follow events and information accumulates, you must be prepared to alter your strategy as new problems and opportunities arise. When you consider the history of the game of chess you see a steady development of strategic innovations. Games are now being won with new concepts. Unlike chess, however, our scope of work can accept no stalemates. The expectations of the client must be met in all their complexity.

A FAST-PACED ACTIVITY

This scope of work puts the full experience and expertise of the team into play. As the application process is a fast-paced activity, the team does not hesitate to develop an initial description of the facility. The safeguard is to make sure you consider this as an hypothesis, to be confirmed, disconfirmed, and modified as the team's deliberations continue. It is expected that team members will suggest as many facility design concepts, schemes, forms, or features as they feel are promising. This is an extremely important point. Team members may at any time suggest a concept for the project or even a candidate preliminary design for the whole facility. People with experience and expertise need not be led by research findings or asked to follow some linear, step-by-step trail. The necessary safeguard, of course, is the discipline of critique; that is, never accept recommendations without justification in terms of value, performance, and image. There will be many points where we will synthesize research findings and design recommendations. The underlying goal is the strategic question: Does every member of the team have a complete image of the facility and how things will work within and around the facility?

Decision Support System: Expert Choice

The value of clearly stated criteria and the application of these are important aspects of the deliberations associated with a project such as the "open entry, open exit" one. In deliberations regarding building value, performance, and image, it will be necessary to specify the criteria that will be used to select design alternatives, weigh the relative importance of criteria, and then systematically apply these to the decisions at hand. Within the context of the "open entry, open exit" project, we will demonstrate how a decision support system facilitates this process. It is not our intention to conduct a training session. Information regarding this system, Expert Choice, and Thomas L. Saaty's (1980) theoretical construct for this application program can be obtained from Decision Support Software, Inc. The goal is to encourage you to review the decision support systems on the market to find what will work for you.

To begin, let's recognize that the "open entry, open exit" project has many stakeholders: technicians concerned with their education and training experience and the setting in which it takes place, faculty responsible for program success, and executives who are protecting their corporation's investment. Each will bring to the project many expectations and requirements, some tangible and some intangible. Likewise, the professionals associated with the project will recognize certain tangible areas of deliberation having to do with building performance and the costs associated with candidate design elements and, simultaneously, need to consider the intangibles associated with building image. Expert Choice is our tool for dealing with these questions: What weight do you give to tangible considerations versus intangible considerations? Can such disparate factors be combined to form one decision? How do you account for the perceived differences in the relative importance of design alternatives? Can a synthesis be developed that accounts for all the factors involved in such a complex deliberation? The decision support system, Expert Choice, provides a positive answer for each of these questions. Here it will be applied to selecting a single facility concept, to site selection, and to a cost/benefit analysis.

Selecting a Facility Concept

For our study vehicle, let's say that there are three alternative concepts for the facility on the table, along with additional concerns for site selection and the possibility of adding additional open-use classrooms and an auditorium. These possibilities were created as the initial focus of the building design and land development team, and reflect preliminary discussions between team members.

The three alternate facility concepts are:

1. Design the facility as one open, two-story space for student workstations, surrounded at the second level by a ring of faculty offices and individual and group study rooms.
2. Design the facility as three separate modules dedicated to the three phases of the instructional program—Technician Levels I, II, and III.
3. Design the facility as three separate, flexible modules generically designed to accommodate any training program.

How do we make the choice? The selection problem is complex, involving the personal and professional views of the entire team. As we undertake this selection, we are aware of the inefficiencies dramatized in the two faulty scenarios. We can avoid most of these problems with our decision support system. Having undertaken a complete Expert Choice application, the relative merits of Alternatives 1, 2, and 3, as shown in Figure 8.1, were derived by a process that identifies decision-making criteria, sets weights for all criteria and subcriteria, and applies these to the three alternatives.

What has actually transpired to produce the conclusion set forth in Figure 8.1? What reliance can we place on these numbers? How was the deliberation conducted? Let's examine the process. Within Expert Choice, we specify selection criteria, determine the relative importance of each, and then apply the weighted criteria to the three facility alternatives. The selection criteria are identified as the encompassing criteria and associated subcriteria. Figure 8.2 shows the encompassing criteria and subcriteria arranged as a hierarchy, a decision-making tree.

Now where do we go? The fundamental rubric of Expert Choice is forced-choice, paired-comparisons or, as called by the program authors, pairwise comparisons. To illustrate this, let's consider the three basic criteria: Building Value, Building Performance, and Building Image. Is each an equally important criteria? If not, we must determine relative importance. Here is

Alternative 1: An open, two-story facility	(0.227)
Alternative 2: A three-module dedicated facility	(0.357)
Alternative 3: A three-module flexible facility.	(0.416)
Total	1.000

Figure 8.1. Relative merits of alternatives.

```
First Level:  Encompassing Criteria
    Second Level:  Selection Subcriteria
        Third Level:  Subcriteria

Building Value
    Conceptual Estimates
        Alternative 1:  An open, two-story facility
        Alternative 2:  A three-module dedicated facility
        Alternative 3:  A three-module flexible facility.
    Staffing Costs
    Occupancy Costs
Building Performance
    Quality of Life
        Students
        Faculty
        Special events
    Workstation Features
    Synergy with other Education and Training Programs
    Expansion Potential
    Replication Potential
    Security
Building Image
    Impact
        Students
        Client Corporation
        Community
    Design Quality
        Exterior Schemes
        Interior Schemes
```

Figure 8.2. Decision-making tree.

the task presented in the Expert Choice application. To cover the three possible pairwise questions, the program asks you to answer the following preliminary questions:

Is Building Cost more important than Building Performance?

Is Building Cost more important than Building Image?

Is Building Performance more important than Building Image?

Further, when making these judgments, the team is asked to state, if more important, how much more important utilizing a nine-point verbal scale. Figure 8.3 contains the results obtained as the team answered the questions automatically posed by Expert Choice. These can be derived as the arithmetic mean of individual assessments or as a group deciding where on the judgment scale

Building Value	**(0.410)**
Building Performance	**(0.327)**
Building Image	**(0.263)**

Figure 8.3. Weights for encompassing criteria.

the appropriate value lies. The relative importance, as depicted in Figure 8.3, indicates the relative weights for each of the three encompassing criteria.

Now, let's illustrate how the weights for subcriteria are derived. Under Building Value within the decision-making tree, we have established these subcriteria: Conceptual Estimates, Staffing Costs, and Occupancy Costs. Figure 8.4 shows the results obtained by the team, which as a group answered the pairwise questions posed by Expert Choice. The relative importance of Conceptual Estimates, Staffing Costs, and Occupancy Costs was derived. Under Conceptual Estimates is another level, which contains the estimates for the three alternatives. Pairwise questioning was applied to examine the willingness of the group to accept the cost implications of their alternatives.

The final step in the Expert Choice application, once the weights for all criteria and subcriteria have been derived, is to make pairwise comparisons in the context of these weighted criteria in terms of the three alternatives. This was the procedure used to derive the final results depicted in Figure 8.1.

The derived weight for the Building Value encompassing criterion is 0.410 (Figure 8.3). This weight is now used as the basis for determining the weights for the subcriteria of this category in the decision-making tree.

Building Value	**(0.410)**
Conceptual Estimates	(0.200)
Alternative 1: An open, two-story facility	(0.040)
Alternative 2: A three-module dedicated facility	(0.055)
Alternative 3: A three-module flexible facility	(0.105)
Staffing Costs	(0.098)
Occupancy Costs	(0.102)
Total	**(0.410)**

Figure 8.4. Weights for subcriteria.

Site Selection

Now that you are developing a sense of the value of decision support systems, we can proceed through this exercise more briefly. The team needs to pick a site for the "open entry, open exit" facility. There are four candidate sites: Roosevelt Road, Hsinghai Road, Wuchuan Road, and a location at the sponsor's manufacturing facility. The selection criteria are Land Value, Value as an Investment, Proximity to Corporate Manufacturing Facility, Proximity to Other Corporations, Distance from Junior College of Technology, Access to Public Transportation, and Quality of Surrounding Neighborhood. Figure 8.5 outlines the application.

Cost/Benefit Analysis

Some project participants wish to add open-use classrooms and an auditorium to the facility. They feel that adding two classrooms with seating for approximately 50 students each and an audito-

---

The goal is to select the site for the "open entry, open exit" facility.

SELECTION CRITERIA AND DERIVED WEIGHTS

Land Value . . . . (0.235)

Value as an Investment . . . . (0.082)

Proximity to Corporate Manufacturing Facility . . . . (0.270)

Proximity to Other Corporations . . . . (0.048)

Distance from Junior College of Technology. . . . . (0.200)

Access to Public Transportation . . . . (0.075)

Quality of Surrounding Neighborhood . . . . (0.090)

RESULTS
When each alternative is evaluated in the context of the established criteria and derived weights the results are:

Candidate site 1: Roosevelt Road . . . . (0.109)

Candidate site 2: Hsinghai Road . . . . (0.385)

Candidate site 3: Wuchuan Road . . . . (0.338)

Candidate site 4: Sponsor's manufacturing facility . . . . (0.168)

These findings indicate that there are two highly acceptable sites, Candidate site 2: Hsinghai Road and Candidate site 3: Wuchuan Road.

Figure 8.5. Site selection for the "open entry, open exit" facility.

rium for 200 people would have great potential. Let's carry out a cost/benefit analysis. The three alternatives considered are: a two-classroom addition, an addition with classrooms and an auditorium, and no addition. First we will assess cost and benefits separately and then conduct the analysis. The process is outlined in Figure 8.6.

COST ANALYSIS
    Economic
        Capital Requirements
        Operating Costs
        Revenue Producing Potential
        Resale Value
    Construction Administration
        Project Delay
        Increased Design Complexity

BENEFIT ANALYSIS
    Educational Advantage
        To Basic Program
        To Sponsor
        To Junior College of Technology
        To Co-sponsors
    Future
        Provides for Basic Program Expansion
        Conference Support
    Social
        Disruption of Basic Program
        Advantage to Community

RESULTS
    Following the Expert Choice application procedure we find that the result of the Cost Analysis is:
        Classrooms . . . . (0.57)
        Classrooms and Auditorium . . . . (0.36)
        No Addition. . . . . (0.07)
    For the Benefit Analysis the result is:
        Classrooms . . . . (0.36)
        Classrooms and Auditorium . . . . (0.58)
        No Addition . . . . (0.05)
    After these analyses, we multiply costs by benefits for each alternative. The results are:
        Two Classroom Addition . . . . (0.57/0.36 = 1.58)
        Two Classroom and Auditorium Addition . . (0.36/0.58 = 0.62)
        No Addition . . . . (0.07/0.05 = 0.01)
The best choice is the Two Classroom Addition.

Figure 8.6. Cost/benefit analysis.

Defining Quality of Life

One additional illustration is the possible utility of a decision support system for deriving stakeholder preferences. Consider the challenge of carrying out a major development project without community support. This is a very common situation. There are political, governmental, business, neighborhood, environmental, grassroots, and individual interests in such developments. How people perceive the impact of the project places us in the world of perception rather than fact. Say all you want, be as analytical as you wish, provide all the numerical and statistical analyses you can, and you will still face the intangibles of preference and apprehension. Before investing in a strategy for persuasion, first discover the preferences that exist and how strongly people feel about these. Then you can form data, information, and project promotion into a targeted effort. We would recommend the application of a decision support system like Expert Choice.

Decision Support System: Relational Database

Consider the amount of data and information that will accrue during our work on the "open entry, open exit" project. Where will this all reside? On note paper, sketch pads, summary reports, in the minds of project participants or, at best, in word processing files. What does this mean for quick access to data, information, and analyses? What does this mean for project history retention and the potential use of this information in the future? With this hodgepodge, we will certainly not be able to immediately apply what we know to any deliberation at hand. If your guiding vision is "fast and simple," the most promising solution is relational database support. Are the advantages of creating and maintaining a relational database worth the man-hour expenditures? Yes. Knowledge developed for one project must be available for use on another project. If we invest in a relational database, what we have learned will never be lost and will always be at our fingertips—on the road or in the office.

We have in mind Borland International Inc.'s relational database program, Paradox for Windows, and their high-performance Windows development tool Delphi. The utility of these programs is proven. The first program, Paradox for Windows, is used to create and manage your project archives. The second program, Delphi, is for those people in your firm with programming skills.

Let them develop a program with data and information of value to your clients. For example, Robin Goodman (1996), while transforming the Malcolm Baldrige Award Criteria into a client assessment knowledge system, furthered her argument by employing Delphi to develop an application program that demonstrated the scope and utility of her knowledge system.

In Chapter 5, it was noted that the 12 sections of the Knowledge Base System and the 54 question items are mutually exclusive information categories that are "addresses" uniquely named and numerically indexed to provide for the precise ordering and storing of data and information. This was done with the expectation that Knowledge Base System applications would be stored as a relational database. This technology is a significant advance in database efficiency. Formerly, a database was dedicated to serve specific information requirements formatted in a fixed prescription. When information needs changed, it was necessary to revise the database. Now, within the relational database logic, we can reformat and add information fields to the parent database at will.

The parent database (Figure 8.7) reflects a possible starting point for the creation of your database. The terms shown are rather formal. By all means, personalize your relational database fields.

CATEGORY ONE: PROJECT IDENTIFICATION INFORMATION

The following fields illustrate the type of scheme needed for information storage and retrieval. Add-on statements, such as "[Char (100)]," indicate the maximum number of characters allowed in a field. You specify how much space you need.

Date (M/D/Y)
This is always an essential reference point.

Project Name [Char (100)]
Here we could use a client's name.

Project Number [Number (5)]
Numbers are efficient for retrieval and can be used uniquely.

Building Type [Char (100)]
This is a basic reference.

Report Name [Char (200)]
Report I.D. Number [Number (5)]
Author [Char (100)]
These three fields provide a way to place under a project reference number all the reports associated with the project that are available in the database, and the author's name.

Reference I.D. Number [Number (3)]
Reference [Word processing file name]
These two fields are used to indicate reference materials that pertain to the project. These might be marketing studies, conceptual estimates, and so forth.

CATEGORY TWO: KNOWLEDGE BASE SYSTEM APPLICATION

This is where we find the full utility of relational databases.

KBS Item Number [Number (5)]

The central information structure used here is the Knowledge Base System. With this field, you can query your relational database with simple questions: What is stored as "2.1"(Facility User Categories) using the project number for "high schools." The result will be 2.1 information for all high school projects.

Adapted Item [Char (1) A or empty]
New Item [Char (1) N or empty]

These two fields provide for adaptations to Knowledge Base System question items or newly created items.

Question Item Name [Char (100)]
Question Item [Char (240)]

You may wish to enter the entire Knowledge Base System so that you will have it to have on hand when developing a report.

Answer I.D. Number [Number (8)]

Space is provided here for question item number plus two digit extension to identify multiple answers to question items.

Answer [Char: (30)]

This field is used to link the relational database with what is residing at directory/program/file name. For instance, we might have a twenty-page report in C:\WINWORD\OSAKA2_1.DOC.

CATEGORY THREE: ANALYSIS AND ISSUES

Reports of deliberations and analyses are associated with every project. The scheme explanations noted in the preceding section apply here.

Analysis Title [Char (100)]

Analysis I.D. Number [Number (5)]

Analysis/Recommendation [Char: (30)] referencing reports found as word-processing files.

Unresolved Issues I.D. Number [Char (5)]

Unresolved Issues [Char: (30)] referencing reports found as word-processing files.

Figure 8.7. Parent database fields and data types.

Virtual Databases

Within the relational database scheme, such as found in Paradox for Windows, the defining feature is the ability to form from the parent database (Figure 8.7) new databases called virtual databases, showing the information needed at a particular time. The term "virtual" refers to something created for the moment whose elements reside in supporting programs and databases. Suppose that a current project will benefit from application of all we have learned about a particular design requirement and its relationship to certain facility user requirements. We can use relational database features to extract the required information, formatted to meet the new manner in which we want this information presented. If you have maintained a relational database within your office formatted to the categories and items listed in Figure 8.7, this can be queried in any number of ways. For example, you have an RFP for a Design Center. Having worked on similar projects in the past, your archives contain information pertaining to Knowledge Base System question items 2.1 listing facility user categories; 2.3 describing facility user activities; and 2.5 containing scenarios highlighting design requirements and expectations. You can query your database by instructing it to form a virtual table containing the following:

Project Names or Building Types

KBS Item Number and all associated answers and analyses/recommendations

When we query the parent relational database with these information requirements, it will form a virtual database table showing this information or any other information we prescribe. This is a remarkable advantage; we can form a virtual database at will as long as we follow a reasoned data entry format, with general regard to future use. Fortunately, relational database technology has advanced in simplicity and is easily learned. We can now add this to our word processing, spread sheet, and Expert Choice programs to form a customized knowledge and decision support system.

To illustrate further the potential of such devices as Expert Choice and Paradox for Windows, let's conclude by briefly considering the National Forest study used as a centerpiece in Chapter 7. The scheme for guiding the development of preference and activity pattern information contained fifteen items from 1. Initial Thoughts, to 15. Final Thoughts. How are you going to handle all this information? How can it be stored for efficient retrieval and application? If placed in a relational database format, we can not only achieve all of this, we can also create virtual tables that answer a number of posed questions regarding what we know about people's preferences for forest recreation opportunities.

The information presented in Chapter 7 can also be read as a number of forest planning objectives associated with conflicting points of views. In this study, there were three major opposing points of view. Developers argued that if there are legitimate commercial uses for the forest, these uses should be allowed. Such groups as the Sierra Club and Isaac Walton clubs favored using the resources of the forest as long as people are carefully educated. The third position was that all development should be stopped and all traces of human activity should be removed—let the forest return to its natural state. When this preservation group was asked, for instance, about providing for the elderly or the disabled, their response was that if these people can no longer handle nature's challenges unaided, their forest experience is over. Expert Choice and Paradox for Windows are the perfect decision support systems for working your way through these subtle and complex issues, providing a place for every point of view in the deliberation.

Insights

Paul R. Neel, F.A.I.A.

A graduate of the University of Southern California, Paul is the 1995 recipient of the Edward C. Kemper Award of the American Institute of Architects, in acknowledgment of his extraordinary leadership and diplomacy in the advancement of the profession. Cal Poly's Dean of the College of Architecture and Environmental Design, Paul has served the profession as California State Architect; President, California Board of Architectural Examiners; and Regional Director, Board of Directors, American Institute of Architects. Recipient of numerous awards and honors for his educational and professional achievements, he has received recognition from President Ronald Reagan and Governor George Deukmejian for his community reconstruction assistance following earthquake disasters.

Comment

Being an architect means being involved in the future and that is what we should be doing. Unfortunately, architects are too often relegated to the same position as those people who do tasks that are brought to them after major decisions are made, so we are really not doing what we should be doing. Architects complain to each other about how we have slipped in position, in our authority in the built environment, to the point where we are only task oriented, but no one ever thinks about trying to fix it. Architects continue to be in their own sort of closed environment and continue to respond to what others are doing to them.

The most important thing for the future of the profession is to elevate the architect to the corporate level. The State of California's facility development process did have something of value. Before making major decisions on space, an agency gets advice from an architect—the State Architect. Now, how many corporate people will go to an architect during the time they are making business decisions? All business decisions eventually end up as space. And who better to be there with you when you make those decisions than the person who knows most about it, the person who has a feeling of what space is and how it responds to people.

This isn't an original idea. The reason that Chuck Luckman was so successful when he left the corporate arena and began to practice architecture is that he stayed right at the executive level. Can you imagine a group of businessmen making a decision on their own to build Madison Square Garden, in the air rights over Pennsylvania Station, while the railroad was operating? That was a decision made by corporate people, but not without being able to get advice from someone like Chuck Luckman. He was on that corporate level, and that's where architects need to be.

Now the next question is, how do architects get there? You get there by acting like a corporate executive. For example, when an agency client came to the State Architect and said they wanted to build a building, the question was asked, "What are your entire space needs and how do these needs address your future? Now is the time to study your total physical assets and then decide what is needed. I'm here to help." Too often people come to the architect and say, "We want a building of so many square feet; here are the parameters, and let's build it." A poor decision may have been made at the beginning and if the building is built, that poor decision is frozen in time as a building. How do we correct that? By elevating the position of the architect to the initial decision-making process in order to leverage the company's physical assets. Every decision that is made regarding space goes to bottom line profit. If a bad decision is made on square footage, and you're planning to keep the building for 30 years, you have a 30-year load that would otherwise go to bottom line profit. What is needed is someone who has knowledge about this important subject. But if that person is absent, and that chair is empty in the corporate boardroom when those decisions are made, the chances are that the decisions will be wrong. Architects must convince people at the corporate level that we should be involved in those decisions, and that architects can help them make the right decisions.

A building is really a machine for making money. If architects can demonstrate that they understand this concept, they can gain the confidence of corporate America. That's the biggest task of all —to change the thinking of corporate America. Corporate boards always have attorneys to advise them on legal matters, and when they discuss capital undertakings, there is usually a financial officer involved. Why not have an architect to help them make decisions about space—a precious corporate asset?

Architects need to develop a new attitude and new viewpoint about who they are and what they do. How do you think the construction managers got into the corporate boardrooms, school board meetings, hospital boards, and so on? They did business development at the front end by selling what they could do for the clients. They created a sales pitch, took it to the people on these boards, and they believed it. Construction managers are making decisions that architects should be making, and they are doing what architects should be doing. Architects have to start doing business development, but first they have to believe that they can do it; they have to believe how important they are.

There's another perspective to this concern with the built environment, which has to do with an opportunity created by the economic downturn. Companies are reorganizing and many major industries are contracting or downsizing. This means that clean site development probably won't take place for a long time because there is so much empty built space available. This provides a new opportunity for the architectural profession, an unbelievable opportunity for the profession to move into the area of: What do you have, how big is it, how old is it, what are you going to do with it, do you need it? Architects can help companies cope with these issues. Let's say that an aircraft company no longer needs its huge hangars, its huge facilities, and another corporation needs more manufacturing space. The corporation will be looking around for potential facilities that are already built into which they can expand. Architects are in an ideal position to help make decisions about how much space is needed and how buildings can be retrofitted, and so forth. This is an area where we have a very definite opportunity—the renovation of older spaces, and redesigning them for new uses. That's recycling, and that's basically where we are headed as we recover from this global adjustment.

Society can certainly use architects but they must place themselves in a position to perform the right kinds of services. I'll give you a scenario that illustrates what can happen when an architect brings a new perspective to his or her practice. I have a friend who had 55 employees in 1991 and his architectural billings were 90 percent. By 1994, he had taken the word "architecture" off the firm's masthead and replaced it with "building services." He still has about 55 architects in the firm, but he has a total of 125 employees. He now has real estate people, attorneys, and financing and costing people. His architectural billings are down to about 40 percent and his corporate profit has increased by 20 percent. He has convinced his clients that he can do everything, and tells them, "If you can't get financing, we'll find the financing; if we can't find it, we'll finance it." That's the kind of client service attitude that architects must have if they are going to be successful.

Some 26 years ago, while writing a master's thesis, I developed a point of view that is as appropriate today as it was almost three decades ago.

A crystal ball is not needed to see that the future of the profession lies with the future clients. The client will rule the actions of the future professionals, and, if they cannot, they will look elsewhere for solutions to their needs. The future client will be: a multi-headed impersonal organization which sets its own ethics—an organization of people who are primarily concerned with the efficiency of the building, the accuracy of estimates, and the dependability of completion dates—an organization which is looking for a service that is well versed in modern technology and management methods.

It is little wonder that most of the major cities in the Western World have "project management services" appearing in the classified sections of the telephone directories in alarmingly increasing numbers. These services would not exist unless there was a client need which has not been satisfied by the architectural profession. Professional isolationism or eloquent article writing and speech making which is supposed to bury the "construction consultants" in abuse will not make the problem disappear. Sad will be the day when the project management consultant becomes the middle man between the architect and the client. No architect wishes to have a middle man as the team leader or decision maker for future building projects.

We, as architectural educators, devoutly believe that the architect's training provides a skill that cannot be supplanted or duplicated. This skill consists of judgment—discriminating between good and bad physical space relationships, between appropriate and unsuitable building products and systems and techniques, and co-ordination—the bringing together of diverse physical elements and systems with efficiency and economy.

Insights

John E. Harrigan, Ph.D.

In his professional setting, as Director of Research, Wolff/Lang/ Christopher Architects, John lives in a world of sophisticated clients and complex design challenges, where he is expert at forming clients, investors, stakeholders, and architects into effective and efficient building design and land development teams. In his academic setting, as Professor of Architecture at Cal Poly and Founding Director of the department's executive program, his main focus is on the unrealized potential of architects whose knowledge is essential for evolving economies, societies, and cultures. A graduate of the University of California, Berkeley, and Fellow of the Human Factors/Ergonomic Society, he learned his psychology, philosophy, and biology in the classroom and his architecture and engineering on the job.

Comment

Unlimited opportunity is the theme of this book. It offers competitive ideas derived mainly from men and women who are working to realize the full potential of architectural services on behalf of their clients. Each contributor looks beyond the everyday aspects of professional practice and engages the client's world to discover new competitive strategies. The concept of the executive architect and the idea of leading the transformation of professional practice is intended to accelerate this effort. If you consider the insights and methodologies developed in this and the preceding chapters, this is a promising model for success. When developing competitive strategies, recall what was said about opportunity and innovation: do not place too much reliance on detailed planning; rather, promote flexibility and enterprise.

The authors and contributors want you to experiment with the concept of the executive architect. As a preliminary step, you should evaluate your firm's assets in terms of the seven executive elements developed in the preceding chapters. What are your capabilities within each of these elements? In terms of what must be accomplished, what can your people do and what are they willing to do? Where must your intellectual capital be renewed? The seven research methods developed in the preceding pages comprise a unique strategy for learning from clients and learning about clients. Where do you find similarities between these methods and your way of working? How can these methods be selectively revised to improve the way you work? Review, in particular, the cases and examples that illustrate how precise, thorough, and comprehensive you must be when establishing expectations and requirements related to quality of life at work, at home, and in the community.

In the next step, identify a candidate market area that holds possibilities for the future. Characterize the client and client organization enterprises typical of this market. Use the Malcolm Baldrige scheme as a diagnostic tool to make sure you have considered every aspect of the challenge in terms that are meaningful to client organizations. Create a client engagement strategy for the most promising opportunity. Use this and the Knowledge Base System to frame the benchmark that will differentiate your firm from your competitors. Verify your thinking by interviewing a number of executives known for success in the selected market area.

When you are comfortable explaining what it is you wish to propose to clients, present yourself at the senior executive level within the corporation, business, or institution you have targeted as an opportunity. Never violate this recommendation! Have your ideas confirmed at the top of the client organization. Never fight an uphill battle. Approach potential clients with two statements: your service concept and its significance in terms of the client's critical success factors. Convince clients that you have a fresh perspective regarding how they can use facility investments to create profit and sustainable advantage.

As you experiment with this entrepreneurial strategy, critically examine your professional philosophy about the meaning of building value, performance, and image. This is the guiding vision that you must continually renew.

REFERENCES

American Institute of Architects (1972). *First report of the national task force.* Washington, DC.

Apgar, M. (1993). Uncovering your hidden occupancy costs. *Harvard Business Review.* May–June, 124–136.

Argyris, C. (1970). *Intervention theory and method.* Reading, MA: Addison-Wesley.

Argyris, C. (1994). Good communication that blocks learning. *Harvard Business Review.* July–August, 77–86.

Ashihara, Y. (1989). *The hidden order: Tokyo through the twentieth century.* Tokyo: Kodansha International.

Barnes, L. B., C. R. Christensen, and A. J. Hansen (1994). *Teaching and the case method.* Boston, MA: Harvard Business School Press.

Bettelheim, B. (1974). *Home for the heart.* New York: Knopf.

Bouchard, T. J. (1976). Field research methods. In M. D. Dunnette (Ed.), *Handbook of industrial organizational psychology.* New York: Rand McNally.

Boulding. K. E. (1974). Planning may seem necessary, but it is hardly ever the essential that we thought. *Technology Review.* 77, 8.

Cannell, C. and R. L. Kahn (1968). Interviewing. In G. Lindzey and E. Aronson (Eds.), *The handbook of social psychology*, 2nd ed., Vol. 2. Reading, MA: Addison-Wesley.

Cooper, J. (1989). Science and design. *Interior Design.* August, 198–203.

Cooper, L. (1994). Louis Agassiz as a teacher. In L. B. Barnes, C. R. Christensen, and A. J. Hansen, *Teaching and the case method.* Boston, MA: Harvard Business School Press.

Crosbie, M. J. (1994). Working in two worlds. *Progressive Architecture.* September, 78–84.

Dorsey, B. W. (1994). Project Rosewood: The Mercedes-Benz siting strategy. *Site Selection.* April, 246–254.

Fairbank, J. K. (1992). *China: A new history.* Cambridge, MA: Harvard University Press.

Fisher, T. (1994). Can this profession be saved? *Progressive Architecture.* February, 45–84.

Flamholtz, E. (1986). *How to make the transition from an entrepreneurship to a professionally managed firm.* San Francisco, CA: Jossey-Bass.

Fleenor, D. (1993). The coming and going of the global corporation. *The Columbia Journal of World Business.* Winter, 6–16.

Freidheim, C. (1993). In D. Fleenor, The coming and going of the global corporation. *The Columbia Journal of World Business.* Winter, 6–16.

George, S. (1992). *The Baldrige Quality System: The do-it-yourself way to transform your business.* New York: Wiley.

Gercik, P. (1992). *On track with the Japanese: A case-by-case approach to building successful relationships.* New York: Kodansha International.

Ghoshal, S. (1993). In D. Fleenor, The coming and going of the global corporation. *The Columbia Journal of World Business.* Winter, 6–16.

Giovannini, J. (1995). Antoine Predock: American visionary. *Architecture.* March, 55–83.

Goodman, R. (1996). Client assessment knowledge system for business industry application. *Facility Management Journal.* In press.

Gragg, C. I. (1940). Because wisdom can't be told. *Harvard Alumni Bulletin.* 19 October, 1–6.

Gross, T., R. Pascale, and A. Athos (1993). The reinvention of the roller coaster: Risking the present for a powerful future. *Harvard Business Review.* November–December, 97–108.

Hamel, G. and C. K. Prahalad (1993). *Competing for the future.* Boston, MA: Harvard Business School Press.

Handy, C. (1994). *The age of paradox.* Boston, MA: Harvard University Press.

Harper, W. R. and D. H. Harris (1975). The application of link analysis to police intelligence. *Human Factors.* 17, 157–164.

Harrigan, J. E. (1987a). *Human factors research: Methods and applications for architects and interior designers.* Amsterdam: Elsevier Science.

Harrigan, J. E. (1987b). Architecture and interior design. In G. Salvendy (Ed.), *The handbook of human factors.* New York: Wiley.

Harrigan, J. E. and A. Chapman (1991). *Building a better product: A knowledge base approach to skilled job performance.* Research report to IBM Corporation.

Hayes, R. H. and G. P. Pisano (1994). Beyond world-class: The new manufacturing strategy. *Harvard Business Review.* January–February, 77–87.

Holleman, E. (1994). In G. P. Zachary, *The Wall Street Journal.* 30 September, A1.

Huey, J. (1993). How McKinsey does it. *Fortune.* 1 November, 56–81.

Itami, H. (1987). *Invisible assets.* Cambridge, MA: Harvard University Press.

Itoh, Y. (1992). *The Nikkei Weekly.* 28 January, 1–2

Keiser, T. C. (1988). Negotiating with a customer you can't afford to lose. *Harvard Business Review.* November–December, 30–37.

Kenichi, O. (1990). *The borderless world: Power and strategy in the interlinked economy.* New York: HarperBusiness.

Kroeber, A. L. (1966). *An anthropologist looks at history*. Princeton, NJ: Princeton Research Press.

Kuhn, T. (1962). *The structure of scientific revolutions*. Chicago: University of Chicago Press.

Lavin, D. (1994). Straight shooter. *The Wall Street Journal*, 10 October, A1.

Lazer, B. (1994). In T. Gross, R. Pascale, and A. Athos. The reinvention of the roller coaster: Risking the present for a powerful future. *Harvard Business Review*. November–December, 97–107.

Levitt, T. (1975). Marketing myopia. *Harvard Business Review*. September–October, 26–48.

Luckman, C. (1988). *Twice in a lifetime*. New York: W. W. Norton.

Mintzberg, H. (1987). Crafting strategy. *Harvard Business Review*. July–August, 66–75.

Mintzberg, H. (1994). The rise and fall of strategic planning. *Harvard Business Review*. January–February, 107–114.

Morita, A. (1988). *Made in Japan*. New York: Penguin.

Nesmith, L. (1990). Model homes: Nexus south, Nexus north. *Architecture*. September, 90–97.

Nihon Keizai Shimbun. (1992). Fitness clubs broaden services to ensure their fiscal health. *The Nikkei Weekly*, 18 January, 18

Nikkei Marketing Journal (1991). Magazines instill pride in housewives. 30 November, 16.

Nishimura, H. (1992). *The Nikkei Weekly*. 3 October, 11.

Ohmae, K. (1982). *The mind of the strategist*. New York: McGraw-Hill.

Ohmae, K. (1990). *The borderless world: Power and strategy in the interlinked economy*. New York: HarperBusiness, 214.

Olson, C. (1992). Chrysler constructs the ultimate advantage. *Building Design & Construction*. 23 September, 16

Peters, T. (1992). *Liberation management*. New York: Knopf

Peterson, C. R. and L. Beach (1967). Man as an intuitive statistician. *Psychological Bulletin*. 68, 29–46.

Porter, M. (1987). The state of strategic thinking. *Economist*. 23 May, 21.

Proshansky, H. M. (1972). Methodology in environmental psychology: Problems and issues. *Human Factors*. 14, 451–460.

Rau, J. (1994). Nothing succeeds like training for success. *The Wall Street Journal*. 12 September, A15.

Rogers, E. and Y. Chen (1990). In M. Von Glinow and S. Mohrman (Eds.), *Managing complexity in high-technology organizations*. New York: Oxford University Presss, 15–36.

Rosenhan, D. L. (1973). On being sane in insane places. *Science*. 179, 250–258.

Rosenthal, R. (1976). *Experimenter effects in behavioral research*. New York: Wiley.

Rosier, M. (1974). Asking silly questions. In N. Armistead (Ed.), *Reconstructing social psychology*. Baltimore, MD: Penguin.

Rothstein, L. R. (1995). The empowerment effort that came undone. *Harvard Business Review*. January–February, 20–32.

Saaty, T. L. (1980). *The analytic hierarchy process: Planning, priority setting, resource allocation*. New York: McGraw-Hill.

Sahlins, M. and E. Service (1960). *Evolution and culture.* Ann Arbor, MI: The University of Michigan Press.

San Diego Union (1991). The new central library. 6 October, E1, E10.

Shellenbarger, S. (1994). Work and family. *The Wall Street Journal.* 20 July, B1.

Slater, R. 1993. *The new GE: How Jack Welch revived an American institution.* New York: Richard D. Irwin.

Sommer, R. (1972). *Design awareness.* San Francisco, CA: Rinehart Press.

Spradley, J. P. (1972). Adaptive strategies of urban nomads: The ethnoscience of tramp culture. In T. Weaver and D. White (Eds.), *The anthropology of urban environments.* Monograph Series, Number II. Washinton, DC: The Society for Applied Anthropology.

Spradley, J. P. (1979). *The enthnographic interview.* New York: Holt, Rinehart, and Winston.

Steiner, G. (1979). *Strategic planning: What every manager must know.* New York: Free Press, 9.

Strebel, P. (1992). *Breakpoints: How managers exploit radical business change.* Boston, MA: Harvard Business School Press.

Terkel, S. (1972). *Working.* New York: Pantheon.

Umlauf, E. (1991). Michigan National's headquarters reflects firm's philosophy toward its staff. *Building Design & Construction.* January, 38–43.

United States Department of Commerce (1995). *The Malcolm Baldrige national quality award.* Gaithersburg, MD: National Institute of Standards and Technology.

Useem, M. (1993). *Executive defense: Shareholder power and corporate reorganization.* Cambridge, MA: Harvard University Press.

Van De Ven, A. H. (1993). Managing the process of organizational innovation. In G. P. Huber and W. H. Glick (Eds.), *Organization change and redesign.* New York: Oxford University Press.

Van Maanen, J. (1973). Observations on the making of policemen. *Human Organization.* 32, 407–418.

Verne, J. (1993). *Twenty thousand leagues under the sea.* Annapolis, MD: Naval Institute Press.

The Wall Street Journal (1994). Staff report. 12 October, A1.

Wolcott, H. (1975). Criteria for an ethnographic approach to research in schools. *Human Organization.* 32, 407–418.

Wright, G. (1989). Distribution center shuns industrial image. *Building Design & Construction.* June, 42–47.

Wright, G. (1991). High-tech campus accommodates variations on a theme. *Building Design & Construction.* August, 33–37.

Yip, G. (1993). In D. Fleenor, The coming and going of the global corporation. *The Columbia Journal of World Business.* Winter, 6–16.

Zabriskie, N. and A. Huellmantel (1994). Marketing research as a strategic tool. *Long Range Planning.* February, 107–115.

NAME INDEX

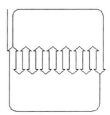

Agassiz, L., 52
Annennberg, L., 130
Annennberg, W., 130
Apgar, M., 88
Argyris, C., 53, 157
Ashihara, Y., 159
Athos, A., 77
Austin, D., 6, 7, 26, 27, 318–
    338

Barnes, L., 206
Beach, L., 313
Bouchard, T., 316
Boulding, K., 165
Brecht, J., 6, 7, 26, 27, 61, 62–74

Cannell, C., 316
Chapman, A., 174
Chen, Y., 120
Chinowsky, P., 6, 7, 26, 257–
    263
Christensen, C., 206
Clark, K., 53
Cooke, G., 3, 4
Cooper, J., 112
Cooper, L., 52
Crosbie, M., 122
Cunard, R., 206

Dorsey, W., 79

Fairbank, J., 57
Feyerabend, P., 52
Fisher, T., 9
Flamholtz, E., 71
Fleenor, D., 83, 84
Foote, F., 6, 7, 26, 61, 88, 127–
    143
Freidheim, C., 83

Gates, B., 55
Gensler, A., 6, 7, 25, 30, 31–
    42, 83
Gensler, D., 6, 7, 26, 264–279
George, S., 77
Gercik, P., 122–123
Ghoshal, S., 84
Giovannini, J., 114
Goodman, R., 108, 352
Gragg, C., 206
Graves, M., 117
Gross, T., 77

Hamel, G., 58
Hansen, A., 206
Harper, W., 292
Harrigan, Janet, 7
Harrigan, J. E., 158, 174, 360–
    361
Harris, D., 292
Hayes, R., 76, 77, 81

Heller, J., 6, 7, 26, 43–51, 88, 256
Hines, J., 44
Honda, K., 122
Huellmantel, A., 54

Itami, H., 15
Itoh, Y., 116

Jahn, H., 131
Johnson, P., 39

Kahn, R., 316
Keiser, T., 53
Kim, T., 122

Lavin, D., 55
Lazer, B., 55
Levitt, T., 55
Luckman, C., 6, 7, 16–20, 21–24

Mallas, L., 127, 137, 138
Matsuda, T., 122
McGlaughlin, H., 323
Mintzberg, H., 55–56
Montgomery, R., 199
Morita, A., 54, 56

Neel, P., 356–359
Nesmith, L., 117
Nishimura, H., 116

Olson, C., 112

Palmer, M., 241, 247
Pascale, R., 77
Pauson, J., 53
Pei, I., 39, 323
Peli, C., 39
Peters, T., 158
Peterson, C., 313
Pisano, G., 76, 77, 81
Poelle, L., 211
Prahalad, C., 58
Predock, A., 114
Proshansky, H., 165

Raiser, J., 85
Rau, J., 55
Reibstock, O., 52
Richert, E., 126
Rogers, E., 120

Rosier, M., 315
Rothstein, L., 208
Rowe, J., 6, 7, 26, 186–205

Saaty, T., 345
Sahlins, M., 57
Service, E., 57
Shellenbarger, S., 210
Simons, L., 61, 62
Sivin, N., 57
Slater, R., 54
Sommer, R., 295
Spradly, J., 113–114
Stafford, J., 9
Strebel, P., 57, 58

Terkel, S., 298
Tigerman, S., 117

Umlaf, E., 112

Van De Ven, A., 85
Van Maanen, J., 298
Verne, J., 206

Ward, W., 212, 309
Watry, N., 108
Welch, J., 54, 88
Willcox, D., 6, 7, 26, 88, 90–105
Wolcott, H., 114
Wolff, L., 148, 241, 247
Wright, G., 112

Yip, G., 83
Young, R., 15

Zabriskie, N., 54
Zeeman, C., 52

SUBJECT INDEX

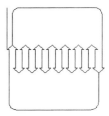

Action plans, 81
Activity analysis, 307–310
  communication matrix, 310
Anchor points, 76
Application possibilities, 13–14
Assets, 81–82
  partnership and alliance,
    83–84
  professional, knowledge,
    and technological, 82–83
  stakeholder, 82

Basic elements of field studies, 207–212
Benchmarks, 77–81
Building Owners and Managers Association, 67

Case study archives, 206–207
Client assessment strategy,
  106–123
Clients:
  critical success factors, 87–88
  evolving needs, 88–89
  learn about, 111–113
  learn from, 113–115
  regard for innovation, 5
  restructuring for the future,
    1–2
  searching for opportunity, 3

unlimited opportunity, 2, 25
world outside the office, 1
Concept phase, 93–94
Contributors:
  Austin, D., 6, 7, 26, 27,
    318–338
  Brecht, J., 6, 7, 26, 27, 61,
    62–74
  Chinowsky, P., 6, 7, 26,
    257–263
  Foote, F., 6, 7, 26, 61, 88,
    127–143
  Gensler, A., 6, 7, 25, 30, 31–
    42, 83
  Gensler, D., 6, 7, 26, 264–279
  Heller, J., 6, 7, 26, 43–51,
    88, 256
  Luckman, C., 6, 7, 16–20,
    21–24
  Rowe, J., 6, 7, 26, 186–205
  Willcox, D., 6, 7, 26, 88, 90–
    105
Critical thinking, 52–58
  mapping challenges, 56–58
  realizing our potential, 54–56

Decision support systems,
  339–353
Delphi development tool, 351
Design guidelines, 84, 157

Eisenhower Medical Center, 90
  Betty Ford Clinic, 90
Entering a new market, 111–
  113
Entrepreneurs, 256
Executive architect, 2
Expert Choice, 339, 346–351

Field studies, 206–253
Financial analyses, 84–85
Fluor Daniel, 79–80
Fukuoka, 116–117

Gensler Information Solu-
  tions, 34, 267–269
Group identification technique, 281–283
  directed group identifica-
    tion, 292
  progressive survey, 283–291

Hsinchu Science Industrial
  Park, 339
Human Factors Advisory
  Service, 122

Innovation, 60, 85–86
Insights and methods, 5–9
International enterprises, 115–
  121

International Facility Managers Association, 29
Interviews, 297–299

Japan Housing Association, 122
Johnson Controls, 77–78

Knowledge Base System:
  basic strategy, 145–146
  commentary, 159–182
  items, 149–156
  specific line of inquiry, 226
  system logos, 148
  twelve-step process, 146–147
Kyoto, 116, 118

Malcolm Baldrige award criteria, 106–111
Mapping the challenges ahead, 56–58
Mexico and America, 111
Minnesota Innovation Research Project, 85–86

National Association of Office and Industrial Parks, 70
National Education Association, 29
National Institute of Standards and Technology, 106

Niagara Gateway Project, 78–79

O.S.I. 9000, 108

Paradox for Windows, 351
Preference assessment, 299–306
Programming, shortcomings, 157

Quality of life, 183–185
Questionnaires, 314–316

Read critically, 20
Readers:
  the corporate reader, 4
  the faculty reader, 4
  the professional reader, 3
  the student reader, 3–4
Realizing our potential, 54–56
Relational database, 355
Research techniques, 280–314

Safeguards, 121–124
Science cities, 111–113
Sense of direction, 255
Society of Manufacturing Engineers, 29
Strategic research, 113
Study sessions, 293–294
  citizen participation, 295–297
  public meetings, 294–295

Systematic observation, 310–314

Taco Bell, 33
The Executive Committee, 333
  Thorough analysis, 75–86
Transformation model, 10
Transformation of professional practice, 9–13
  ahead of convential wisdom, 61
  cash flow and profit margins, 29–30
  a high performance practice, 26
  hustle, 28–29
  intellectual capital, 27
  a new language, 2
  a practical strategic prescription, 10–11
Tsukuba Science City, 120
Two pathways: Insights and methods, 5–9
Typical two weeks of research, 281

Unlimited opportunity, 25–26
Urban Land Institute, 70

Young Presidents Organization, 333–334